Pharo by Example

Andrew P. Black   Stéphane Ducasse

Oscar Nierstrasz   Damien Pollet

with Damien Cassou and Marcus Denker

Version of 2010-02-01

This book is available as a free download from http://PharoByExample.org.

Published by Square Bracket Associates, Switzerland. http://SquareBracketAssociates.org
ISBN 978-3-9523341-4-0
First Edition, October, 2009. Cover art by Samuel Morello.

Contents

Preface   **ix**

I   **Getting Started**

1   **A quick tour of Pharo**   **3**
1.1   Getting started 3
1.2   The World menu 7
1.3   Sending messages 8
1.4   Saving, quitting and restarting a Pharo session 10
1.5   Workspaces and Transcripts 11
1.6   Keyboard shortcuts 12
1.7   The Class Browser 14
1.8   Finding classes 16
1.9   Finding methods 18
1.10   Defining a new method 20
1.11   Chapter summary 25

2   **A first application**   **27**
2.1   The Lights Out game 27
2.2   Creating a new Package 28
2.3   Defining the class LOCell 29
2.4   Adding methods to a class 31
2.5   Inspecting an object 33
2.6   Defining the class LOGame 34
2.7   Organizing methods into protocols 37

2.8	Let's try our code	40
2.9	Saving and sharing Smalltalk code.	43
2.10	Chapter summary.	47

3	**Syntax in a nutshell**	**49**
3.1	Syntactic elements	49
3.2	Pseudo-variables	52
3.3	Message sends	53
3.4	Method syntax	54
3.5	Block syntax.	55
3.6	Conditionals and loops in a nutshell	56
3.7	Primitives and pragmas	58
3.8	Chapter summary.	58

4	**Understanding message syntax**	**61**
4.1	Identifying messages	61
4.2	Three kinds of messages	63
4.3	Message composition	65
4.4	Hints for identifying keyword messages	71
4.5	Expression sequences	73
4.6	Cascaded messages	73
4.7	Chapter summary.	74

II	**Developing in Pharo**	

5	**The Smalltalk object model**	**77**
5.1	The rules of the model	77
5.2	Everything is an Object	77
5.3	Every object is an instance of a class	78
5.4	Every class has a superclass	85
5.5	Everything happens by sending messages	89
5.6	Method lookup follows the inheritance chain	90
5.7	Shared variables	96
5.8	Chapter summary.	101

6	**The Pharo programming environment**	**103**
6.1	Overview	104
6.2	The Browser	105
6.3	Monticello	117
6.4	The Inspector and the Explorer	124
6.5	The Debugger	126
6.6	The Process Browser	135
6.7	Finding methods	136
6.8	Change sets and the Change Sorter	136
6.9	The File List Browser	139
6.10	In Smalltalk, you can't lose code	141
6.11	Chapter summary	142

7	**SUnit**	**145**
7.1	Introduction	145
7.2	Why testing is important	146
7.3	What makes a good test?	147
7.4	SUnit by example	148
7.5	The SUnit cook book	152
7.6	The SUnit framework	153
7.7	Advanced features of SUnit	156
7.8	The implementation of SUnit	157
7.9	Some advice on testing	160
7.10	Chapter summary	161

8	**Basic Classes**	**163**
8.1	Object	163
8.2	Numbers	172
8.3	Characters	175
8.4	Strings	176
8.5	Booleans	177
8.6	Chapter summary	179

9   Collections   181

9.1   Introduction 181

9.2   The varieties of collections 182

9.3   Implementations of collections 184

9.4   Examples of key classes 186

9.5   Collection iterators 195

9.6   Some hints for using collections 199

9.7   Chapter summary 200

10   Streams   203

10.1   Two sequences of elements 203

10.2   Streams vs. collections 204

10.3   Streaming over collections 205

10.4   Using streams for file access 213

10.5   Chapter summary 215

11   Morphic   217

11.1   The history of Morphic 217

11.2   Manipulating morphs 219

11.3   Composing morphs 220

11.4   Creating and drawing your own morphs 220

11.5   Interaction and animation 224

11.6   Interactors 227

11.7   Drag-and-drop 228

11.8   A complete example 230

11.9   More about the canvas 234

11.10 Chapter summary 235

12   Seaside by Example   237

12.1   Why do we need Seaside? 237

12.2   Getting started 238

12.3   Seaside components 242

12.4   Rendering XHTML 246

12.5   CSS: Cascading style sheets 252

12.6   Managing control flow 254

12.7   A complete tutorial example 261

12.8   A quick look at AJAX 267

12.9   Chapter summary. 270

III   Advanced Pharo

13   **Classes and metaclasses**   **275**

13.1   Rules for classes and metaclasses 275

13.2   Revisiting the Smalltalk object model. 276

13.3   Every class is an instance of a metaclass 278

13.4   The metaclass hierarchy parallels the class hierarchy 279

13.5   Every metaclass Inherits from Class and Behavior 281

13.6   Every metaclass is an instance of Metaclass 284

13.7   The metaclass of Metaclass is an Instance of Metaclass 284

13.8   Chapter summary. 286

14   **Reflection**   **287**

14.1   Introspection 288

14.2   Browsing code 292

14.3   Classes, method dictionaries and methods 295

14.4   Browsing environments 297

14.5   Accessing the run-time context 298

14.6   Intercepting messages not understood 301

14.7   Objects as method wrappers 305

14.8   Pragmas 308

14.9   Chapter summary. 309

IV   Appendices

A   **Frequently Asked Questions**   **315**

A.1   Getting started 315

A.2   Collections 315

A.3   Browsing the system. 316

A.4   Using Monticello and SqueakSource 318

A.5   Tools 319
A.6   Regular expressions and parsing 319

Bibliography   **321**

Index   **322**

Preface

What is Pharo?

Pharo is a modern, open source, fully-featured implementation of the Smalltalk programming language and environment. Pharo is derived from Squeak[1], a re-implementation of the classic Smalltalk-80 system. Whereas Squeak was developed mainly as a platform for developing experimental educational software, Pharo strives to offer a lean, open-source platform for professional software development, and a robust and stable platform for research and development into dynamic languages and environments. Pharo serves as the reference implementation for the Seaside web development framework.

Pharo resolves some licensing issues with Squeak. Unlike previous versions of Squeak, the Pharo core contains only code that has been contributed under the MIT license. The Pharo project started in March 2008 as a fork of Squeak 3.9, and the first 1.0 beta version was released on July 31, 2009.

Although Pharo removes many packages from Squeak, it also includes numerous features that are optional in Squeak. For example, true type fonts are bundled into Pharo. Pharo also includes support for true block closures. The user interfaces has been simplified and revised.

Pharo is highly portable — even its virtual machine is written entirely in Smalltalk, making it easy to debug, analyze, and change. Pharo is the vehicle for a wide range of innovative projects from multimedia applications and educational platforms to commercial web development environments.

There is an important aspect behind Pharo: Pharo should not just be a copy of the past but really *reinvent* Smalltalk. Big-bang approaches rarely succeed. Pharo will really favor evolutionary and incremental changes. We want to

---

[1]Dan Ingalls et al., Back to the Future: The Story of Squeak, a Practical Smalltalk Written in Itself. In Proceedings of the 12th ACM SIGPLAN conference on Object-oriented programming, systems, languages, and applications (OOPSLA'97). ACM Press, November 1997 ⟨URL: http://www.cosc.canterbury.ac.nz/~wolfgang/cosc205/squeak.html⟩.

be able to experiment with important new features or libraries. Evolution means that Pharo accepts mistakes and is not aiming for the next perfect solution in one big step — even if we would love it. Pharo will favor small incremental changes but a multitude of them. The success of Pharo depends on the contributions of its community.

Who should read this book?

This book is based on *Squeak by Example*[2], an open-source introduction to Squeak. The book has been liberally adapted and revised to reflect the differences between Pharo and Squeak. This book presents the various aspects of Pharo, starting with the basics, and proceeding to more advanced topics.

This book will not teach you how to program. The reader should have some familiarity with programming languages. Some background with object-oriented programming would be helpful.

This book will introduce the Pharo programming environment, the language and the associated tools. You will be exposed to common idioms and practices, but the focus is on the technology, not on object-oriented design. Wherever possible, we will show you lots of examples. (We have been inspired by Alec Sharp's excellent book on Smalltalk[3].)

There are numerous other books on Smalltalk freely available on the web but none of these focuses specifically on Pharo. See for example: http://stephane.ducasse.free.fr/FreeBooks.html

A word of advice

Do not be frustrated by parts of Smalltalk that you do not immediately understand. You do not have to know everything! Alan Knight expresses this principle as follows[4]:

---

[2] http://SqueakByExample.org

[3] Alec Sharp, *Smalltalk by Example*. McGraw-Hill, 1997 ⟨URL: http://stephane.ducasse.free.fr/FreeBooks/ByExample/⟩.

[4] http://www.surfscranton.com/architecture/KnightsPrinciples.htm

> **Try not to care.** Beginning Smalltalk programmers often have trouble because they think they need to understand all the details of how a thing works before they can use it. This means it takes quite a while before they can master Transcript show: 'Hello World'. One of the great leaps in OO is to be able to answer the question "How does this work?" with "I don't care".

An open book

This book is an open book in the following senses:

- The content of this book is released under the Creative Commons Attribution-ShareAlike (by-sa) license. In short, you are allowed to freely share and adapt this book, as long as you respect the conditions of the license available at the following URL: http://creativecommons.org/licenses/by-sa/3.0/.

- This book just describes the core of Pharo. Ideally we would like to encourage others to contribute chapters on the parts of Pharo that we have not described. If you would like to participate in this effort, please contact us. We would like to see this book grow!

For more details, visit http://PharoByExample.org.

The Pharo community

The Pharo community is friendly and active. Here is a short list of resources that you may find useful:

- http://www.pharo-project.org is the main web site of Pharo.

- http://www.squeaksource.com is the equivalent of SourceForge for Pharo projects. Many optional packages for Pharo live here.

Examples and exercises

We make use of two special conventions in this book.

We have tried to provide as many examples as possible. In particular, there are many examples that show a fragment of code which can be evaluated. We use the symbol $\longrightarrow$ to indicate the result that you obtain when you select an expression and `print it`:

```
3 + 4   ⟶   7   "if you select 3+4 and 'print it', you will see 7"
```

In case you want to play in Pharo with these code snippets, you can download a plain text file with all the example code from the book's web site: http://PharoByExample.org.

The second convention that we use is to display the icon ☾ to indicate when there is something for you to do:

☾   *Go ahead and read the next chapter!*

Acknowledgments

We would first like to thank the original developers of Squeak for making this amazing Smalltalk development environment available as an open source project.

We would also like to thank Hilaire Fernandes and Serge Stinckwich who allowed us to translate parts of their columns on Smalltalk, and Damien Cassou for contributing the chapter on streams.

We especially thank Alexandre Bergel, Orla Greevy, Fabrizio Perin, Lukas Renggli, Jorge Ressia and Erwann Wernli for their detailed reviews.

We thank the University of Bern, Switzerland, for graciously supporting this open-source project and for hosting the web site of this book.

We also thank the Squeak community for their enthusiastic support of this book project, and for informing us of the errors found in the first edition of this book.

Part I

Getting Started

Chapter 1

A quick tour of Pharo

In this chapter we will give you a high-level tour of Pharo to help you get comfortable with the environment. There will be plenty of opportunities to try things out, so it would be a good idea if you have a computer handy when you read this chapter.

We will use this icon: 🕗 to mark places in the text where you should try something out in Pharo. In particular, you will fire up Pharo, learn about the different ways of interacting with the system, and discover some of the basic tools. You will also learn how to define a new method, create an object and send it messages.

1.1 Getting started

Pharo is available as a free download from http://pharo-project.org. There are three parts that you will need to download, consisting of four files (see Figure 1.1).

1. The *virtual machine* (VM) is the only part of the system that is different for each operating system and processor. Pre-compiled virtual machines are available for all the major computing environments. In Figure 1.1 we see the VM for the selected platform is called *Pharo.exe*.

2. The *sources* file contains the source code for all of the parts of Pharo that don't change very frequently. In Figure 1.1 it is called *SqueakV39.sources*.[1]

3. The current *system image* is a snapshot of a running Pharo system, frozen in time. It consists of two files: an *.image* file, which contains the

---

[1]Pharo is derived from Squeak 3.9, and presently shares the VM with Squeak.

Squeak 4.0.1beta1U.app

SqueakV39.sources

PBE.image

PBE.changes

Virtual Machine   **Shared Sources**   **User-specific system files**

Pharo.exe
Pharo Virtual Machine
pharo-project.org

SqueakV39.sources
SOURCES-Datei
17.173 KB

pharo.image
IMAGE-Datei
29.975 KB

pharo.changes
CHANGES-Datei
27.708 KB

Virtual Machine   **Shared Sources**   **User-specific system files**

Figure 1.1: The Pharo download files for one of the supported platforms.

state of all of the objects in the system (including classes and methods, since they are objects too), and a *.changes* file, which contains a log of all of the changes to the source code of the system. In Figure 1.1, these files are called *pharo.image* and *pharo.changes*.

☝ *Download and install Pharo on your computer.*

We recommend that you use the image provided on the Pharo by Example web page.[2]

Most of the introductory material in this book will work with any version, so if you already have one installed, you may as well continue to use it. However, if you notice differences between the appearance or behaviour of your system and what is described here, do not be surprised.

As you work in Pharo, the image and changes files are modified, so you need to make sure that they are writable. Always keep these two files together. Never edit them directly with a text editor, as Pharo uses them to store the objects you work with and to log the changes you make to the source code. It is a good idea to keep a backup copy of the downloaded image and changes files so you can always start from a fresh image and reload your code.

The *sources* file and the VM can be read-only — they can be shared between different users. All of these files can be placed in the same directory, but it is also possible to put the Virtual Machine and sources file in separate directory where everyone has access to them. Do whatever works best for your style of working and your operating system.

---

[2]http://PharoByExample.org

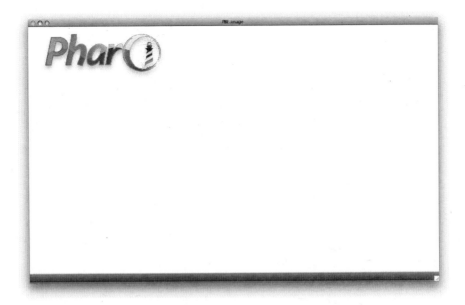

Figure 1.2: A fresh http://PharoByExample.org image.

Launching. To start Pharo, do whatever your operating system expects: drag the *.image* file onto the icon of the virtual machine, or double-click the *.image* file, or at the command line type the name of the virtual machine followed by the path to the *.image* file. (When you have multiple VMs installed on your machine the operating system may not automatically pick the right one; in this case it is safer to drag and drop the image onto the virtual machine, or to use the command line.)

Once Pharo is running, you should see a single large window, possibly containing some open workspace windows (see Figure 1.2), and it's not obvious how to proceed! You might notice a menu bar, but Pharo mainly makes use of context-dependent pop-up menus.

🔦 *Start Pharo. You can dismiss any open workspaces by clicking on the red button in the top left corner of the workspace window.*

You can minimize windows (so that they move to the dock on the bottom of the screen) by clicking on the orange button. Clicking on the green button will cause the window to take up the entire screen.

First Interaction. A good place to get started is the world menu shown in Figure 1.3 (a).

🔦 *Click with the mouse on the background of the main window to show the world menu, then choose* Workspace *to create a new workspace.*

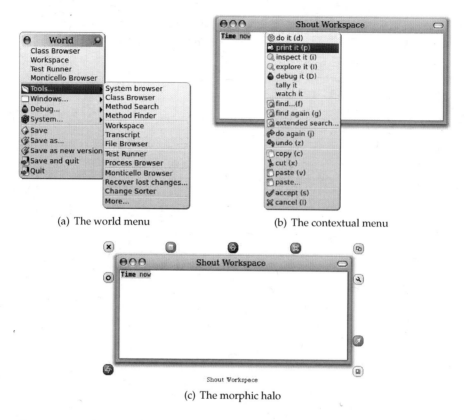

(a) The world menu   (b) The contextual menu

(c) The morphic halo

Figure 1.3: The world menu (brought up by clicking), a contextual menu (action-clicking), and a morphic halo (meta-clicking).

Smalltalk was originally designed for a computer with a three button mouse. If your mouse has fewer than three buttons, you will have to press extra keys while clicking the mouse to simulate the extra buttons. A two-button mouse works quite well with Pharo, but if you have only a single-button mouse, you should seriously consider buying a two-button mouse with a clickable scroll wheel: it will make working with Pharo much more pleasant.

Pharo avoids terms like "left mouse click" because different computers, mice, keyboards and personal configurations mean that different users will need to press different physical buttons to achieve the same effect. Originally Smalltalk introduced colours to stand for the different mouse buttons.[3] Since

---

[3]The button colours were *red, yellow* and *blue*. The authors of this book could never remember which colour referred to which button.

many users will use various modifiers keys (*control*, *ALT*, *meta* etc.) to achieve the same effect, we will instead use the following terms:

click: this is the most often used mouse button, and is normally equivalent to clicking a single-mouse button without any modifier key; click on the image to bring up the "World" menu (Figure 1.3 (a)).

action-click: this is the next most used button; it is used to bring up a contextual menu, that is, a menu that offers different sets of actions depending on where the mouse is pointing; see Figure 1.3 (b). If you do not have a multi-button mouse, then normally you will configure the *control* modifier key to action-click with the mouse button.

meta-click: Finally, you may meta-click on any object displayed in the image to activate the "morphic halo", an array of handles that are used to perform operations on the on-screen objects themselves, such as rotating them or resizing them; see Figure 1.3 (c).[4] If you let the mouse linger over a handle, a help balloon will explain its function. In Pharo, how you meta-click depends on your operating system: either you must hold SHIFT *ctrl* or SHIFT *option* while clicking.

Type Time now *in the workspace. Now action-click in the workspace. Select* print it.

We recommend that right-handed people configure their mouse to click with the left button, action-click with the right button, and meta-click with the clickable scroll wheel, if one is available. If you are using a Macintosh without a second mouse button, you can simulate one by holding down the ⌘ key while clicking the mouse. However, if you are going to be using Pharo at all often, we recommend investing in a mouse with at least two buttons.

You can configure your mouse to work the way you want by using the preferences of your operating system and mouse driver. Pharo has some preferences for customising the mouse and the meta keys on your keyboard. In the preference browser (System ... ▷ Preferences ... ▷ Preference Browser...), the keyboard category contains an option swapControlAndAltKeys that switches the action-click and meta-click functions. There are also options to duplicate the various command keys.

1.2 The World menu

Click again on the Pharo background.

---

[4]Note that the morphic handles are inactive by default in Pharo, but you can turn them on using the Preferences Browser, which we will see shortly.

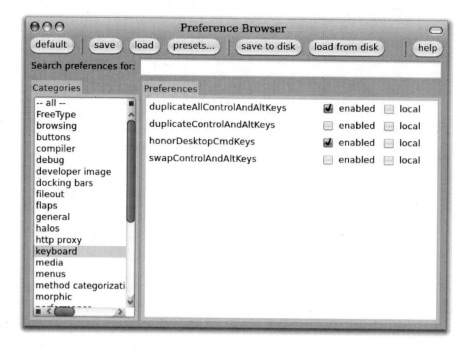

Figure 1.4: The Preference Browser.

You will see the World menu again. Most Pharo menus are not modal; you can leave them on the screen for as long as you wish by clicking the push pin icon in the top-right corner. Do this.

The world menu provides you a simple means to access many of the tools that Pharo offers.

Have a closer look at the World *and* Tools ... *menus. (Figure 1.3 (a))*

You will see a list of several of the core tools in Pharo, including the browser and the workspace. We will encounter most of them in the coming chapters.

1.3   Sending messages

Open a workspace. Type in the following text:

BouncingAtomsMorph new openInWorld

Now action-click. A menu should appear. Select do it (d). *(See Figure 1.5.)*

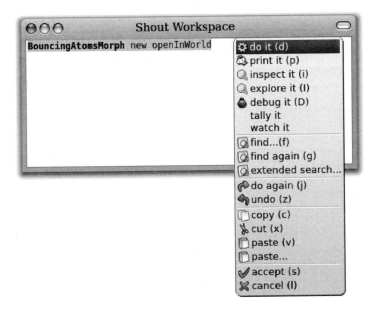

Figure 1.5: "Doing" an expression

A window containing a large number of bouncing atoms should open in the top left of the Pharo image.

You have just evaluated your first Smalltalk expression! You just sent the message new to the BouncingAtomsMorph class, resulting in a new BouncingAtomsMorph instance, followed by the message openInWorld to this instance. The BouncingAtomsMorph class decided what to do with the new message, that is, it looked up its *methods* for handling new message and reacted appropriately. Similarly the BouncingAtomsMorph instance looked up its method for responding to openInWorld and took appropriate action.

If you talk to Smalltalkers for a while, you will quickly notice that they generally do not use expressions like "call an operation" or "invoke a method", but instead they will say "send a message". This reflects the idea that objects are responsible for their own actions. You never *tell* an object what to do—instead you politely *ask* it to do something by sending it a message. The object, not you, selects the appropriate method for responding to your message.

1.4   Saving, quitting and restarting a Pharo session

ⓘ   *Now click on the bouncing atoms window and drag it anywhere you like. You now have the demo "in hand". Put it down by clicking anywhere.*

Figure 1.6: A BouncingAtomsMorph.   Figure 1.7: The save as ... dialogue.

ⓘ   *Select* World ▷ Save as ... *, enter the name "myPharo", and click on the* OK *button. Now select* World ▷ Save and quit.

Now if you go to the location where the original image and changes files were, you will find two new files called "myPharo.image" and "myPharo.changes" that represent the working state of the Pharo image at the moment before you told Pharo to Save and quit. If you wish, you can move these two files anywhere that you like on your disk, but if you do so you may (depending on your operating system) need to also move, copy or link to the virtual machine and the *sources* file.

ⓘ   *Start up Pharo from the newly created "myPharo.image" file.*

Now you should find yourself in precisely the state you were when you quit Pharo. The BouncingAtomsMorph is there again and the atoms continue to bounce from where they were when you quit.

When you start Pharo for the first time, the Pharo virtual machine loads the image file that you provide. This file contains a snapshot of a large number of objects, including a vast amount of pre-existing code and a large number of programming tools (all of which are objects). As you work with Pharo, you will send messages to these objects, you will create new objects, and some of these objects will die and their memory will be reclaimed (*i.e.,* garbage-collected).

When you quit Pharo, you will normally save a snapshot that contains all of your objects. If you save normally, you will overwrite your old image file with the new snapshot. Alternatively, you may save the image under a new name, as we just did.

In addition to the *.image* file, there is also a *.changes* file. This file contains a log of all the changes to the source code that you have made using the standard tools. Most of the time you do not need to worry about this file at all. As we shall see, however, the *.changes* file can be very useful for recovering from errors, or replaying lost changes. More about this later!

The image that you have been working with is a descendant of the original Smalltalk-80 image created in the late 1970s. Some of these objects have been around for decades!

You might think that the image is the key mechanism for storing and managing software projects, but you would be wrong. As we shall see very soon, there are much better tools for managing code and sharing software developed by teams. Images are very useful, but you should learn to be very cavalier about creating and throwing away images, since tools like Monticello offer much better ways to manage versions and share code amongst developers.

☺ *Using the mouse (and the appropriate modifier keys), meta-click on the* Bounc-ingAtomsMorph.[5]

You will see a collection of colored circles that are collectively called the BouncingAtomsMorph's morphic halo. Each circle is called a *handle*. Click in the pink handle containing the cross; the BouncingAtomsMorph should go away.

1.5 Workspaces and Transcripts

☺ *Close all open windows. Open a transcript and a workspace. (The transcript can be opened from the* World ▷ Tools ... *submenu.)*

☺ *Position and resize the transcript and workspace windows so that the workspace just overlaps the transcript.*

You can resize windows either by dragging one of the corners, or by meta-clicking the window to bring up the morphic halo, and dragging the yellow (bottom right) handle.

At any time only one window is active; it is in front and has its border highlighted.

The transcript is an object that is often used for logging system messages. It is a kind of "system console".

Workspaces are useful for typing snippets of Smalltalk code that you would like to experiment with. You can also use workspaces simply for

---

[5]Remember, you may have to set the halosEnabled option in the Preferences Browser.

typing arbitrarily text that you would like to remember, such as to-do lists or instructions for anyone who will use your image. Workspaces are often used to hold documentation about a captured image, as is the case with the standard image that we downloaded earlier (see Figure 1.2).

⚠ *Type the following text into the workspace:*

Transcript show: 'hello world'; cr.

Try double-clicking in the workspace at various points in the text you have just typed. Notice how an entire word, entire string, or the whole text is selected, depending on whether you click within a word, at the end of the string, or at the end of the entire expression.

⚠ *Select the text you have typed and action-click. Select* do it (d) .

Notice how the text "hello world" appears in the transcript window (Figure 1.8). Do it again. (The (d) in the menu item do it (d) tells you that the keyboard shortcut to *do it* is CMD−d. More on this in the next section!)

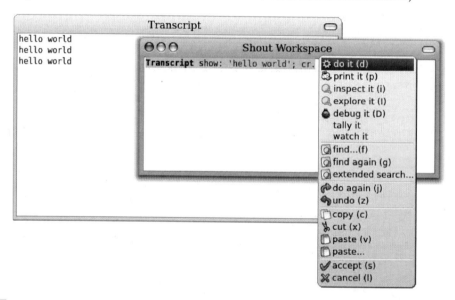

Figure 1.8: Overlapping windows. The workspace is active.

1.6   Keyboard shortcuts

If you want to evaluate an expression, you do not always have to action-click. Instead, you can use keyboard shortcuts. These are the parenthesized expressions in the menu. Depending on your platform, you may have to press one of the modifier keys (control, alt, command, or meta). (We will indicate these generically as CMD–*key*.)

⚉ *Evaluate the expression in the workspace again, but using the keyboard shortcut:* CMD–*d*.

In addition to do it, you will have noticed print it, inspect it and explore it. Let's have a quick look at each of these.

⚉ *Type the expression* 3 + 4 *into the workspace. Now* do it *with the keyboard shortcut.*

Do not be surprised if you saw nothing happen! What you just did is send the message + with argument 4 to the number 3. Normally the result 7 will have been computed and returned to you, but since the workspace did not know what to do with this answer, it simply threw the answer away. If you want to see the result, you should print it instead. print it actually compiles the expression, executes it, sends the message printString to the result, and displays the resulting string.

⚉ *Select* 3+4 *and* print it *(CMD–p).*

This time we see the result we expect (Figure 1.9).

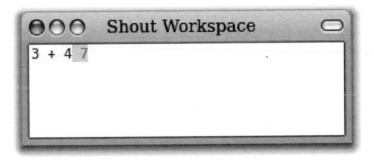

Figure 1.9: "Print it" rather than "do it".

3 + 4 $\longrightarrow$ 7

We use the notation $\longrightarrow$ as a convention in this book to indicate that a particular Pharo expression yields a given result when you print it.

⚉ *Delete the highlighted text "7" (Pharo should have selected it for you, so you can just press the delete key). Select* 3+4 *again and this time* inspect it *(CMD–i).*

Now you should see a new window, called an *inspector*, with the heading SmallInteger: 7 (Figure 1.10). The inspector is an extremely useful tool that will allow you to browse and interact with any object in the system. The title tells us that 7 is an instance of the class SmallInteger. The left panel allows us to browse the instance variables of an object, the values of which are shown in the right panel. The bottom panel can be used to write expressions to send messages to the object.

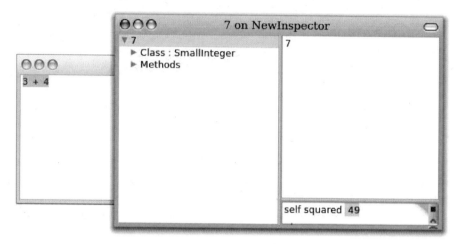

Figure 1.10: Inspecting an object.

(!) *Type* self squared *in the bottom panel of the inspector on* 7 *and* print it.

(!) *Close the inspector. Type the expression* Object *in a workspace and this time* explore it (CMD−*I, uppercased i*).

This time you should see a window labelled Object containing the text ▷ root: Object. Click on the triangle to open it up (Figure 1.11).

The explorer is similar to the inspector, but it offers a tree view of a complex object. In this case the object we are looking at is the Object class. We can see directly all the information stored in this class, and we can easily navigate to all its parts.

1.7   The Class Browser

The class browser[6] is one of the key tools used for programming. As we shall see, there are several interesting browsers available for Pharo, but this is the

---

[6]Confusingly, this is variously referred to as the "system browser" or the "code browser". Pharo uses the OmniBrowser implementation of the browser, which may also be variously known as "OB" or the "Package browser". In this book we will simply use the term "browser", or, in case of ambiguity, the "class browser".

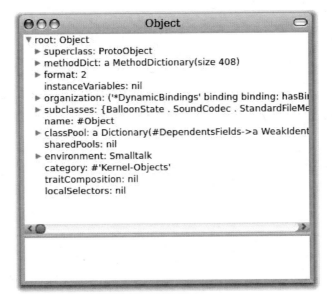

Figure 1.11: Exploring Object.

basic one you will find in any image.

⬤ *Open a browser by selecting* World ▷ Class browser .[7]

We can see a browser in Figure 1.12. The title bar indicates that we are browsing the class Object.

When the browser first opens, all panes are empty but the leftmost one. This first pane lists all known *packages*, which contain groups of related classes.

⬤ *Click on the* Kernel *package.*

This causes the second pane to show a list of all of the classes in the selected package.

⬤ *Select the class* Object.

Now the remaining two panes will be filled with text. The third pane displays the *protocols* of the currently selected class. These are convenient groupings of related methods. If no protocol is selected you should see all methods in the fourth pane.

⬤ *Select the* printing *protocol.*

---

[7]If the browser you get does not look like the one shown in Figure 1.12, then you may need to change the default browser. See FAQ 5, p. 316.

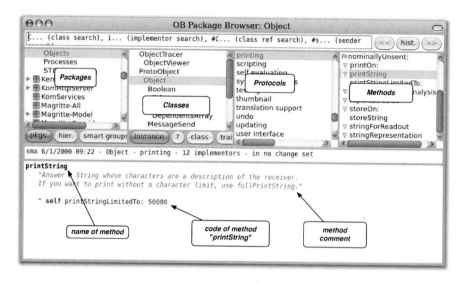

Figure 1.12: The browser showing the printString method of class object.

You may have to scroll down to find it. Now you will see in the fourth pane only methods related to printing.

Select the printString *method.*

Now we see in the bottom pane the source code of the printString method, shared by all objects in the system (except those that override it).

1.8 Finding classes

There are several ways to find a class in Pharo. The first, as we have just seen above, is to know (or guess) what category it is in, and to navigate to it using the browser.

A second way is to send the browse message to the class, asking it to open a browser on itself. Suppose we want to browse the class Boolean.

Type Boolean browse *into a workspace and* do it.

A browser will open on the Boolean class (Figure 1.13). There is also a keyboard shortcut CMD−b (browse) that you can use in any tool where you find a class name; select the name and type CMD−b.

Use the keyboard shortcut to browse the class Boolean.

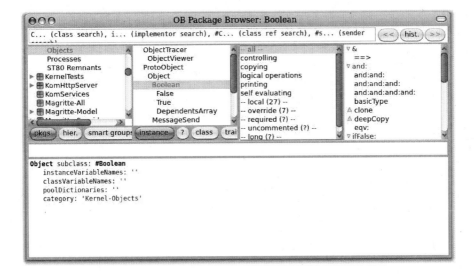

Figure 1.13: The browser showing the definition of class Boolean.

Notice that when the Boolean class is selected but no protocol or method is selected, instead of the source code of a method, we see a *class definition* (Figure 1.13). This is nothing more than an ordinary Smalltalk message that is sent to the parent class, asking it to create a subclass. Here we see that the class Object is being asked to create a subclass named Boolean with no instance variables, class variables or "pool dictionaries", and to put the class Boolean in the *Kernel-Objects* category. If you click on the ? at the bottom of the class pane, you can see the class comment in a dedicated pane (see Figure 1.14).

Often, the fastest way to find a class is to search for it by name. For example, suppose that you are looking for some unknown class that represents dates and times.

Put the mouse in the package pane of the browser and type CMD–f, *or select* find class ... (f) *by action-clicking. Type "time" in the dialog box and accept it.*

You will be presented with a list of classes whose names contain "time" (see Figure 1.15). Choose one, say, Time, and the browser will show it, along with a class comment that suggests other classes that might be useful. If you want to browse one of the others, select its name (in any text pane), and type CMD–b.

Note that if you type the complete (and correctly capitalized) name of a class in the find dialog, the browser will go directly to that class without showing you the list of options.

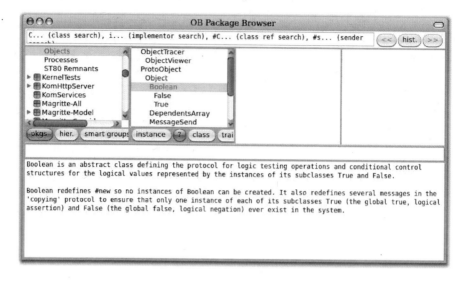

Figure 1.14: The class comment for Boolean.

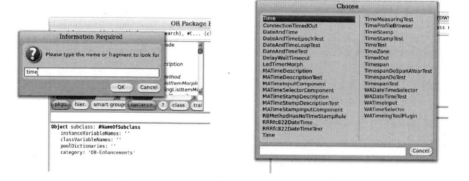

Figure 1.15: Searching for a class by name.

1.9 Finding methods

Sometimes you can guess the name of a method, or at least part of the name
of a method, more easily than the name of a class. For example, if you are
interested in the current time, you might expect that there would be a method
called "now", or containing "now" as a substring. But where might it be?
The *method finder* can help you.

(icon) *Select* World ▷ Tools ... ▷ Method finder . *Type "now" in the top left pane, and*
accept *it (or just press the* RETURN *key).*

The method finder will display a list of all the method names that contain the substring "now". To scroll to now itself, move the cursor to the list and type "n"; this trick works in all scrolling windows. Select "now" and the right-hand pane shows you the classes that define a method with this name, as shown in Figure 1.16. Selecting any one of them will open a browser on it.

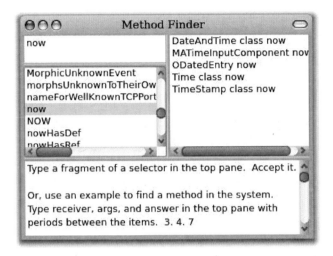

Figure 1.16: The method finder showing all classes defining a method named now.

At other times you may have a good idea that a method exists, but will have no idea what it might be called. The method finder can still help! For example, suppose that you would like to find a method that turns a string into upper case, for example, it would translate 'eureka' into 'EUREKA'.

Type 'eureka' . 'EUREKA' *into the method finder and press the* RETURN *key, as shown in Figure 1.17.*

The method finder will suggest a method that does what you want.[8]

An asterisk at the beginning of a line in the right pane of the method finder indicates that this method is the one that was actually used to obtain the requested result. So, the asterisk in front of String asUppercase lets us know that the method asUppercase defined on the class String was executed and returned the result we wanted. The methods that do not have an asterisk are just the other methods that have the same name as the ones that returned the expected result. So Character»asUppercase was not executed on our example, because 'eureka' is not a Character object.

You can also use the method finder for methods with arguments; for

---

[8]If a window pops up with a warning about a deprecated method, don't panic — the method finder is simply trying out all likely candidates, including deprecated methods. Just click Proceed.

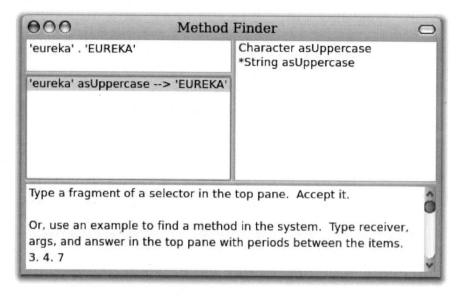

Figure 1.17: Finding a method by example.

example, if you are looking for a method that will find the greatest common factor of two integers, you might try 25. 35. 5 as an example. You can also give the method finder multiple examples to narrow the search space; the help text in the bottom pane explains how.

1.10 Defining a new method

The advent of Test Driven Development[9] (TDD) has changed the way that we write code. The idea behind TDD is that we write a test that defines the desired behaviour of our code *before* we write the code itself. Only then do we write the code that satisfies the test.

Suppose that our assignment is to write a method that "says something loudly and with emphasis". What exactly could that mean? What would be a good name for such a method? How can we make sure that programmers who may have to maintain our method in the future have an unambiguous description of what it should do? We can answer all of these questions by giving an example:

When we send the message shout to the string "Don't panic" the result should be "DON'T PANIC!".

[9]Kent Beck, *Test Driven Development: By Example.* Addison-Wesley, 2003, ISBN 0–321–14653–0.

To make this example into something that the system can use, we turn it into a test method:

Method 1.1: *A test for a shout method*

```
testShout
    self assert: ('Don''t panic' shout = 'DON''T PANIC!')
```

How do we create a new method in Pharo? First, we have to decide which class the method should belong to. In this case, the shout method that we are testing will go in class String, so the corresponding test will, by convention, go in a class called StringTest.

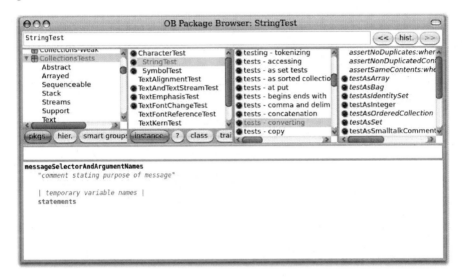

Figure 1.18: The new method template in class StringTest.

Open a browser on the class StringTest, *and select an appropriate protocol for our method, in this case* tests - converting*, as shown in Figure 1.18. The highlighted text in the bottom pane is a template that reminds you what a Smalltalk method looks like. Delete this and enter the code from method 1.1.*

Once you have typed the text into the browser, notice that the bottom pane is outlined in red. This is a reminder that the pane contains unsaved changes. So select accept (s) by action-clicking in the bottom pane, or just type CMD−s, to compile and save your method.

If this is the first time you have accepted any code in your image, you will likely be prompted to enter your name. Since many people have contributed code to the image, it is important to keep track of everyone who creates or modifies methods. Simply enter your first and last names, without any spaces, or separated by a dot.

Because there is as yet no method called shout, the browser will ask you to confirm that this is the name that you really want — and it will suggest some other names that you might have intended (Figure 1.20). This can be quite useful if you have merely made a typing mistake, but in this case, we really *do* mean shout, since that is the method we are about to create, so we have to confirm this by selecting the first option from the menu of choices, as shown in Figure 1.20.

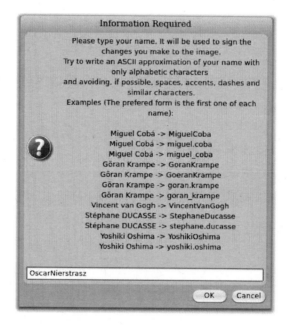

Figure 1.19: Entering your name.

ⓘ *Run your newly created test: open the SUnit TestRunner from the* World *menu.*

The leftmost two panes are a bit like the top panes in the browser. The left pane contains a list of categories, but it's restricted to those categories that contain test classes.

ⓘ *Select* CollectionsTests-Text *and the pane to the right will show all of the test classes in that category, which includes the class* StringTest. *The names of the classes are already selected, so click* Run Selected *to run all these tests.*

You should see a message like that shown in Figure 1.21, which indicates that there was an error in running the tests. The list of tests that gave rise to errors is shown in the bottom right pane; as you can see, StringTest»#testShout is the culprit. (Note that StringTest>>#testShout is the Smalltalk way of identifying the testShout method of the StringTest class.) If you click on that line of text, the

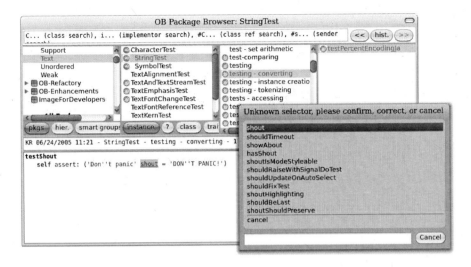

Figure 1.20: Accepting the StringTest method testShout.

erroneous test will run again, this time in such a way that you see the error happen: "MessageNotUnderstood: ByteString»shout".

The window that opens with the error message is the Smalltalk debugger (see Figure 1.22). We will look at the debugger and how to use it in Chapter 6.

The error is, of course, exactly what we expected: running the test generates an error because we haven't yet written a method that tells strings how to shout. Nevertheless, it's good practice to make sure that the test fails because this confirms that we have set up the testing machinery correctly and that the new test is actually being run. Once you have seen the error, you can Abandon the running test, which will close the debugger window. Note that often with Smalltalk you can define the missing method using the Create button, edit the newly-created method in the debugger, and then Proceed with the test.

Now let's define the method that will make the test succeed!

(!) *Select class* String *in the browser, select the* converting *protocol, type the text in method 1.2 over the method creation template, and* accept *it. (Note: to get a ↑, type ^).*

Method 1.2: *The shout method*

```
shout
    ↑ self asUppercase, '!'
```

The comma is the string concatenation operation, so the body of this method appends an exclamation mark to an upper-case version of whatever

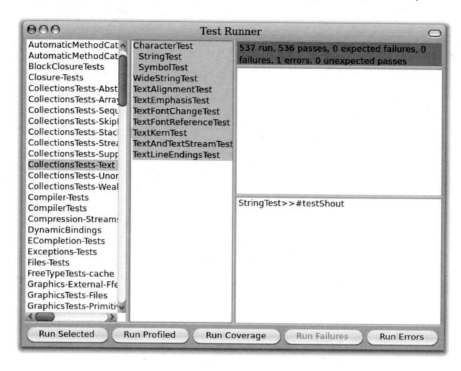

Figure 1.21: Running the String tests.

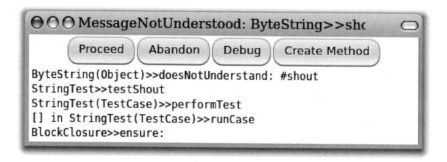

Figure 1.22: The (pre-)debugger.

String object the shout message was sent to. The ↑ tells Pharo that the expression that follows is the answer to be returned from the method, in this case the new concatenated string.

Does this method work? Let's run the tests and see.

(!) *Click on* Run Selected *again in the test runner, and this time you should see a green bar and text indicating that all of the tests ran with no failures and no errors.*

When you get to a green bar[10], it's a good idea to save your work and take a break. So do that right now!

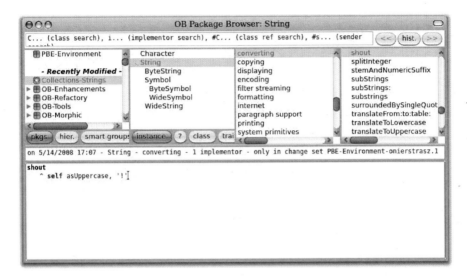

Figure 1.23: The shout method defined on class String.

1.11   Chapter summary

This chapter has introduced you to the Pharo environment and shown you how to use some of the major tools, such as the browser, the method finder, and the test runner. You have also seen a little of Pharo's syntax, even though you may not understand it all yet.

- A running Pharo system consists of a *virtual machine*, a *sources* file, and *image* and *changes* files. Only these last two change, as they record a snapshot of the running system.

- When you restore a Pharo image, you will find yourself in exactly the same state — with the same running objects — that you had when you last saved that image.

- Pharo is designed to work with a three-button mouse to click, action-click or meta-click. If you don't have a three-button mouse, you can use modifier keys to obtain the same effect.

- You click on the Pharo background to bring up the *World menu* and launch various tools.

- A *workspace* is a tool for writing and evaluating snippets of code. You can also use it to store arbitrary text.

- You can use keyboard shortcuts on text in the workspace, or any other tool, to evaluate code. The most important of these are do it (CMD–d), print it (CMD–p), inspect it (CMD–i), explore it (CMD–I) and browse it (CMD–b).

- The *browser* is the main tool for browsing Pharo code, and for developing new code.

- The *test runner* is a tool for running unit tests. It also supports Test Driven Development.

Chapter 2

A first application

In this chapter, we will develop a simple game: Lights Out.[1] Along the way we will demonstrate most of the tools that Pharo programmers use to construct and debug their programs, and show how programs are exchanged with other developers. We will see the browser, the object inspector, the debugger and the Monticello package browser. Development in Smalltalk is efficient: you will find that you spend far more time actually writing code and far less managing the development process. This is partly because the Smalltalk language is very simple, and partly because the tools that make up the programming environment are very well integrated with the language.

2.1 The Lights Out game

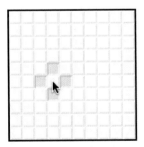

Figure 2.1: The Lights Out game board. The user has just clicked the mouse as shown by the cursor.

To show you how to use Pharo's programming tools, we will build a simple game called *Lights Out*. The game board is shown in Figure 2.1; it

---

[1] http://en.wikipedia.org/wiki/Lights_Out_(game)

consists of rectangular array of light yellow *cells*. When you click on one of the cells with the mouse, the four surrounding cells turn blue. Click again, and they toggle back to light yellow. The object of the game is to turn blue as many cells as possible.

The Lights Out game shown in Figure 2.1 is made up of two kinds of objects: the game board itself, and 100 individual cell objects. The Pharo code to implement the game will contain two classes: one for the game and one for the cells. We will now show you how to define these classes using the Pharo programming tools.

2.2 Creating a new Package

We have already seen the browser in Chapter 1, where we learned how to navigate to classes and methods, and saw how to define new methods. Now we will see how to create packages, categories and classes.

Open a browser and action-click in the package pane. Select create package .[2]

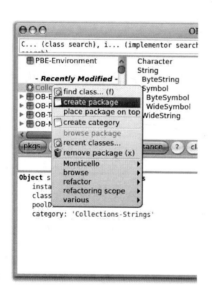

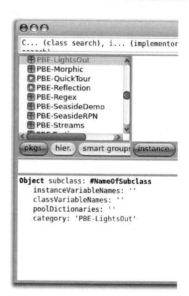

Figure 2.2: Adding a package.   Figure 2.3: The class template.

Type the name of the new package (we will use *PBE-LightsOut*) in the dialog box and click accept (or just press the return key); the new package is created,

---

[2]We are assuming that the Package Browser is installed as the default browser, which should normally be the case. If the browser you get does not look like the one shown in Figure 2.2, then you may need to change the default browser. See FAQ 5, p. 316.

and positioned alphabetically in the list of packages.

2.3 Defining the class LOCell

As yet there are of course no classes in the new package. However, the main editing pane displays a template to make it easy to create a new class (see Figure 2.3).

This template shows us a Smalltalk expression that sends a message to a class called Object, asking it to create a subclass called NameOfSubClass. The new class has no variables, and should belong to the category *PBE-LightsOut*.

On Categories and Packages

Historically, Smalltalk only knows about *categories*, not packages. You may well ask, what is the difference? A category is simply a collection of related classes in a Smalltalk image. A *package* is a collection of related classes *and extension methods* that may be versioned using the Monticello versioning tool. By convention, package names and category names are the same. For most purposes we do not care about the difference, but we will be careful to use the correct terminology in this book since there are points where the difference is crucial. We will learn more when we start working with Monticello.

Creating a new class

We simply modify the template to create the class that we really want.

(✏) *Modify the class creation template as follows:*

- Replace Object by SimpleSwitchMorph.

- Replace NameOfSubClass by LOCell.

- Add mouseAction to the list of instance variables.

The result should look like class 2.1.

Class 2.1: *Defining the class* LOCell

```
SimpleSwitchMorph subclass: #LOCell
    instanceVariableNames: 'mouseAction'
    classVariableNames: ''
    poolDictionaries: ''
    category: 'PBE-LightsOut'
```

This new definition consists of a Smalltalk expression that sends a message to the existing class SimpleSwitchMorph, asking it to create a subclass called LOCell. (Actually, since LOCell does not exist yet, we passed as an argument the *symbol* #LOCell which stands for the name of the class to create.) We also tell it that instances of the new class should have a mouseAction instance variable, which we will use to define what action the cell should take if the mouse should click over it.

At this point you still have not created anything. Note that the border of the class template pane has changed to red (Figure 2.4). This means that there are *unsaved changes.* To actually send this message, you must accept it.

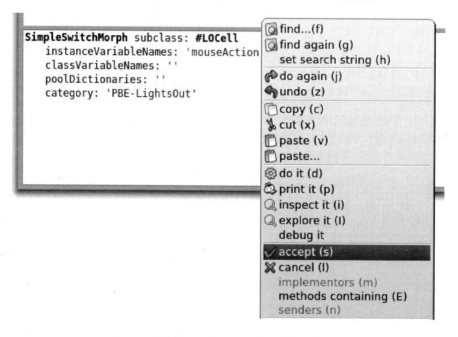

Figure 2.4: The class-creation Template.

🕹 *Accept the new class definition.*

Either action-click and select accept, or use the shortcut CMD−s (for "save"). The message will be sent to SimpleSwitchMorph, which will cause the new class to be compiled.

Once the class definition is accepted, the class will be created and appear in the classes pane of the browser (Figure 2.5). The editing pane now shows the class definition, and a small pane below it will remind you to write a few words describing the purpose of the class. This is called a *class comment,* and it is quite important to write one that will give other programmers a high-level overview of the purpose of this class. Smalltalkers put a very high value on the readability of their code, and detailed comments in methods are unusual: the philosophy is that the code should speak for itself. (If it doesn't, you should refactor it until it does!) A class comment need not contain a detailed description of the class, but a few words describing its overall purpose are vital if programmers who come after you are to know whether to spend time looking at this class.

Type a class comment for LOCell *and accept it; you can always improve it later.*

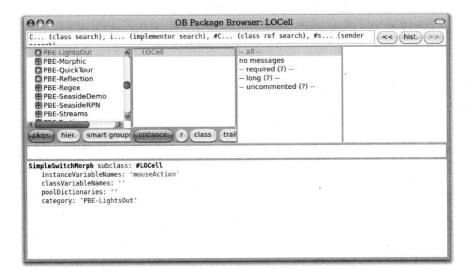

Figure 2.5: The newly-created class LOCell

2.4 Adding methods to a class

Now let's add some methods to our class.

Select the protocol --all-- *in the protocol pane.*

You will see a template for method creation in the editing pane. Select it, and replace it by the text of method 2.2.

Method 2.2: *Initializing instances of* LOCell

```
1   initialize
2      super initialize.
3      self label: ''.
4      self borderWidth: 2.
5      bounds := 0@0 corner: 16@16.
6      offColor := Color paleYellow.
7      onColor := Color paleBlue darker.
8      self useSquareCorners.
9      self turnOff
```

Note that the characters " on line 3 are two separate single quotes with nothing between them, not a double quote! " denotes the empty string.

(☝) Accept *this method definition.*

What does the above code do? We won't go into all of the details here (that's what the rest of the book is for!), but we will give you a quick preview. Let's take it line by line.

Notice that the method is called initialize. The name is very significant! By convention, if a class defines a method named initialize, it will be called right after the object is created. So, when we evaluate LOCell new, the message initialize will be sent automatically to this newly created object. Initialize methods are used to set up the state of objects, typically to set their instance variables; this is exactly what we are doing here.

The first thing that this method does (line 2) is to execute the initialize method of its superclass, SimpleSwitchMorph. The idea here is that any inherited state will be properly initialized by the initialize method of the superclass. It is always a good idea to initialize inherited state by sending super initialize before doing anything else; we don't know exactly what SimpleSwitchMorph's initialize method will do, and we don't care, but it's a fair bet that it will set up some instance variables to hold reasonable default values, so we had better call it, or we risk starting in an unclean state.

The rest of the method sets up the state of this object. Sending self label: '', for example, sets the label of this object to the empty string.

The expression 0@0 corner: 16@16 probably needs some explanation. 0@0 represents a Point object with x and y coordinates both set to 0. In fact, 0 @0 sends the message @ to the number 0 with argument 0. The effect will be that the number 0 will ask the Point class to create a new instance with coordinates (0,0). Now we send this newly created point the message corner: 16@16, which causes it to create a Rectangle with corners 0@0 and 16@16. This newly created rectangle will be assigned to the bounds variable, inherited from the superclass.

Note that the origin of the Pharo screen is the *top left*, and the y coordinate increases *downwards.*

The rest of the method should be self-explanatory. Part of the art of writing good Smalltalk code is to pick good method names so that Smalltalk code can be read like a kind of pidgin English. You should be able to imagine the object talking to itself and saying "Self use square corners!", "Self turn off!".

2.5 Inspecting an object

You can test the effect of the code you have written by creating a new LOCell object and inspecting it.

(✏) *Open a workspace. Type the expression* LOCell new *and* inspect it .

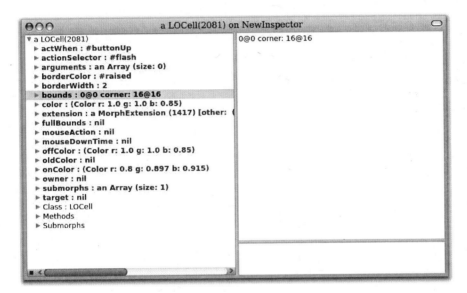

Figure 2.6: The inspector used to examine a LOCell object.

The left-hand pane of the inspector shows a list of instance variables; if you select one (try bounds), the value of the instance variable is shown in the right pane.

The bottom pane of the inspector is a mini-workspace. It's useful because in this workspace the pseudo-variable self is bound to the object selected.

(✏) *Select the LOCell at the root of the inspector window. Type the text* self bounds: (200@200 corner: 250@250) *in the bottom pane and* do it . *The* bounds *variable should change in the inspector. Now type the text* self openInWorld *in the mini-workspace and* do it .

The cell should appear near the top left-hand corner of the screen, indeed, exactly where its bounds say that it should appear. meta-click on the cell to bring up the morphic halo. Move the cell with the brown (next to top-right) handle and resize it with the yellow (bottom-right) handle. Notice how the bounds reported by the inspector also change. (You may have to action-click refresh to see the new bounds value.)

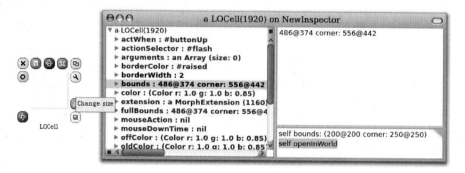

Figure 2.7: Resizing the cell.

Delete the cell by clicking on the x *in the pink handle.*

2.6 Defining the class LOGame

Now let's create the other class that we need for the game, which we will call LOGame.

Make the class definition template visible in the browser main window.

Do this by clicking on the package name. Edit the code so that it reads as follows, and accept it.

Class 2.3: *Defining the* LOGame *class*

```
BorderedMorph subclass: #LOGame
   instanceVariableNames: ''
   classVariableNames: ''
   poolDictionaries: ''
   category: 'PBE-LightsOut'
```

Here we subclass BorderedMorph; Morph is the superclass of all of the graphical shapes in Pharo, and (surprise!) a BorderedMorph is a Morph with a border. We could also insert the names of the instance variables between the quotes on the second line, but for now, let's just leave that list empty.

Now let's define an initialize method for LOGame.

(!) *Type the following into the browser as a method for* LOGame *and try to* accept *it:*

Method 2.4: *Initializing the game*

```
1   initialize
2      | sampleCell width height n |
3      super initialize.
4      n := self cellsPerSide.
5      sampleCell := LOCell new.
6      width := sampleCell width.
7      height := sampleCell height.
8      self bounds: (5@5 extent: ((width*n) @(height*n)) + (2 * self borderWidth)).
9      cells := Matrix new: n tabulate: [ :i :j | self newCellAt: i at: j ].
```

Pharo will complain that it doesn't know the meaning of some of the terms. Pharo tells you that it doesn't know of a message cellsPerSide, and suggests a number of corrections, in case it was a spelling mistake.

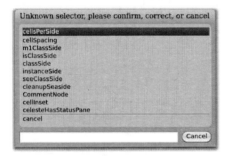

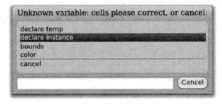

Figure 2.9: Declaring a new instance variable.

Figure 2.8: Pharo detecting an unknown selector.

But cellsPerSide is not a mistake — it is just a method that we haven't yet defined — we will do so in a minute or two.

(!) *So just select the first item from the menu, which confirms that we really meant* cellsPerSide.

Next, Pharo will complain that it doesn't know the meaning of cells. It offers you a number of ways of fixing this.

(!) *Choose* declare instance *because we want* cells *to be an instance variable.*

Finally, Pharo will complain about the message newCellAt:at: sent on the last line; this is also not a mistake, so confirm that message too.

If you now look at the class definition once again (which you can do by clicking on the [instance] button), you will see that the browser has modified it to include the instance variable cells.

Let's look at this initialize method. The line | sampleCell width height n | declares 4 temporary variables. They are called temporary variables because their scope and lifetime are limited to this method. Temporary variables with explanatory names are helpful in making code more readable. Smalltalk has no special syntax to distinguish constants and variables, and in fact all four of these "variables" are really constants. Lines 4–7 define these constants.

How big should our game board be? Big enough to hold some integral number of cells, and big enough to draw a border around them. How many cells is the right number? 5? 10? 100? We don't know yet, and if we did, we would probably change our minds later. So we delegate the responsibility for knowing that number to another method, which we will call cellsPerSide, and which we will write in a minute or two. It's because we are sending the cellsPerSide message before we define a method with that name that Pharo asked us to "confirm, correct, or cancel" when we accepted the method body for initialize. Don't be put off by this: it is actually good practice to write in terms of other methods that we haven't yet defined. Why? Well, it wasn't until we started writing the initialize method that we realized that we needed it, and at that point, we can give it a meaningful name, and move on, without interrupting our flow.

The fourth line uses this method: the Smalltalk self cellsPerSide sends the message cellsPerSide to self, i.e., to this very object. The response, which will be the number of cells per side of the game board, is assigned to n.

The next three lines create a new LOCell object, and assign its width and height to the appropriate temporary variables.

Line 8 sets the bounds of the new object. Without worrying too much about the details just yet, just believe us that the expression in parentheses creates a square with its origin (*i.e.*, its top-left corner) at the point (5,5) and its bottom-right corner far enough away to allow space for the right number of cells.

The last line sets the LOGame object's instance variable cells to a newly created Matrix with the right number of rows and columns. We do this by sending the message new:tabulate: to the Matrix class (classes are objects too, so we can send them messages). We know that new:tabulate: takes two arguments because it has two colons (:) in its name. The arguments go right after the colons. If you are used to languages that put all of the arguments together inside parentheses, this may seem weird at first. Don't panic, it's only syntax! It turns out to be a very good syntax because the name of the method can be used to explain the roles of the arguments. For example, it is pretty clear that Matrix rows: 5 columns: 2 has 5 rows and 2 columns, and not 2 rows and 5 columns.

Matrix new: n tabulate: [:i :j | self newCellAt: i at: j] creates a new n×n matrix and initializes its elements. The initial value of each element will depend on its coordinates. The (i,j)th element will be initialized to the result of evaluating self newCellAt: i at: j.

2.7   Organizing methods into protocols

Before we define any more methods, let's take a quick look at the third pane at the top of the browser. In the same way that the first pane of the browser lets us categorize classes into packages so we are not overwhelmed by a very long list of class names in the second pane, so the third pane lets us categorize methods so that we are not overwhelmed by a very long list of method names in the fourth pane. These categories of methods are called "protocols".

If there are only a few methods in a class, the extra level of hierarchy provided by protocols is not really necessary. This is why the browser also offers us the *--all--* virtual protocol, which, you will not be surprised to learn, contains all of the methods in the class.

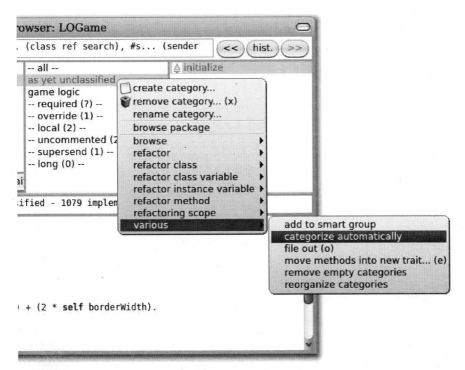

Figure 2.10: Automatically categorize all uncategorized methods.

If you have followed along with this example, the third pane may well contain the protocol *as yet unclassified*.

🔔 *Action-click in the protocol pane and select* various ▷ categorize automatically *to fix this, and move the* initialize *methods to a new protocol called* initialization.

How does Pharo know that this is the right protocol? Well, in general Pharo can't know, but in this case there is also an initialize method in a superclass, and Pharo assumes that our initialize method should go in the same category as the one that it overrides.

A typographic convention. Smalltalkers frequently use the notation ">>" to identify the class to which a method belongs, so, for example, the cellsPerSide method in class LOGame would be referred to as LOGame>> cellsPerSide. To indicate that this is *not* Smalltalk syntax, we will use the special symbol » instead, so this method will appear in the text as LOGame» cellsPerSide

From now on, when we show a method in this book, we will write the name of the method in this form. Of course, when you actually type the code into the browser, you don't have to type the class name or the »; instead, you just make sure that the appropriate class is selected in the class pane.

Now let's define the other two methods that are used by the LOGame» initialize method. Both of them can go in the *initialization* protocol.

Method 2.5: *A constant method.*

```
LOGame»cellsPerSide
  "The number of cells along each side of the game"
  ↑ 10
```

This method could hardly be simpler: it answers the constant 10. One advantage of representing constants as methods is that if the program evolves so that the constant then depends on some other features, the method can be changed to calculate this value.

Method 2.6: *An initialization helper method*

```
LOGame»newCellAt: i at: j
  "Create a cell for position (i,j) and add it to my on–screen
  representation at the appropriate screen position.  Answer the new cell"
  | c origin |
  c := LOCell new.
  origin := self innerBounds origin.
  self addMorph: c.
  c position: ((i – 1) * c width) @ ((j – 1) * c height) + origin.
  c mouseAction: [self toggleNeighboursOfCellAt: i at: j]
```

☝ *Add the methods* LOGame»cellsPerSide *and* LOGame»newCellAt:at:.

Confirm the spelling of the new selectors toggleNeighboursOfCellAt:at: and mouseAction:.

Method 2.6 answers a new LOCell, specialized to position (i, j) in the Matrix of cells. The last line defines the new cell's mouseAction to be the *block* [self toggleNeighboursOfCellAt: i at: j]. In effect, this defines the callback behaviour to perform when the mouse is clicked. The corresponding method also needs to be defined.

Method 2.7: *The callback method*

```
LOGame»toggleNeighboursOfCellAt: i at: j
    (i > 1) ifTrue: [ (cells at: i – 1 at: j ) toggleState].
    (i < self cellsPerSide) ifTrue: [ (cells at: i + 1 at: j) toggleState].
    (j > 1) ifTrue: [ (cells at: i  at: j – 1) toggleState].
    (j < self cellsPerSide) ifTrue: [ (cells at: i at: j + 1) toggleState].
```

Method 2.7 toggles the state of the four cells to the north, south, west and east of cell (i, j). The only complication is that the board is finite, so we have to make sure that a neighboring cell exists before we toggle its state.

☝ *Place this method in a new protocol called* game logic. *(Action-click in the protocol pane to add a new protocol.)*

To move the method, you can simply click on its name and drag it to the newly-created protocol (Figure 2.11).

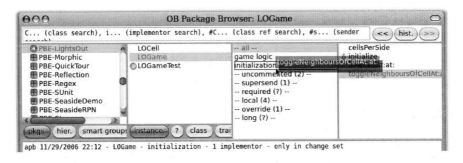

Figure 2.11: Drag a method to a protocol.

To complete the Lights Out game, we need to define two more methods in class LOCell to handle mouse events.

Method 2.8: *A typical setter method*

```
LOCell»mouseAction: aBlock
    ↑ mouseAction := aBlock
```

Method 2.8 does nothing more than set the cell's mouseAction variable to the argument, and then answers the new value. Any method that *changes* the value of an instance variable in this way is called a *setter method*; a method that *answers* the current value of an instance variable is called a *getter method*.

If you are used to getters and setters in other programming languages, you might expect these methods to be called setmouseAction and getmouseAction. The Smalltalk convention is different. A getter always has the same name as the variable it gets, and a setter is named similarly, but with a trailing ":", hence mouseAction and mouseAction:.

Collectively, setters and getters are called *accessor* methods, and by convention they should be placed in the *accessing* protocol. In Smalltalk, *all* instance variables are private to the object that owns them, so the only way for another object to read or write those variables in the Smalltalk language is through accessor methods like this one[3].

✒ *Go to the class* LOCell, *define* LOCell»mouseAction: *and put it in the* accessing *protocol.*

Finally, we need to define a method mouseUp:; this will be called automatically by the GUI framework if the mouse button is released while the mouse is over this cell on the screen.

Method 2.9: *An event handler*

```
LOCell»mouseUp: anEvent
  mouseAction value
```

✒ *Add the method* LOCell»mouseUp: *and then* categorize automatically *methods.*

What this method does is to send the message value to the object stored in the instance variable mouseAction. Recall that in LOGame»newCellAt: i at: j we assigned the following code fragment to mouseAction:

```
[self toggleNeighboursOfCellAt: i at: j ]
```

Sending the value message causes this code fragment to be evaluated, and consequently the state of the cells will toggle.

2.8   Let's try our code

That's it: the Lights Out game is complete!

If you have followed all of the steps, you should be able to play the game, consisting of just 2 classes and 7 methods.

---

[3]In fact, the instance variables can be accessed in subclasses too.

🕭 *In a workspace, type* LOGame new openInWorld *and* do it.

The game will open, and you should be able to click on the cells and see how it works.

Well, so much for theory... When you click on a cell, a *notifier* window called the PreDebugWindow window appears with an error message! As depicted in Figure 2.12, it says MessageNotUnderstood: LOGame»toggleState.

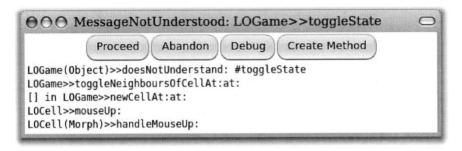

Figure 2.12: There is a bug in our game when a cell is clicked!

What happened? To find out, let's use one of Smalltalk's more powerful tools: the debugger.

🕭 *Click on the* debug *button in the notifer window.*

The debugger will appear. In the upper part of the debugger window you can see the execution stack, showing all the active methods; selecting any one of them will show, in the middle pane, the Smalltalk code being executed in that method, with the part that triggered the error highlighted.

🕭 *Click on the line labelled* LOGame»toggleNeighboursOfCellAt:at: *(near the top).*

The debugger will show you the execution context within this method where the error occurred (Figure 2.13).

At the bottom of the debugger are two small inspector windows. On the left, you can inspect the object that is the receiver of the message that caused the selected method to execute, so you can look here to see the values of the instance variables. On the right you can inspect an object that represents the currently executing method itself, so you can look here to see the values of the method's parameters and temporary variables.

Using the debugger, you can execute code step by step, inspect objects in parameters and local variables, evaluate code just as you can in a workspace, and, most surprisingly to those used to other debuggers, change the code while it is being debugged! Some Smalltalkers program in the debugger almost all the time, rather than in the browser. The advantage of this is that

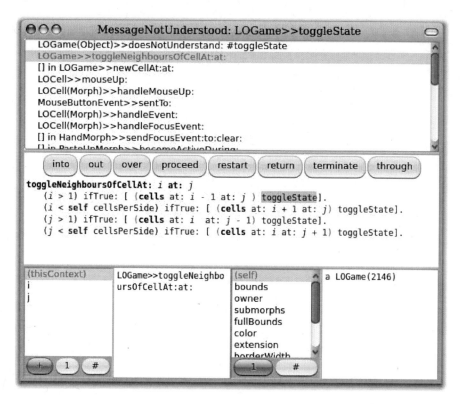

Figure 2.13: The debugger, with the method toggleNeighboursOfCell:at: selected.

you see the method that you are writing as it will be executed, with real parameters in the actual execution context.

In this case we can see in the first line of the top panel that the toggleState message has been sent to an instance of LOGame, while it should clearly have been an instance of LOCell. The problem is most likely with the initialization of the cells matrix. Browsing the code of LOGame»initialize shows that cells is filled with the return values of newCellAt:at:, but when we look at that method, we see that there is no return statement there! By default, a method returns self, which in the case of newCellAt:at: is indeed an instance of LOGame.

Ⓓ   *Close the debugger window. Add the expression "↑ c" to the end of the method* LOGame»newCellAt:at: *so that it returns c. (See method 2.10.)*

Method 2.10: *Fixing the bug.*

```
LOGame»newCellAt: i at: j
  "Create a cell for position (i,j) and add it to my on-screen
  representation at the appropriate screen position.  Answer the new cell"
```

```
| c origin |
c := LOCell new.
origin := self innerBounds origin.
self addMorph: c.
c position: ((i – 1) * c width) @ ((j – 1) * c height) + origin.
c mouseAction: [self toggleNeighboursOfCellAt: i at: j].
↑ c
```

Recall from Chapter 1 that the construct to return a value from a method in Smalltalk is ↑, which you obtain by typing ^.

Often, you can fix the code directly in the debugger window and click Proceed to continue running the application. In our case, because the bug was in the initialization of an object, rather than in the method that failed, the easiest thing to do is to close the debugger window, destroy the running instance of the game (with the halo), and create a new one.

(!) *Do:* LOGame new openInWorld *again.*

Now the game should work properly ... or nearly so. If we happen to move the mouse between clicking and releasing, then the cell the mouse is over will also be toggled. This turns out to be behavior that we inherit from SimpleSwitchMorph. We can fix this simply by overriding mouseMove: to do nothing:

Method 2.11: *Overriding mouse move actions.*

LOGame»mouseMove: anEvent

Finally we are done!

2.9   Saving and sharing Smalltalk code

Now that you have the Lights Out game working, you probably want to save it somewhere so that you can share it with your friends. Of course, you can save your whole Pharo image, and show off your first program by running it, but your friends probably have their own code in their images, and don't want to give that up to use your image. What you need is a way of getting source code out of your Pharo image so that other programmers can bring it into theirs.

The simplest way of doing this is by *filing out* the code. The action-click menu in the Package pane will give you the option to various ▷ file out the whole of package *PBE-LightsOut*. The resulting file is more or less human readable, but is really intended for computers, not humans. You can email this file to your friends, and they can file it into their own Pharo images using the file list browser.

(!) *Action-click on the* PBE-LightsOut *package and* various ▷ file out *the contents.*

You should now find a file called "PBE-LightsOut.st" in the same folder on disk where your image is saved. Have a look at this file with a text editor.

(!) *Open a fresh Pharo image and use the File Browser tool* (Tools ... ▷ File Browser) *to* file in *the PBE-LightsOut.st fileout. Verify that the game now works in the new image.*

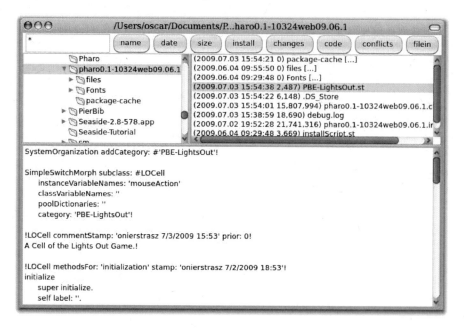

Figure 2.14: Filing in Pharo source code.

Monticello packages

Although fileouts are a convenient way of making a snapshot of the code you have written, they are decidedly "old school". Just as most open-source projects find it much more convenient to maintain their code in a repository using CVS[4] or Subversion[5], so Pharo programmers find it more convenient to manage their code using Monticello packages. These packages are represented as files with names ending in .mcz; they are actually zip-compressed bundles that contain the complete code of your package.

Using the Monticello package browser, you can save packages to repositories on various types of server, including FTP and HTTP servers; you can

---

[4]http://www.nongnu.org/cvs
[5]http://subversion.tigris.org

also just write the packages to a repository in a local file system directory. A copy of your package is also always cached on your local hard-disk in the *package-cache* folder. Monticello lets you save multiple versions of your program, merge versions, go back to an old version, and browse the differences between versions. In fact, Monticello is a distributed revision control system; this means it allows developers to save their work on different places, not on a single repository as it is the case with CVS or Subversion.

You can also send a .mcz file by email. The recipient will have to place it in her *package-cache* folder; she will then be able to use Monticello to browse and load it.

Open the Monticello browser from the World menu.

In the right-hand pane of the browser (see Figure 2.15) is a list of Monticello repositories, which will include all of the repositories from which code has been loaded into the image that you are using.

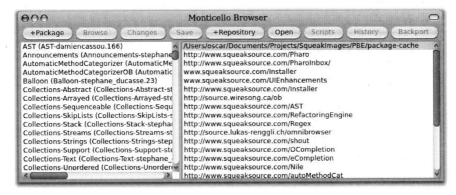

Figure 2.15: The Monticello browser.

At the top of the list in the Monticello browser is a repository in a local directory called the *package cache*, which caches copies of the packages that you have loaded or published over the network. This local cache is really handy because it lets you keep your own local history; it also allows you to work in places where you do not have internet access, or where access is slow enough that you do not want to save to a remote repository very frequently.

Saving and loading code with Monticello.

On the left-hand side of the Monticello browser is a list of packages that have a version loaded into the image; packages that have been modified since they were loaded are marked with an asterisk. (These are sometimes referred to as dirty packages.) If you select a package, the list of repositories is restricted to just those repositories that contain a copy of the selected package.

ⓘ   *Add the* PBE–LightsOut *package to your Monticello browser using the* +Package
button and type PBE–LightsOut.

SqueakSource : a SourceForge for Pharo.

We think that the best way to save your code and share it is to create an
account for your project on a SqueakSource server. SqueakSource is like
SourceForge[6]: it is a web front-end to a HTTP Monticello server that lets
you manage your projects. There is a public SqueakSource server at http:
//www.squeaksource.com, and a copy of the code related to this book is stored
there at http://www.squeaksource.com/PharoByExample.html. You can look at this
project with a web browser, but it's a lot more productive to do so from inside
Pharo, using the Monticello browser, which lets you manage your packages.

ⓘ   *Open a web browser to* http:// www.squeaksource.com. *Create an account for
yourself and then create (i.e., "register") a project for the Lights Out game.*

SqueakSource will show you the information that you should use when
adding a repository using the Monticello browser.

Once your project has been created on SqueakSource, you have to tell
your Pharo system to use it.

ⓘ   *With the* PBE–LightsOut *package selected, click the* +Repository *button in the
Monticello browser.*

You will see a list of the different types of Repository that are available; to
add a SqueakSource repository select HTTP . You will be presented with a dialog in which you can provide the necessary information about the server. You
should copy the presented template to identify your SqueakSource project,
paste it into Monticello and supply your initials and password:

```
MCHttpRepository
    location: 'http://www.squeaksource.com/YourProject'
    user: 'yourInitials'
    password: 'yourPassword'
```

If you provide empty initials and password strings, you can still load the
project, but you will not be able to update it:

```
MCHttpRepository
    location: 'http://www.squeaksource.com/YourProject'
    user: ''
    password: ''
```

---

[6]http://sourceforge.net

Once you have accepted this template, your new repository should be listed on the right-hand side of the Monticello browser.

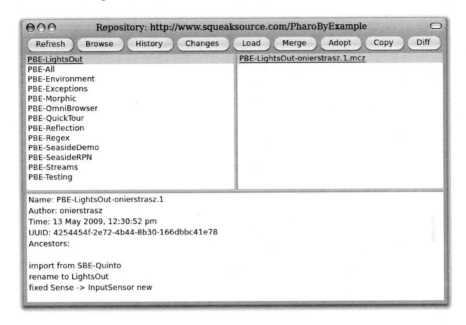

Figure 2.16: Browsing a Monticello Repository

☝ *Click on the* Save *button to save a first version of your Lights Out game on SqueakSource.*

To load a package into your image, you must first select a particular version. You can do this in the repository browser, which you can open using the Open button or the action-click menu. Once you have selected a version, you can load it onto your image.

☝ *Open the* PBE–LightsOut *repository you have just saved.*

Monticello has many more capabilities, which will be discussed in depth in Chapter 6. You can also look at the on-line documentation for Monticello at http://www.wiresong.ca/Monticello/.

2.10 Chapter summary

In this chapter you have seen how to create categories, classes and methods. You have see how to use the browser, the inspector, the debugger and the Monticello browser.

- Categories are groups of related classes.

- A new class is created by sending a message to its superclass.

- Protocols are groups of related methods.

- A new method is created or modified by editing its definition in the browser and then *accepting* the changes.

- The inspector offers a simple, general-purpose GUI for inspecting and interacting with arbitrary objects.

- The browser detects usage of undeclared methods and variables, and offers possible corrections.

- The initialize method is automatically executed after an object is created in Pharo. You can put any initialization code there.

- The debugger provides a high-level GUI to inspect and modify the state of a running program.

- You can share source code *filing out* a category.

- A better way to share code is to use Monticello to manage an external repository, for example defined as a SqueakSource project.

Chapter 3

Syntax in a nutshell

Pharo, like most modern Smalltalk dialects, adopts a syntax very close to that of Smalltalk-80. The syntax is designed so that program text can be read aloud as though it were a kind of pidgin English:

```
(Smalltalk includes: Class) ifTrue: [ Transcript show: Class superclass ]
```

Pharo's syntax is minimal. Essentially there is syntax only for *sending messages* (*i.e.*, expressions) . Expressions are built up from a very small number of primitive elements. There are only 6 keywords, and there is no syntax for control structures or declaring new classes. Instead, nearly everything is achieved by sending messages to objects. For instance, instead of an if-then-else control structure, Smalltalk sends messages like ifTrue: to Boolean objects. New (sub-)classes are created by sending a message to their superclass.

3.1 Syntactic elements

Expressions are composed of the following building blocks: (i) six reserved keywords, or *pseudo-variables*: self, super, nil, true, false, and thisContext, (ii) constant expressions for *literal objects* including numbers, characters, strings, symbols and arrays, (iii) variable declarations, (iv) assignments, (v) block closures, and (vi) messages.

We can see examples of the various syntactic elements in Table 3.1.

Local variables startPoint is a variable name, or identifier. By convention, identifiers are composed of words in "camelCase" (*i.e.*, each word except the first starting with an upper case letter). The first letter of an instance variable, method or block argument, or temporary variable must be lower case. This indicates to the reader that the variable has a private

Syntax	What it represents
startPoint	a variable name
Transcript	a global variable name
self	pseudo-variable
1	decimal integer
2r101	binary integer
1.5	floating point number
2.4e7	exponential notation
$a	the character 'a'
'Hello'	the string "Hello"
#Hello	the symbol #Hello
#(1 2 3)	a literal array
{1. 2. 1+2}	a dynamic array
"a comment"	a comment
| x y |	declaration of variables x and y
x := 1	assign 1 to x
[x + y]	a block that evaluates to x+y
<primitive: 1>	virtual machine primitive or annotation
3 factorial	unary message
3+4	binary messages
2 raisedTo: 6 modulo: 10	keyword message
↑ true	return the value true
Transcript show: 'hello'. Transcript cr	expression separator (.)
Transcript show: 'hello'; cr	message cascade (;)

Table 3.1: Pharo Syntax in a Nutshell

scope.

Shared variables Identifiers that start with upper case letters are global variables, class variables, pool dictionaries or class names. Transcript is a global variable, an instance of the class TranscriptStream.

The receiver. self is a keyword that refers to the object inside which the current method is executing. We call it "the receiver" because this object will normally have received the message that caused the method to execute. self is called a "pseudo-variable" since we cannot assign to it.

Integers. In addition to ordinary decimal integers like 42, Pharo also provides a radix notation. 2r101 is 101 in radix 2 (*i.e.*, binary), which is equal to decimal 5.

Floating point numbers can be specified with their base-ten exponent: 2.4e7 is 2.4×10^7.

Characters. A dollar sign introduces a literal character: $a is the literal for 'a'. Instances of non-printing characters can be obtained by sending appropriately named messages to the Character class, such as Character space and Character tab.

Strings. Single quotes are used to define a literal string. If you want a string with a quote inside, just double the quote, as in 'G"day'.

Symbols are like Strings, in that they contain a sequence of characters. However, unlike a string, a literal symbol is guaranteed to be globally unique. There is only one Symbol object #Hello but there may be multiple String objects with the value 'Hello'.

Compile-time arrays are defined by #( ), surrounding space-separated literals. Everything within the parentheses must be a compile-time constant. For example, #(27 (true false) abc) is a literal array of three elements: the integer 27, the compile-time array containing the two booleans, and the symbol #abc. (Note that this is the same as #(27 #(true false) #abc).)

Run-time arrays. Curly braces { } define a (dynamic) array at run-time. Elements are expressions separated by periods. So { 1. 2. 1+2 } defines an array with elements 1, 2, and the result of evaluating 1+2. (The curly-brace notation is peculiar to the Pharo and Squeak dialects of Smalltalk! In other Smalltalks you must build up dynamic arrays explicitly.)

Comments are enclosed in double quotes. *"hello"* is a comment, not a string, and is ignored by the Pharo compiler. Comments may span multiple lines.

Local variable definitions. Vertical bars | | enclose the declaration of one or more local variables in a method (and also in a block).

Assignment. := assigns an object to a variable.

Blocks. Square brackets [ ] define a block, also known as a block closure or a lexical closure, which is a first-class object representing a function. As we shall see, blocks may take arguments and can have local variables.

Primitives. <primitive: ...> denotes an invocation of a virtual machine primitive. (<primitive: 1> is the VM primitive for SmallInteger»+.) Any code following the primitive is executed only if the primitive fails. The same syntax is also used for method annotations.

Unary messages consist of a single word (like factorial) sent to a receiver (like 3).

Binary messages are operators (like +) sent to a receiver and taking a single argument. In 3+4, the receiver is 3 and the argument is 4.

Keyword messages consist of multiple keywords (like raisedTo:modulo:), each ending with a colon and taking a single argument. In the expression 2 raisedTo: 6 modulo: 10, the *message selector* raisedTo:modulo: takes the two arguments 6 and 10, one following each colon. We send the message to the receiver 2.

Method return. ↑ is used to *return* a value from a method. (You must type ^ to obtain the ↑ character.)

Sequences of statements. A period or full-stop (.) is the *statement separator*. Putting a period between two expressions turns them into independent statements.

Cascades. Semicolons can be used to send a *cascade* of messages to a single receiver. In Transcript show: 'hello'; cr we first send the keyword message show: 'hello' to the receiver Transcript, and then we send the unary message cr to the same receiver.

The classes Number, Character, String and Boolean are described in more detail in Chapter 8.

3.2 Pseudo-variables

In Smalltalk, there are 6 reserved keywords, or *pseudo-variables*: nil, true, false, self, super, and thisContext. They are called pseudo-variables because they are predefined and cannot be assigned to. true, false, and nil are constants while the values of self, super, and thisContext vary dynamically as code is executed.

true and false are the unique instances of the Boolean classes True and False. See Chapter 8 for more details.

self always refers to the receiver of the currently executing method.

super also refers to the receiver of the current method, but when you send a message to super, the method-lookup changes so that it starts from the superclass of the class containing the method that uses super. For further details see Chapter 5.

nil is the undefined object. It is the unique instance of the class UndefinedObject. Instance variables, class variables and local variables are initialized to nil.

thisContext is a pseudo-variable that represents the top frame of the run-time stack. In other words, it represents the currently executing MethodContext or BlockClosure. thisContext is normally not of interest to most programmers, but it is essential for implementing development tools like the debugger and it is also used to implement exception handling and continuations.

3.3 Message sends

There are three kinds of messages in Pharo.

1. *Unary* messages take no argument. 1 factorial sends the message factorial to the object 1.

2. *Binary* messages take exactly one argument. 1 + 2 sends the message + with argument 2 to the object 1.

3. *Keyword* messages take an arbitrary number of arguments. 2 raisedTo: 6 modulo: 10 sends the message consisting of the message selector raisedTo:modulo: and the arguments 6 and 10 to the object 2.

Unary message selectors consist of alphanumeric characters, and start with a lower case letter.

Binary message selectors consist of one or more characters from the following set:

```
+ - / \ * ~ < > = @ % | & ? ,
```

Keyword message selectors consist of a series of alphanumeric keywords, where each keyword starts with a lower-case letter and ends with a colon.

Unary messages have the highest precedence, then binary messages, and finally keyword messages, so:

```
2 raisedTo: 1 + 3 factorial   ⟶   128
```

(First we send factorial to 3, then we send + 6 to 1, and finally we send raisedTo: 7 to 2.) Recall that we use the notation *expression* ⟶ *result* to show the result of evaluating an expression.

Precedence aside, evaluation is strictly from left to right, so

```
1 + 2 * 3   ⟶   9
```

not 7. Parentheses must be used to alter the order of evaluation:

```
1 + (2 * 3)   ⟶   7
```

Message sends may be composed with periods and semi-colons. A period-separated sequence of expressions causes each expression in the series to be evaluated as a *statement*, one after the other.

```
Transcript cr.
Transcript show: 'hello world'.
Transcript cr
```

This will send cr to the Transcript object, then send it show: 'hello world', and finally send it another cr.

When a series of messages is being sent to the *same* receiver, then this can be expressed more succinctly as a *cascade*. The receiver is specified just once, and the sequence of messages is separated by semi-colons:

```
Transcript cr;
    show: 'hello world';
    cr
```

This has precisely the same effect as the previous example.

3.4   Method syntax

Whereas expressions may be evaluated anywhere in Pharo (for example, in a workspace, in a debugger, or in a browser), methods are normally defined in a browser window, or in the debugger. (Methods can also be filed in from an external medium, but this is not the usual way to program in Pharo.)

Programs are developed one method at a time, in the context of a given class. (A class is defined by sending a message to an existing class, asking it to create a subclass, so there is no special syntax required for defining classes.)

Here is the method lineCount in the class String. (The usual convention is to refer to methods as ClassName»methodName, so we call this method String» lineCount.)

Method 3.1: *Line count*

```
String»lineCount
    "Answer the number of lines represented by the receiver,
    where every cr adds one line."
    | cr count |
    cr := Character cr.
    count := 1 min: self size.
    self do:
        [:c | c == cr ifTrue: [count := count + 1]].
    ↑ count
```

Syntactically, a method consists of:

1. the method pattern, containing the name (*i.e.*, lineCount) and any arguments (none in this example);

2. comments (these may occur anywhere, but the convention is to put one at the top that explains what the method does);

3. declarations of local variables (*i.e.*, cr and count); and

4. any number of expressions separated by dots; here there are four.

The evaluation of any expression preceded by a ↑ (typed as ^) will cause the method to exit at that point, returning the value of that expression. A method that terminates without explicitly returning some expression will implicitly return self.

Arguments and local variables should always start with lower case letters. Names starting with upper-case letters are assumed to be global variables. Class names, like Character, for example, are simply global variables referring to the object representing that class.

3.5 Block syntax

Blocks provide a mechanism to defer the evaluation of expressions. A block is essentially an anonymous function. A block is evaluated by sending it the message value. The block answers the value of the last expression in its body, unless there is an explicit return (with ↑), in which case it does not answer any value.

```
[ 1 + 2 ] value  ⟶  3
```

Blocks may take parameters, each of which is declared with a leading colon. A vertical bar separates the parameter declaration(s) from the body of the block. To evaluate a block with one parameter, you must send it the message value: with one argument. A two-parameter block must be sent value:value:, and so on, up to 4 arguments.

```
[ :x | 1 + x ] value: 2  ⟶  3
[ :x :y | x + y ] value: 1 value: 2  ⟶  3
```

If you have a block with more than four parameters, you must use valueWithArguments: and pass the arguments in an array. (A block with a large number of parameters is often a sign of a design problem.)

Blocks may also declare local variables, which are surrounded by vertical bars, just like local variable declarations in a method. Locals are declared after any arguments:

```
[ :x :y | | z | z := x+ y. z ] value: 1 value: 2  ⟶  3
```

Blocks are actually lexical *closures*, since they can refer to variables of the surrounding environment. The following block refers to the variable x of its enclosing environment:

```
| x |
x := 1.
[ :y | x + y ] value: 2     ⟶     3
```

Blocks are instances of the class BlockClosure. This means that they are objects, so they can be assigned to variables and passed as arguments just like any other object.

3.6 Conditionals and loops in a nutshell

Smalltalk offers no special syntax for control constructs. Instead, these are typically expressed by sending messages to booleans, numbers and collections, with blocks as arguments.

Conditionals are expressed by sending one of the messages ifTrue:, ifFalse: or ifTrue:ifFalse: to the result of a boolean expression. See Chapter 8 for more about booleans.

```
(17 * 13 > 220)
   ifTrue: [ 'bigger' ]
   ifFalse: [ 'smaller' ]     ⟶     'bigger'
```

Loops are typically expressed by sending messages to blocks, integers or collections. Since the exit condition for a loop may be repeatedly evaluated, it should be a block rather than a boolean value. Here is an example of a very procedural loop:

```
n := 1.
[ n < 1000 ] whileTrue: [ n := n*2 ].
n     ⟶     1024
```

whileFalse: reverses the exit condition.

```
n := 1.
[ n > 1000 ] whileFalse: [ n := n*2 ].
n     ⟶     1024
```

timesRepeat: offers a simple way to implement a fixed iteration:

```
n := 1.
10 timesRepeat: [ n := n*2 ].
n     ⟶     1024
```

We can also send the message to:do: to a number which then acts as the initial value of a loop counter. The two arguments are the upper bound, and a block that takes the current value of the loop counter as its argument:

```
result := String new.
1 to: 10 do: [:n | result := result, n printString, ' '].
result      ⟶    '1 2 3 4 5 6 7 8 9 10 '
```

High-Order Iterators. Collections comprise a large number of different classes, many of which support the same protocol. The most important messages for iterating over collections include do:, collect:, select:, reject:, detect: and inject:into:. These messages define high-level iterators that allow one to write very compact code.

An Interval is a collection that lets one iterate over a sequence of numbers from the starting point to the end. 1 to: 10 represents the interval from 1 to 10. Since it is a collection, we can send the message do: to it. The argument is a block that is evaluated for each element of the collection.

```
result := String new.
(1 to: 10) do: [:n | result := result, n printString, ' '].
result      ⟶    '1 2 3 4 5 6 7 8 9 10 '
```

collect: builds a new collection of the same size, transforming each element.

```
(1 to: 10) collect: [ :each | each * each ]    ⟶    #(1 4 9 16 25 36 49 64 81 100)
```

select: and reject: build new collections, each containing a subset of the elements satisfying (or not) the boolean block condition. detect: returns the first element satisfying the condition. Don't forget that strings are also collections, so you can iterate over all the characters.

```
'hello there' select: [ :char | char isVowel ]    ⟶    'eoee'
'hello there' reject: [ :char | char isVowel ]    ⟶    'hll thr'
'hello there' detect: [ :char | char isVowel ]    ⟶    $e
```

Finally, you should be aware that collections also support a functional-style *fold* operator in the inject:into: method. This lets you generate a cumulative result using an expression that starts with a seed value and injects each element of the collection. Sums and products are typical examples.

```
(1 to: 10) inject: 0 into: [ :sum :each | sum + each ]    ⟶    55
```

This is equivalent to 0+1+2+3+4+5+6+7+8+9+10.

More about collections can be found in Chapter 9.

3.7   Primitives and pragmas

In Smalltalk everything is an object, and everything happens by sending messages. Nevertheless, at certain points we hit rock bottom. Certain objects can only get work done by invoking virtual machine primitives.

For example, the following are all implemented as primitives: memory allocation (new, new:), bit manipulation (bitAnd:, bitOr:, bitShift:), pointer and integer arithmetic (+, −, <, >, *, / , =, ==...), and array access (at:, at:put:).

Primitives are invoked with the syntax <primitive: aNumber>. A method that invokes such a primitive may also include Smalltalk code, which will be evaluated *only* if the primitive fails.

Here we see the code for SmallInteger»+. If the primitive fails, the expression super + aNumber will be evaluated and returned.

Method 3.2: *A primitive method*

```
+ aNumber
   "Primitive. Add the receiver to the argument and answer with the result
   if it is a SmallInteger. Fail if the argument or the result is not a
   SmallInteger  Essential  No Lookup. See Object documentation whatIsAPrimitive."

   <primitive: 1>
   ↑ super + aNumber
```

In Pharo, the angle bracket syntax is also used for method annotations called pragmas.

3.8   Chapter summary

- Pharo has (only) six reserved identifiers also called *pseudo-variables*: true, false, nil, self, super, and thisContext.

- There are five kinds of literal objects: numbers (5, 2.5, 1.9e15, 2r111), characters ($a), strings ('hello'), symbols (#hello), and arrays (#('hello' #hi))

- Strings are delimited by single quotes, comments by double quotes. To get a quote inside a string, double it.

- Unlike strings, symbols are guaranteed to be globally unique.

- Use #(...) to define a literal array. Use { ... } to define a dynamic array. Note that #(1 + 2) size $\longrightarrow$ 3, but { 1 + 2 } size $\longrightarrow$ 1

- There are three kinds of messages: *unary* (e.g., 1 asString, Array new), *binary* (e.g., 3 + 4, 'hi' , ' there'), and *keyword* (e.g., 'hi' at: 2 put: $o)

- A *cascaded* message send is a sequence of messages sent to the same target, separated by semi-colons: OrderedCollection new add: #calvin; add: #hobbes; size $\longrightarrow$ 2

- Local variables are declared with vertical bars. Use := for assignment.
  |x| x:=1

- Expressions consist of message sends, cascades and assignments, possibly grouped with parentheses. *Statements* are expressions separated by periods.

- Block closures are expressions enclosed in square brackets. Blocks may take arguments and can contain temporary variables. The expressions in the block are not evaluated until you send the block a value... message with the correct number of arguments.
  [:x | x + 2] value: 4 $\longrightarrow$ 6.

- There is no dedicated syntax for control constructs, just messages that conditionally evaluate blocks.
  (Smalltalk includes: Class) ifTrue: [Transcript show: Class superclass]

Chapter 4

Understanding message syntax

Although Smalltalk's message syntax is extremely simple, it is unconventional and can take some time getting used to. This chapter offers some guidance to help you get acclimatized to this special syntax for sending messages. If you already feel comfortable with the syntax, you may choose to skip this chapter, or come back to it later.

4.1 Identifying messages

In Smalltalk, except for the syntactic elements listed in Chapter 3 (:= ↑ . ; # () {} [: |]), everything is a message send. As in C++, you can define operators like + for your own classes, but all operators have the same precedence. Moreover, you cannot change the arity of a method. "−" is always a binary message; there is no way to have a unary "−" with a different overloading.

In Smalltalk the order in which messages are sent is determined by the kind of message. There are just three kinds of messages: *unary*, *binary*, and *keyword* messages. Unary messages are always sent first, then binary messages and finally keyword ones. As in most languages, parentheses can be used to change the order of evaluation. These rules make Smalltalk code as easy to read as possible. And most of the time you do not have to think about the rules.

As most computation in Smalltalk is done by message passing, correctly identifying messages is crucial. The following terminology will help us:

- A message is composed of the message *selector* and the optional message arguments.

- A message is sent to a *receiver*.

- The combination of a message and its receiver is called a *message send* as shown in Figure 4.1.

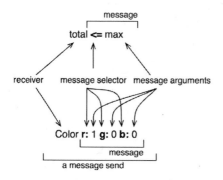

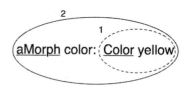

Figure 4.2: aMorph color: Color yellow is composed of two message sends: Color yellow and aMorph color: Color yellow.

Figure 4.1: Two messages composed of a receiver, a method selector, and a set of arguments.

> A message is always sent to a receiver, which can be a single literal, a block or a variable or the result of evaluating another message.

To help you identify the receiver of a message, we will underline it for you. We will also surround each message send with an ellipse and number message sends starting from the first one that will be sent to help you see the order in which messages are sent.

Figure 4.2 represents two message sends, Color yellow and aMorph color: Color yellow, hence there are two ellipses. The message send Color yellow is executed first so its ellipse is numbered 1. There are two receivers: aMorph which receives the message color: ... and Color which receives the message yellow. Both receivers are underlined.

A receiver can be the first element of a message, such as 100 in the message send 100 + 200 or Color in the message send Color yellow. However, a receiver can also be the result of other messages. For example in the message Pen new go: 100, the receiver of the message go: 100 is the object returned by the message send Pen new. In all the cases, a message is sent to an object called the *receiver* which may be the result of another message send.

Table 4.1 shows several examples of message sends. You should note that not all message sends have arguments. Unary messages like open do

Message send	Message type	Result
Color yellow	unary	Creates a color.
aPen go: 100.	keyword	The receiving pen moves forward 100 pixels.
100 + 20	binary	The number 100 receives the message + with the number 20.
Browser open	unary	Opens a new browser.
Pen new go: 100	unary and keyword	A pen is created and moved 100 pixels.
aPen go: 100 + 20	keyword and binary	The receiving pen moves forward 120 pixels.

Table 4.1: Examples of Message Sends and their Types

not have arguments. Single keyword and binary messages like go: 100 and + 20 each have one argument. There are also simple messages and composed ones. Color yellow and 100 + 20 are simple: a message is sent to an object, while the message send aPen go: 100 + 20 is composed of two messages: + 20 is sent to 100 and go: is sent to aPen with the argument being the result of the first message. A receiver can be an expression (such as an assignment, a message send or a literal) which returns an object. In Pen new go: 100, the message go: 100 is sent to the object that results from the execution of the message send Pen new.

4.2   Three kinds of messages

Smalltalk defines a few simple rules to determine the order in which the messages are sent. These rules are based on the distinction between 3 different kinds of messages:

- *Unary messages* are messages that are sent to an object without any other information. For example in 3 factorial, factorial is a unary message.

- *Binary messages* are messages consisting of operators (often arithmetic). They are binary because they always involve only two objects: the receiver and the argument object. For example in 10 + 20, + is a binary message sent to the receiver 10 with argument 20.

- *Keyword messages* are messages consisting of one or more keywords, each ending with a colon (:) and taking an argument. For example in anArray at: 1 put: 10, the keyword at: takes the argument 1 and the keyword put: takes the argument 10.

Unary messages

Unary messages are messages that do not require any argument. They follow
the syntactic template: receiver messageName. The selector is simply made up
of a succession of characters not containing : (*e.g.*, factorial, open, class).

```
89 sin              ⟶    0.860069405812453
3 sqrt              ⟶    1.732050807568877
Float pi            ⟶    3.141592653589793
'blop' size         ⟶    4
true not            ⟶    false
Object class   ⟶    Object class  "The class of Object is Object class (!)"
```

> Unary messages are messages that do not require any
> argument.
> They follow the syntactic template: receiver **selector**

Binary messages

Binary messages are messages that require exactly one argument *and* whose
selector consists of a sequence of one or more characters from the set: +, −, *, /,
&, =, >, |, <, ~, and @. Note that −− is not allowed for parsing reasons.

```
100@100             ⟶    100@100 "creates a Point object"
3 + 4               ⟶    7
10 − 1              ⟶    9
4 <= 3              ⟶    false
(4/3) * 3 = 4       ⟶    true  "equality is just a binary message, and Fractions are exact"
(3/4) == (3/4)      ⟶    false "two equal Fractions are not the same object"
```

> Binary messages are messages that require exactly one
> argument *and* whose selector is composed of a sequence
> of characters from: +, −, *, /, &, =, >, |, <, ~, and @. −− is not
> possible.
> They follow the syntactic template: receiver **selector** argu-
> ment

Keyword messages

Keyword messages are messages that require one or more arguments and
whose selector consists of one or more keywords each ending in :. Keyword

messages follow the syntactic template: receiver **selectorWordOne:** argumentOne **wordTwo:** argumentTwo

Each keyword takes an argument. Hence r:g:b: is a method with three arguments, playFileNamed: and at: are methods with one argument, and at:put: is a method with two arguments. To create an instance of the class Color one can use the method r:g:b: as in Color r: 1 g: 0 b: 0, which creates the color red. Note that the colons are part of the selector.

> In Java or C++, the Smalltalk method invocation Color r: 1 g: 0 b: 0 would be written Color.rgb(1,0,0).

```
1 to: 10                    ⟶    (1 to: 10)  "creates an interval"
Color r: 1 g: 0 b: 0        ⟶    Color red "creates a new color"
12 between: 8 and: 15   ⟶    true

nums := Array newFrom: (1 to: 5).
nums at: 1 put: 6.
nums      ⟶     #(6 2 3 4 5)
```

> Keyword based messages are messages that require one or more arguments. Their selector consists of one or more keywords each ending in a colon (:). They follow the syntactic template:
> receiver **selectorWordOne:** argumentOne **wordTwo:** argumentTwo

4.3 Message composition

The three kinds of messages each have different precedence, which allows them to be composed in an elegant way.

1. Unary messages are always sent first, then binary messages and finally keyword messages.

2. Messages in parentheses are sent prior to any kind of messages.

3. Messages of the same kind are evaluated from left to right.

These rules lead to a very natural reading order. Now if you want to be sure that your messages are sent in the order that you want you can always

put more parentheses as shown in Figure 4.3. In this figure, the message yellow
is an unary message and the message color: a keyword message, therefore
the message send Color yellow is sent first. However as message sends in
parentheses are sent first, putting (unnecessary) parentheses around Color
yellow just emphasizes that it will be sent first. The rest of the section illustrates
each of these points.

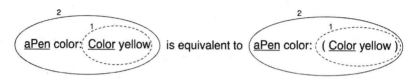

Figure 4.3: Unary messages are sent first so Color yellow is sent. This returns a
color object which is passed as argument of the message aPen color:.

Unary > Binary > Keywords

Unary messages are sent first, then binary messages, and finally keyword
messages. We also say that unary messages have a higher priority over the
other kinds of messages.

> **Rule One.** Unary messages are sent first, then binary
> messages, and finally keyword based messages.
> Unary > Binary > Keyword

As these examples show, Smalltalk's syntax rules generally ensure that
message sends can be read in a natural way:

```
1000 factorial / 999 factorial    ⟶    1000
2 raisedTo: 1 + 3 factorial       ⟶    128
```

Unfortunately the rules are a bit too simplistic for arithmetic message
sends, so you need to introduce parentheses whenever you want to impose a
priority over binary operators:

```
1 + 2 * 3      ⟶   9
1 + (2 * 3)    ⟶   7
```

The following example, which is a bit more complex (!), offers a nice
illustration that even complicated Smalltalk expressions can be read in a
natural way:

```
[:aClass | aClass methodDict keys select: [:aMethod | (aClass>>aMethod) isAbstract ]]
    value: Boolean   ⟶   an IdentitySet(#or: #| #and: #& #ifTrue: #ifTrue:ifFalse:
    #ifFalse: #not #ifFalse:ifTrue:)
```

Here we want to know which methods of the Boolean class are abstract[1]. We ask some argument class, aClass, for the keys of its method dictionary, and select those methods of that class that are abstract. Then we bind the argument aClass to the concrete value Boolean. We need parentheses only to send the binary message >>, which selects a method from a class, before sending the unary message isAbstract to that method. The result shows us which methods must be implemented by Boolean's concrete subclasses True and False.

Example. In the message aPen color: Color yellow, there is one *unary* message yellow sent to the class Color and a *keyword* message color: sent to aPen. Unary messages are sent first so the message send Color yellow is sent (1). This returns a color object which is passed as argument of the message aPen color: aColor (2) as shown in example 4.1. Figure 4.3 shows graphically how messages are sent.

Example 4.1: *Decomposing the evaluation of* aPen color: Color yellow

```
      aPen color: Color yellow
(1)              Color yellow      "unary message is sent first"
                 ⟶    aColor
(2)  aPen color: aColor            "keyword message is sent next"
```

Example. In the message aPen go: 100 + 20, there is a *binary* message + 20 and a *keyword* message go:. Binary messages are sent prior to keyword messages so 100 + 20 is sent first (1): the message + 20 is sent to the object 100 and returns the number 120. Then the message aPen go: 120 is sent with 120 as argument (2). Example 4.2 shows how the message send is executed.

Example 4.2: *Decomposing* aPen go: 100 + 20

```
      aPen go: 100 + 20
(1)            100 + 20          "binary message first"
               ⟶    120
(2)  aPen go: 120               "then keyword message"
```

Example. As an exercise we let you decompose the evaluation of the message Pen new go: 100 + 20 which is composed of one unary, one keyword and one binary message (see Figure 4.5).

---

[1]In fact, we could also have written the equivalent but simpler expression: Boolean methodDict select: #isAbstract thenCollect: #selector

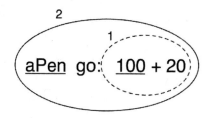

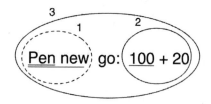

Figure 4.4: Binary messages are sent before keyword messages.

Figure 4.5: Decomposing Pen new go: 100 + 20

Parentheses first

> **Rule Two.** Parenthesised messages are sent prior to other messages.
>
> (Msg) > Unary > Binary > Keyword

1.5 tan rounded asString = (((1.5 tan) rounded) asString)   ⟶   true   *"parentheses not needed here"*
3 + 4 factorial   ⟶   27   *"(not 5040)"*
(3 + 4) factorial   ⟶   5040

Here we need the parentheses to force sending lowMajorScaleOn: before play.

(FMSound lowMajorScaleOn: FMSound clarinet) play
"(1) send the message clarinet to the FMSound class to create a clarinet sound.
(2) send this sound to FMSound as argument to the lowMajorScaleOn: keyword
  message.
(3) play the resulting sound."

Example. The message (65@325 extent: 134 @ 100) center returns the center of a rectangle whose top left point is $(65, 325)$ and whose size is 134×100. Example 4.3 shows how the message is decomposed and sent. First the message between parentheses is sent: it contains two binary messages 65@325 and 134@100 that are sent first and return points, and a keyword message extent: which is then sent and returns a rectangle. Finally the unary message center is sent to the rectangle and a point is returned. Evaluating the message without parentheses would lead to an error because the object 100 does not understand the message center.

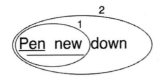

Figure 4.6: Decomposing Pen new down

Example 4.3: *Example of Parentheses.*

```
    (65 @ 325 extent: 134 @ 100) center
(1) 65@325                              "binary"
    ⟶     aPoint
(2)                  134@100            "binary"
          ⟶     anotherPoint
(3) aPoint extent: anotherPoint         "keyword"
    ⟶     aRectangle
(4) aRectangle center                   "unary"
    ⟶     132@375
```

From left to right

Now we know how messages of different kinds or priorities are handled. The final question to be addressed is how messages with the same priority are sent. They are sent from the left to the right. Note that you already saw this behaviour in example 4.3 where the two point creation messages (@) were sent first.

> **Rule Three.** When the messages are of the same kind, the order of evaluation is from left to right.

Example. In the message sends Pen new down all messages are unary messages, so the leftmost one, Pen new, is sent first. This returns a newly created pen to which the second message down is sent, as shown in Figure 4.6.

Arithmetic inconsistencies

The message composition rules are simple but they result in inconsistency for the execution of arithmetic message sends expressed in terms of binary messages. Here we see the common situations where extra parentheses are needed.

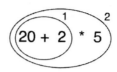

3 + 4 * 5	⟶ 35	*"(not 23) Binary messages sent from left to right"*
3 + (4 * 5)	⟶ 23	
1 + 1/3	⟶ (2/3)	*"and not 4/3"*
1 + (1/3)	⟶ (4/3)	
1/3 + 2/3	⟶ (7/9)	*"and not 1"*
(1/3) + (2/3)	⟶ 1	

Example.   In the message sends 20 + 2 * 5, there are only binary messages + and *. However in Smalltalk there is no specific priority for the operations + and *. They are just binary messages, hence * does not have priority over +. Here the leftmost message + is sent first (1) and then the * is sent to the result as shown in example 4.4.

Example 4.4: *Decomposing* 20 + 2 * 5

*"As there is no priority among binary messages, the leftmost message + is evaluated first even if by the rules of arithmetic the * should be sent first."*

```
      20 + 2 * 5
(1)  20 + 2    ⟶    22
(2)  22      * 5   ⟶    110
```

As shown in example 4.4 the result of this message send is not 30 but 110. This result is perhaps unexpected but follows directly from the rules used to send messages. This is somehow the price to pay for the simplicity of the Smalltalk model. To get the correct result, we should use parentheses. When messages are enclosed in parentheses, they are evaluated first. Hence the message send 20 + (2 * 5) returns the result as shown in example 4.5.

Example 4.5: *Decomposing* 20 + (2 * 5)

*"The messages surrounded by parentheses are evaluated first therefore * is sent prior to + which produces the correct behaviour."*

```
      20 + (2 * 5)
(1)      (2 * 5)   ⟶    10
(2)  20 + 10    ⟶    30
```

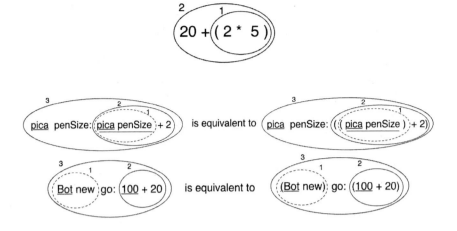

Figure 4.7: Equivalent messages using parentheses.

Implicit precedence	Explicitly parenthesized equivalent
aPen color: Color yellow	aPen color: (Color yellow)
aPen go: 100 + 20	aPen go: (100 + 20)
aPen penSize: aPen penSize + 2	aPen penSize: ((aPen penSize) + 2)
2 factorial + 4	(2 factorial) + 4

Figure 4.8: Message sends and their fully parenthesized equivalents

> In Smalltalk, arithmetic operators such as + and * do not have different priority. + and * are just binary messages, therefore * does not have priority over +. Use parentheses to obtain the desired result.

Note that the first rule stating that unary messages are sent prior to binary and keyword messages avoids the need to put explicit parentheses around them. Table 4.8 shows message sends written following the rules and equivalent message sends if the rules would not exist. Both message sends result in the same effect or return the same value.

4.4   Hints for identifying keyword messages

Often beginners have problems understanding when they need to add parentheses. Let's see how keywords messages are recognized by the compiler.

Parentheses or not?

The characters [,], (and) delimit distinct areas. Within such an area, a keyword message is the longest sequence of words terminated by : that is not cut by the characters ., or ;. When the characters [,], (and) surround some words with colons, these words participate in the keyword message *local* to the area defined.

In this example, there are two distinct keyword messages: rotatedBy:magnify:smoothing: and at:put:.

```
aDict
  at: (rotatingForm
        rotateBy: angle
        magnify: 2
        smoothing: 1)
  put: 3
```

> The characters [,], (and) delimit distinct areas. Within such an area, a keyword message is the longest sequence of words terminated by : that is not cut by the characters ., or ;. When the characters [,], (and) surround some words with colons, these words participate in the keyword message local to the area defined.

Hints. If you have problems with these precedence rules, you may start simply by putting parentheses whenever you want to distinguish two messages having the same precedence.

The following piece of code does not require parentheses because the message send x isNil is unary hence is sent prior to the keyword message ifTrue:.

```
(x isNil)
  ifTrue:[...]
```

The following piece of code requires parentheses because the messages includes: and ifTrue: are both keyword messages.

```
ord := OrderedCollection new.
(ord includes: $a)
  ifTrue:[...]
```

Without parentheses the unknown message includes:ifTrue: would be sent to the collection!

When to use [ ] or ( )

You may also have problems understanding when to use square brackets rather than parentheses. The basic principle is that you should use [ ] when you do not know how many times, potentially zero, an expression should be evaluated. [*expression*] will create a block closure (*i.e.*, an object) from *expression*, which may be evaluated any number of times (possibly zero), depending on the context. Here note that an expression can either be a message send, a variable, a literal, an assignment or a block.

Hence the conditional branches of ifTrue: or ifTrue:ifFalse: require blocks. Following the same principle both the receiver and the argument of a whileTrue: message require the use of square brackets since we do not know how many times either the receiver or the argument should be evaluated.

Parentheses, on the other hand, only affect the order of sending messages. So in (*expression*), the *expression* will *always* be evaluated exactly once.

```
[ x isReady ] whileTrue: [ y doSomething ]    "both the receiver and the argument must be
        blocks"
4 timesRepeat: [ Beeper beep ]                "the argument is evaluated more than once,
        so must be a block"
(x isReady) ifTrue: [ y doSomething ]         "receiver is evaluated once, so is not a block"
```

4.5 Expression sequences

Expressions (*i.e.*, messages sends, assignments...) separated by periods are evaluated in sequence. Note that there is no period between a variable definition and the following expression. The value of a sequence is the value of the last expression. The values returned by all the expressions except the last one are ignored. Note that the period is a separator and not a terminator. Therefore a final period is optional.

```
| box |
box := 20@30 corner: 60@90.
box containsPoint: 40@50    ⟶    true
```

4.6 Cascaded messages

Smalltalk offers a way to send multiple messages to the same receiver using a semicolon (;). This is called the *cascade* in Smalltalk jargon.

Expression Msg1 ; Msg2

Transcript show: 'Pharo is '.
Transcript show: 'fun '.
Transcript cr.
	is equivalent to:	Transcript
		    show: 'Pharo is';
		    show: 'fun ';
		    cr

Note that the object receiving the cascaded messages can itself be the result of a message send. In fact the receiver of all the cascaded messages is the receiver of the first message involved in a cascade. In the following example, the first cascaded message is setX:setY: since it is followed by a cascade. The receiver of the cascaded message setX:setY: is the newly created point resulting from the evaluation of Point new, and *not* Point. The subsequent message isZero is sent to that same receiver.

Point new setX: 25 setY: 35; isZero $\longrightarrow$ false

4.7   Chapter summary

- A message is always sent to an object named the *receiver* which may be the result of other message sends.

- Unary messages are messages that do not require any argument. They are of the form of receiver **selector**.

- Binary messages are messages that involve two objects, the receiver and another object *and* whose selector is composed of one or more characters from the following list: +, −, *, /, |, &, =, >, <, ~, and @. They are of the form: receiver **selector** argument

- Keyword messages are messages that involve more than one object and that contain at least one colon character (:). They are of the form: receiver **selectorWordOne:** argumentOne **wordTwo:** argumentTwo

- **Rule One.** Unary messages are sent first, then binary messages, and finally keyword messages.

- **Rule Two.** Messages in parentheses are sent before any others.

- **Rule Three.** When the messages are of the same kind, the order of evaluation is from left to right.

- In Smalltalk, traditional arithmetic operators such as + and * have the same priority. + and * are just binary messages, therefore * does not have priority over +. You must use parentheses to obtain a different result.

Part II

Developing in Pharo

Chapter 5

The Smalltalk object model

Smalltalk's programming model is simple and uniform: everything is an object, and objects communicate only by sending each other messages. However, this simplicity and uniformity can be a source of difficulty for programmers used to other languages. In this chapter we present the core concepts of the Smalltalk object model; in particular we discuss the consequences of representing classes as objects.

5.1   The rules of the model

The Smalltalk object model is based on a set of simple rules that are applied *uniformly*. The rules are as follows:

Rule 1. Everything is an object.

Rule 2. Every object is an instance of a class.

Rule 3. Every class has a superclass.

Rule 4. Everything happens by sending messages.

Rule 5. Method lookup follows the inheritance chain.

Let us look at each of these rules in some detail.

5.2   Everything is an Object

The mantra "everything is an object" is highly contagious. After only a short while working with Smalltalk, you will start to be surprised at how this rule simplifes everything you do. Integers, for example, are truly objects, so you can send messages to them, just as you do to any other object.

```
3 + 4            ⟶   7    "send '+ 4' to 3, yielding 7"
20 factorial     ⟶   2432902008176640000   "send factorial, yielding a big number"
```

The representation of 20 factorial is certainly different from the representation of 7, but because they are both objects, none of the code — not even the implementation of factorial — needs to now about this.

Perhaps the most fundamental consequence of this rule is the following:

> Classes are objects too.

Furthermore, classes are not second-class objects: they are really first-class objects that you can send messages to, inspect, and so on. This means that Pharo is a truly reflective system, which gives a great deal of expressive power to developers.

Deep in the implementation of Smalltalk, there are three different kinds of objects. There are (1) ordinary objects with instance variables that are passed by references, there are (2) *small integers* that are passed by value, and there are (3) indexable objects like arrays that hold a contiguous portion of memory. The beauty of Smalltalk is that you normally don't need to care about the differences between these three kinds of object.

5.3   Every object is an instance of a class

Every object has a class; you can find out which by sending it the message class.

```
1 class                ⟶   SmallInteger
20 factorial class     ⟶   LargePositiveInteger
'hello' class          ⟶   ByteString
#(1 2 3) class         ⟶   Array
(4@5) class            ⟶   Point
Object new class       ⟶   Object
```

A class defines the *structure* of its instances via instance variables, and the *behavior* of its instances via methods. Each method has a name, called its *selector*, which is unique within the class.

Since *classes are objects*, and *every object is an instance of a class*, it follows that classes must also be instances of classes. A class whose instances are classes is called a *metaclass*. Whenever you create a class, the system automatically creates a metaclass for you. The metaclass defines the structure and behavior of the class that is its instance. 99% of the time you will not need to think about metaclasses, and may happily ignore them. (We will have a closer look at metaclasses in Chapter 13.)

Instance variables

Instance variables in Smalltalk are private to the *instance* itself. This is in contrast to Java and C++, which allow instance variables (also known as "fields" or "member variables") to be accessed by any other instance that happens to be of the same class. We say that the *encapsulation boundary* of objects in Java and C++ is the class, whereas in Smalltalk it is the instance.

In Smalltalk, two instances of the same class cannot access each other's instance variables unless the class defines "accessor methods". There is no language syntax that provides direct access to the instance variables of any other object. (Actually, a mechanism called reflection does provide a way to ask another object for the values of its instance variables; meta-programming is intended for writing tools like the object inspector, whose sole purpose is to look inside other objects.)

Instance variables can be accessed by name in any of the instance methods of the class that defines them, and also in the methods defined in its subclasses. This means that Smalltalk instance variables are similar to *protected* variables in C++ and Java. However, we prefer to say that they are private, because it is considered bad style in Smalltalk to access an instance variable directly from a subclass.

Example

Method Point»dist: (method 5.1) computes the distance between the receiver and another point. The instance variables x and y of the receiver are accessed directly by the method body. However, the instance variables of the other point must be accessed by sending it the messages x and y.

Method 5.1: *the distance between two points*

```
Point»dist: aPoint
    "Answer the distance between aPoint and the receiver."
    | dx dy |
    dx := aPoint x - x.
    dy := aPoint y - y.
    ↑ ((dx * dx) + (dy * dy)) sqrt
```

1@1 dist: 4@5 ⟶ 5.0

The key reason to prefer instance-based encapsulation to class-based encapsulation is that it enables different implementations of the same abstraction to coexist. For example, method point»dist:, need not know or care whether the argument aPoint is an instance of the same class as the receiver. The argument object might be represented in polar coordinates, or as a record in a database, or on another computer in a distributed system; as long as it can respond to the messages x and y, the code in method 5.1 will still work.

Methods

All methods are public.[1] Methods are grouped into protocols that indicate their intent. Some common protocol names have been established by convention, for example, *accessing* for all accessor methods, and *initialization* for establishing a consistent initial state for the object. The protocol *private* is sometimes used to group methods that should not be seen from outside. Nothing, however, prevents you from sending a message that is implemented by such a "private" method.

Methods can access all instance variables of the object. Some Smalltalk developers prefer to access instance variables only through accessors. This practice has some value, but it also clutters the interface of your classes, and worse, exposes private state to the world.

The instance side and the class side

Since classes are objects, they can have their own instance variables and their own methods. We call these *class instance variables* and *class methods*, but they are really no different from ordinary instance variables and methods: class instance variables are just instance variables defined by a metaclass, and class methods are just methods defined by a metaclass.

A class and its metaclass are two separate classes, even though the former is an instance of the latter. However, this is largely irrelevant to you as a programmer: you are concerned with defining the behavior of your objects and the classes that create them.

For this reason, the browser helps you to browse both class and metaclass as if they were a single thing with two "sides": the "instance side" and the "class side", as shown in Figure 5.1. Clicking on the instance button browses the class Color, *i.e.*, you browse the methods that are executed when messages are sent to an instance of Color, like the blue color. Pressing the class button browses the class Color class, *i.e.*, you see the methods that will be executed when messages are sent to the class Color itself. For example, Color blue sends

---

[1] Well, almost all. In Pharo, methods whose selectors start with the string pvt are private: a pvt message can be sent *only* to self. However, pvt methods are not used very much.

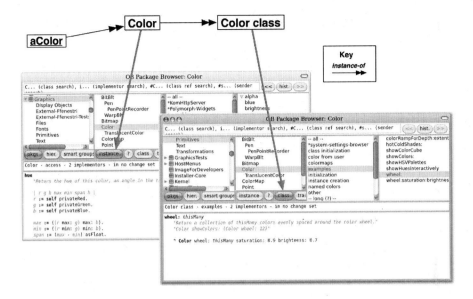

Figure 5.1: Browsing a class and its metaclass.

the message blue to the class Color. You will therefore find the method blue defined on the class side of Color, not on the instance side.

aColor := Color blue.		*"Class side method blue"*
aColor	$\longrightarrow$ Color blue	
aColor red	$\longrightarrow$ 0.0	*"Instance side accessor method red"*
aColor blue	$\longrightarrow$ 1.0	*"Instance side accessor method blue"*

You define a class by filling in the template proposed on the instance side. When you accept this template, the system creates not just the class that you defined, but also the corresponding metaclass. You can browse the metaclass by clicking on the |class| button. The only part of the metaclass creation template that makes sense for you to edit directly is the list of instance variable names.

Once a class has been created, clicking the |instance| button lets you edit and browse the methods that will be possessed by instances of that class (and of its subclasses). For example, we can see in Figure 5.1 that the method hue is defined on instances of the class Color. In contrast, the |class| button lets you browse and edit the metaclass (in this case Color class).

Class methods

Class methods can be quite useful; browse Color class for some good examples. You will see that there are two kinds of method defined on a class: those that create instances of the class, like Color class»blue and those that perform a utility function, like Color class»showColorCube. This is typical, although you will occasionally find class methods used in other ways.

It is convenient to place utility methods on the class side because they can be executed without having to create any additional objects first. Indeed, many of them will contain a comment designed to make it easy to execute them.

(!) *Browse method* Color class»showColorCube, *double-click just inside the quotes on the comment* "Color showColorCube" *and type* CMD−d.

You will see the effect of executing this method.   (Select World ▷ restore display (r) to undo the effects.)

For those familiar with Java and C++, class methods may seem similar to static methods. However, the uniformity of Smalltalk means that they are somewhat different: whereas Java static methods are really just statically-resolved procedures, Smalltalk class methods are dynamically-dispatched methods. This means that inheritance, overriding and super-sends work for class methods in Smalltalk, whereas they don't work for static methods in Java.

Class instance variables

With ordinary instance variables, all the instances of a class have the same set of variable names, and the instances of its subclasses inherit those names; however, each instance has its own private set of values. The story is exactly the same with class instance variables: each class has its own private class instance variables. A subclass will inherit those class instance variables, *but it has its own private copies of those variables.* Just as objects don't share instance variables, neither do classes and their subclasses share class instance variables.

You could use a class instance variable called count to keep track of how many instances you create of a given class. However, any subclass would have its own count variable, so subclass instances would be counted separately.

Example: class instance variables are not shared with subclasses. Suppose we define classes Dog and Hyena, where Hyena inherits the class instance variable count from Dog.

Class 5.2: *Dogs and Hyenas*

```
Object subclass: #Dog
    instanceVariableNames: "
    classVariableNames: "
    poolDictionaries: "
    category: 'PBE-CIV'

Dog class
    instanceVariableNames: 'count'

Dog subclass: #Hyena
    instanceVariableNames: "
    classVariableNames: "
    poolDictionaries: "
    category: 'PBE-CIV'
```

Now suppose we define class methods for Dog to initialize its count to 0, and to increment it when new instances are created:

Method 5.3: *Keeping count of new dogs*

```
Dog class»initialize
    super initialize.
    count := 0.

Dog class»new
    count := count +1.
    ↑ super new

Dog class»count
    ↑ count
```

Now when we create a new Dog its count is incremented, and so is that of every Hyena, but they are counted separately:

```
Dog initialize.
Hyena initialize.
Dog count       ⟶   0
Hyena count     ⟶   0
Dog new.
Dog count       ⟶   1
Dog new.
Dog count       ⟶   2
Hyena new.
Hyena count     ⟶   1
```

Note also that class instance variables are private to a class in exactly the same way that instance variables are private to the instance. Since classes and their instances are different objects, this has the following immediate consequences:

> A class does not have access to the instance variables of its own instances.

> An instance of a class does not have access to the class instance variables of its class.

For this reason, instance initialization methods must always be defined on the instance side — the class side has no access to instance variables, so cannot initialize them! All that the class can do is to send initialization messages, possibly using accessors, to newly created instances.

Similarly, instances can only access class instance variables indirectly, by sending accessor messages to their class.

Java has nothing equivalent to class instance variables. Java and C++ static variables are more like Smalltalk class variables, which we will discuss in Section 5.7: all of the subclasses and all of their instances share the same static variable.

Example: Defining a Singleton.   The Singleton pattern[2] provides a typical example of the use of class instance variables and class methods. Imagine that we would like to implement a class WebServer and use the Singleton pattern to ensure that it has only one instance.

Clicking on the instance button in the browser, we define the class WebServer as follows (class 5.4).

Class 5.4: *A singleton class*

```
Object subclass: #WebServer
  instanceVariableNames: 'sessions'
  classVariableNames: ''
  poolDictionaries: ''
  category: 'Web'
```

Then, clicking on the class button, we add the instance variable uniqueInstance to the class side.

Class 5.5: *The class side of the singleton class*

```
WebServer class
  instanceVariableNames: 'uniqueInstance'
```

---

[2]Sherman R. Alpert, Kyle Brown and Bobby Woolf, *The Design Patterns Smalltalk Companion.* Addison Wesley, 1998, ISBN 0–201–18462–1.

The consequence of this is that the class WebServer now has another instance variable, in addition to the variables that it inherits, such as superclass and methodDict.

We can now define a class method named uniqueInstance as shown in method 5.6. This method first checks whether uniqueInstance has been initialized. If it has not, the method creates an instance and assigns it to the class instance variable uniqueInstance. Finally the value of uniqueInstance is returned. Since uniqueInstance is a class instance variable, this method can directly access it.

Method 5.6: *uniqueInstance (on the class side)*

```
WebServer class»uniqueInstance
    uniqueInstance ifNil: [uniqueInstance := self new].
    ↑ uniqueInstance
```

The first time that WebServer uniqueInstance is executed, an instance of the class WebServer will be created and assigned to the uniqueInstance variable. The next time, the previously created instance will be returned instead of creating a new one.

Note that the instance creation code inside the conditional in method 5.6 is written as self new and not as WebServer new. What is the difference? Since the uniqueInstance method is defined in WebServer class, you might think that they were the same. And indeed, until someone creates a subclass of WebServer, they are the same. But suppose that ReliableWebServer is a subclass of WebServer, and inherits the uniqueInstance method. We would clearly expect ReliableWebServer uniqueInstance to answer a ReliableWebServer:. Using self ensures that this will happen, since it will be bound to the respective class. Note also that WebServer and ReliableWebServer will each have their own class instance variable called uniqueInstance. These two variables will of course have different values.

5.4 Every class has a superclass

Each class in Smalltalk inherits its behaviour and the description of its structure from a single *superclass*. This means that Smalltalk has single inheritance.

SmallInteger superclass	⟶	Integer
Integer superclass	⟶	Number
Number superclass	⟶	Magnitude
Magnitude superclass	⟶	Object
Object superclass	⟶	ProtoObject
ProtoObject superclass	⟶	nil

Traditionally the root of the Smalltalk inheritance hierarchy is the class Object (since everything is an object). In Pharo, the root is actually a class called ProtoObject, but you will normally not pay any attention to this class. ProtoObject encapsulates the minimal set of messages that all objects *must* have. However, most classes inherit from Object, which defines many additional messages that almost all objects ought to understand and respond to. Unless you have a very good reason to do otherwise, when creating application classes you should normally subclass Object, or one of its subclasses.

🕮 *A new class is normally created by sending the message* subclass: instanceVariableNames: ... *to an existing class. There are a few other methods to create classes. Have a look at the protocol* Kernel-Classes ▷ Class ▷ subclass creation *to see what they are.*

Although Pharo does not provide multiple inheritance, it supports a mechanism called *traits* for sharing behaviour across unrelated classes. Traits are collections of methods that can be reused by multiple classes that are not related by inheritance. Using traits allows one to share code between different classes without duplicating code.

Abstract methods and abstract classes

An abstract class is a class that exists to be subclassed, rather than to be instantiated. An abstract class is usually incomplete, in the sense that it does not define all of the methods that it uses. The "missing" methods — those that the other methods assume, but which are not themselves defined — are called abstract methods.

Smalltalk has no dedicated syntax to specify that a method or a class is abstract. By convention, the body of an abstract method consists of the expression self subclassResponsibility. This is known as a "marker method", and indicates that subclasses have the responsibility to define a concrete version of the method. self subclassResponsibility methods should always be overridden, and thus should never be executed. If you forget to override one, and it is executed, an exception will be raised.

A class is considered abstract if one of its methods is abstract. Nothing actually prevents you from creating an instance of an abstract class; everything will work until an abstract method is invoked.

Example: the class Magnitude.

Magnitude is an abstract class that helps us to define objects that can be compared to each other. Subclasses of Magnitude should implement the methods <, = and hash. Using such messages Magnitude defines other methods such as >, >=, <=, max:, min: between:and: and others for comparing objects. Such methods are inherited by subclasses. The method < is abstract and defined as shown in method 5.7.

Method 5.7: Magnitude»<

```
Magnitude»< aMagnitude
    "Answer whether the receiver is less than the argument."
    ↑self subclassResponsibility
```

By contrast, the method >= is concrete; it is defined in terms of <:

Method 5.8: Magnitude»>=

```
>= aMagnitude
    "Answer whether the receiver is greater than or equal to the argument."
    ↑(self < aMagnitude) not
```

The same is true of the other comparison methods.

Character is a subclass of Magnitude; it overrides the subclassResponsibility method for < with its own version of < (see method 5.9). Character also defines methods = and hash; it inherits from Magnitude the methods >=, <=, ~= and others.

Method 5.9: Character»<

```
Character»< aCharacter
    "Answer true if the receiver's value < aCharacter's value."
    ↑self asciiValue < aCharacter asciiValue
```

Traits

A *trait* is a collection of methods that can be included in the behaviour of a class without the need for inheritance. This makes it easy for classes to have a unique superclass, yet still share useful methods with otherwise unrelated classes.

To define a new trait, simply replace the subclass creation template by a message to the class Trait.

Class 5.10: *Defining a new trait*

```
Trait named: #TAuthor
    uses: { }
    category: 'PBE–LightsOut'
```

Here we define the trait TAuthor in the category *PBE-LightsOut*. This trait does not *use* any other existing traits. In general we can specify a *trait composition expression* of other traits to use as part of the uses: keyword argument. Here we simply provide an empty array.

Traits may contain methods, but no instance variables. Suppose we would like to be able to add an author method to various classes, independent of where they occur in the hierarchy. We might do this as follows:

Method 5.11: *An author method*

```
TAuthor»author
    "Returns author initials"
    ↑ 'on'   "oscar nierstrasz"
```

Now we can use this trait in a class that already has its own superclass, for instance the LOGame class that we defined in Chapter 2. We simply modify the class creation template for LOGame to include a uses: keyword argument that specifies that TAuthor should be used.

Class 5.12: *Using a trait*

```
BorderedMorph subclass: #LOGame
    uses: TAuthor
    instanceVariableNames: 'cells'
    classVariableNames: ''
    poolDictionaries: ''
    category: 'PBE–LightsOut'
```

If we now instantiate LOGame, it will respond to the author message as expected.

```
LOGame new author   ⟶   'on'
```

Trait composition expressions may combine multiple traits using the + operator. In case of conflicts (*i.e.*, if multiple traits define methods with the same name), these conflicts can be resolved by explicitly removing these methods (with –), or by redefining these methods in the class or trait that you are defining. It is also possible to *alias* methods (with @), providing a new name for them.

Traits are used in the system kernel. One good example is the class Behavior.

Class 5.13: Behavior *defined using traits*

```
Object subclass: #Behavior
    uses: TPureBehavior @ {#basicAddTraitSelector:withMethod:–>
        #addTraitSelector:withMethod:}
    instanceVariableNames: 'superclass methodDict format'
    classVariableNames: 'ObsoleteSubclasses'
    poolDictionaries: ''
    category: 'Kernel–Classes'
```

Here we see that the method addTraitSelector:withMethod: defined in the trait TPureBehavior has been aliased to basicAddTraitSelector:withMethod:. Support for traits is currently being added to the browsers.

5.5 Everything happens by sending messages

This rule captures the essence of programming in Smalltalk.

In procedural programming, the choice of which piece of code to execute when a procedure is called is made by the caller. The caller chooses the procedure or function to execute *statically*, by name.

In object-oriented programming, we do *not* "call methods": we "send messages." The choice of terminology is significant. Each object has its own responsibilities. We do not *tell* an object what to do by applying some procedure to it. Instead, we politely *ask* an object to do something for us by sending it a message. The message is *not* a piece of code: it is nothing but a name and a list of arguments. The receiver then decides how to respond by selecting its own *method* for doing what was asked. Since different objects may have different methods for responding to the same message, the method must be chosen *dynamically*, when the message is received.

```
3 + 4        ⟶    7      "send message + with argument 4 to integer 3"
(1@2) + 4    ⟶    5@6    "send message + with argument 4 to point (1@2)"
```

As a consequence, we can send the *same message* to different objects, each of which may have *its own method* for responding to the message. We do not tell the SmallInteger 3 or the Point 1@2 how to respond to the message + 4. Each has its own method for +, and responds to + 4 accordingly.

One of the consequences of Smalltalk's model of message sending is that it encourages a style in which objects tend to have very small methods and delegate tasks to other objects, rather than implementing huge, procedural methods that assume too much responsibility. Joseph Pelrine expresses this principle succinctly as follows:

> Don't do anything that you can push off onto someone else.

Many object-oriented languages provide both static and dynamic operations for objects; in Smalltalk there are only dynamic message sends. Instead of providing static class operations, for instance, classes are objects and we simply send messages to classes.

Nearly everything in Smalltalk happens by sending messages. At some point action must take place:

- *Variable declarations* are not message sends. In fact, variable declarations are not even executable. Declaring a variable just causes space to be allocated for an object reference.

- *Assignments* are not message sends. An assignment to a variable causes that variable name to be freshly bound in the scope of its definition.

- *Returns* are not message sends. A return simply causes the computed result to be returned to the sender.

- *Primitives* are not message sends. They are implemented in the virtual machine.

Other than these few exceptions, pretty much everything else does truly happen by sending messages. In particular, since there are no "public fields" in Smalltalk, the only way to update an instance variable of another object is to send it a message asking that it update its own field. Of course, providing setter and getter methods for all the instance variables of an object is not good object-oriented style. Joseph Pelrine also states this very nicely:

> Don't let anyone else play with your data.

5.6   Method lookup follows the inheritance chain

What exactly happens when an object receives a message?

The process is quite simple: the class of the receiver looks up the method to use to handle the message. If this class does not have a method, it asks its superclass, and so on, up the inheritance chain. When the method is found, the arguments are bound to the parameters of the method, and the virtual machine executes it.

It is essentially as simple as this. Nevertheless there are a few questions that need some care to answer:

- *What happens when a method does not explicitly return a value?*

- *What happens when a class reimplements a superclass method?*

- *What is the difference between* self *and* super *sends?*

- *What happens when no method is found?*

The rules for method lookup that we present here are conceptual: virtual machine implementors use all kinds of tricks and optimizations to speed-up method lookup. That's their job, but you should never be able to detect that they are doing something different from our rules.

First let us look at the basic lookup strategy, and then consider these . further questions.

Method lookup

Suppose we create an instance of EllipseMorph.

anEllipse := EllipseMorph new.

If we now send this object the message defaultColor, we get the result Color yellow:

anEllipse defaultColor $\longrightarrow$ Color yellow

The class EllipseMorph implements defaultColor, so the appropriate method is found immediately.

Method 5.14: *A locally implemented method*

EllipseMorph»defaultColor
  "answer the default color/fill style for the receiver"
  ↑ Color yellow

In contrast, if we send the message openInWorld to anEllipse, the method is not immediately found, since the class EllipseMorph does not implement openInWorld. The search therefore continues in the superclass, BorderedMorph, and so on, until an openInWorld method is found in the class Morph (see Figure 5.2).

Method 5.15: *An inherited method*

Morph»openInWorld
  "Add this morph to the world."

  self openInWorld: self currentWorld

Returning self

Notice that EllipseMorph»defaultColor (method 5.14) explicitly returns Color yellow whereas Morph»openInWorld (method 5.15) does not appear to return anything.

Actually a method *always* answers a message with a value — which is, of course, an object. The answer may be defined by the ↑ construct in the method, but if execution reaches the end of the method without executing a ↑, the method still answers a value: it answers the object that received the

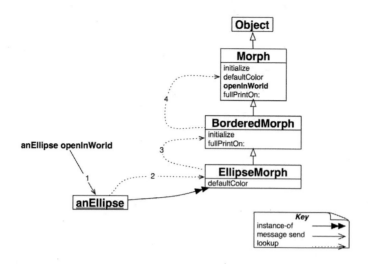

Figure 5.2: Method lookup follows the inheritance hierarchy.

message. We usually say that the method "answers self", because in Smalltalk the pseudo-variable self represents the receiver of the message, rather like this in Java.

This suggests that method 5.15 is equivalent to method 5.16:

Method 5.16: *Explicitly returning self*

```
Morph»openInWorld
   "Add this morph to the world."

   self openInWorld: self currentWorld
   ↑ self      "Don't do this unless you mean it"
```

Why is writing ↑ self explicitly not a good thing to do? Well, when you return something explicitly, you are communicating that you are returning something of interest to the sender. When you explicitly return self, you are saying that you expect the sender to use the returned value. This is not the case here, so it is best not to explicitly return self.

This is a common idiom in Smalltalk, which Kent Beck refers to as "Interesting return value"[3]:

> Return a value only when you intend for the sender to use the value.

---
[3]Kent Beck, *Smalltalk Best Practice Patterns*. Prentice-Hall, 1997.

Overriding and extension

If we look again at the EllipseMorph class hierarchy in Figure 5.2, we see that the classes Morph and EllipseMorph both implement defaultColor. In fact, if we open a new morph (Morph new openInWorld) we see that we get a blue morph, whereas an ellipse will be yellow by default.

We say that EllipseMorph *overrides* the defaultColor method that it inherits from Morph. The inherited method no longer exists from the point of view of anEllipse.

Sometimes we do not want to override inherited methods, but rather *extend* them with some new functionality, that is, we would like to be able to invoke the overridden method *in addition to* the new functionality we are defining in the subclass. In Smalltalk, as in many object-oriented languages that support single inheritance, this can be done with the help of super sends.

The most important application of this mechanism is in the initialize method. Whenever a new instance of a class is initialized, it is critical to also initialize any inherited instance variables. However, the knowledge of how to do this is already captured in the initialize methods of each of the superclass in the inheritance chain. The subclass has no business even trying to initialize inherited instance variables!

It is therefore good practice whenever implementing an initialize method to send super initialize before performing any further initialization:

Method 5.17: *Super initialize*

```
BorderedMorph»initialize
    "initialize the state of the receiver"
    super initialize.
    self borderInitialize
```

> An initialize method should always start by sending super initialize.

Self sends and super sends

We need super sends to compose inherited behaviour that would otherwise be overridden. The usual way to compose methods, whether inherited or not, however, is by means of self sends.

How do self sends differ from super sends? Like self, super represents the receiver of the message. The only thing that changes is the method lookup. Instead of lookup starting in the class of the receiver, it starts in the superclass of the class of the method where the super send occurs.

Note that super is *not* the superclass! It is a common and natural mistake to think this. It is also a mistake to think that lookup starts in the superclass of the receiver. We shall see with the following example precisely how this works.

Consider the message constructorString, which we can send to any morph:

anEllipse constructorString   ⟶   '((EllipseMorph newBounds: (0@0 corner: 50@40)
    color: Color yellow) setBorderWidth: 1 borderColor: Color black)'

The return value is a string that can be evaluated to recreate the morph.

How exactly is this result obtained through a combination of self and super sends? First, anEllipse constructorString will cause the method constructorString to be found in the class Morph, as shown in Figure 5.3.

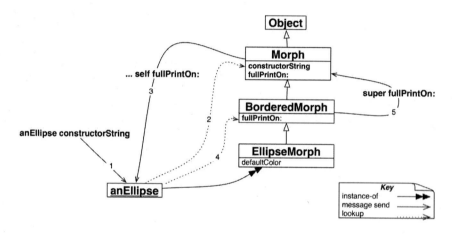

Figure 5.3: self and super sends

Method 5.18: *A self send*

Morph»constructorString
   ↑ String streamContents: [:s | self printConstructorOn: s indent: 0].

The method Morph»constructorString performs a self send of printConstruc-torOn:indent:. This message is also looked up, starting in the class Ellipse-Morph, and found in Morph. This method in turn does a self send of print-ConstructorOn:indent:nodeDict:, which does a self send of fullPrintOn:. Once again, fullPrintOn: is looked up starting in the class EllipseMorph, and fullPrintOn: is found in BorderedMorph (see Figure 5.3 once again). What is critical to notice is that the self send causes the method lookup to start again in the class of the receiver, namely the class of anEllipse.

> A self send triggers a *dynamic* method lookup starting in the class of the receiver.

Method 5.19: *Combining* super *and* self *sends*

```
BorderedMorph»fullPrintOn: aStream
    aStream nextPutAll: '('.
    super fullPrintOn: aStream.
    aStream nextPutAll: ') setBorderWidth: '; print: borderWidth;
        nextPutAll: ' borderColor: ' , (self colorString: borderColor)
```

At this point, BorderedMorph»fullPrintOn: does a super send to extend the fullPrintOn: behaviour it inherits from its superclass. Because this is a super send, the lookup now starts in the superclass of the class where the super send occurs, namely in Morph. We then immediately find and evaluate Morph» fullPrintOn:.

Note that the super lookup did not start in the superclass of the receiver. This would have caused lookup to start from BorderedMorph, resulting in an infinite loop!

> A super send triggers a *static* method lookup starting in the superclass of the class of the method performing the super send.

If you think carefully about super send and Figure 5.3, you will realize that super bindings are static: all that matters is the class in which the text of the super send is found. By contrast, the meaning of self is dynamic: it always represents the receiver of the currently executing message. This means that *all* messages sent to self are looked-up by starting in the receiver's class.

Message not understood

What happens if the method we are looking for is not found?

Suppose we send the message foo to our ellipse. First the normal method lookup would go through the inheritance chain all the way up to Object (or rather ProtoObject) looking for this method. When this method is not found, the virtual machine will cause the object to send self doesNotUnderstand: #foo. (See Figure 5.4.)

Now, this is a perfectly ordinary, dynamic message send, so the lookup starts again from the class EllipseMorph, but this time searching for the method doesNotUnderstand:. As it turns out, Object implements doesNotUnderstand:. This

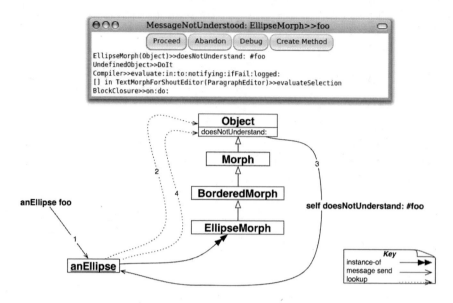

Figure 5.4: Message foo is not understood

method will create a new MessageNotUnderstood object which is capable of starting a Debugger in the current execution context.

Why do we take this convoluted path to handle such an obvious error? Well, this offers developers an easy way to intercept such errors and take alternative action. One could easily override the method doesNotUnderstand: in any subclass of Object and provide a different way of handling the error.

In fact, this can be an easy way to implement automatic delegation of messages from one object to another. A Delegator object could simply delegate all messages it does not understand to another object whose responsibility it is to handle them, or raise an error itself!

5.7   Shared variables

Now we will look at an aspect of Smalltalk that is not so easily covered by our five rules: shared variables.

Smalltalk provides three kinds of shared variables: (1) *globally* shared variables; (2) variables shared between instances and classes (*class variables*), and (3) variables shared amongst a group of classes (*pool variables*). The names of all of these shared variables start with a capital letter, to warn us that they are indeed shared between multiple objects.

Global variables

In Pharo, all global variables are stored in a namespace called Smalltalk, which is implemented as an instance of the class SystemDictionary. Global variables are accessible everywhere. Every class is named by a global variable; in addition, a few globals are used to name special or commonly useful objects.

The variable Transcript names an instance of TranscriptStream, a stream that writes to a scrolling window. The following code displays some information and then goes to the next line in the Transcript.

```
Transcript show: 'Pharo is fun and powerful' ; cr
```

Before you do it, open a transcript by selecting World ▷ Tools ... ▷ Transcript.

HINT *Writing to the Transcript is slow, especially when the transcript window is open. So, if you experience some sluggishness and are writing to the Transcript, think about collapsing it.*

Other useful global variables

- Smalltalk is the instance of SystemDictionary that defines all of the globals — including Smalltalk itself. The keys to this dictionary are the symbols that name the global objects in Smalltalk code. So, for example,

```
Smalltalk at: #Boolean    ⟶    Boolean
```

  Since Smalltalk is itself a global variable,

```
Smalltalk at: #Smalltalk    ⟶    a SystemDictionary(lots of globals)}
```

  and

```
(Smalltalk at: #Smalltalk) == Smalltalk    ⟶    true
```

- Sensor is an instance of EventSensor, and represents input to Pharo. For example, Sensor keyboard answers the next character input on the keyboard, and Sensor leftShiftDown answers true if the left shift key is being held down, while Sensor mousePoint answers a Point indicating the current mouse location.

- World is an instance of PasteUpMorph that represents the screen. World bounds answers a rectangle that defines the whole screen space; all Morphs on the screen are submorphs of World.

- ActiveHand is the current instance of HandMorph, the graphical representation of the cursor. ActiveHand's submorphs hold anything being dragged by the mouse.

- Undeclared is another dictionary — it contains all the undeclared variables. If you write a method that references an undeclared variable, the browser will normally prompt you to declare it, for example, as a global or as an instance variable of the class. However, if you later delete the declaration, the code will then reference an undeclared variable. Inspecting Undeclared can sometimes help explain strange behaviour!

- SystemOrganization is an instance of SystemOrganizer: it records the organization of classes into packages. More precisely, it categorizes the *names* of classes, so

SystemOrganization categoryOfElement: #Magnitude   ⟶   #'Kernel–Numbers'

Current practice is to strictly limit the use of global variables; it is usually better to use class instance variables or class variables, and to provide class methods to access them. Indeed, if Pharo were to be implemented from scratch today, most of the global variables that are not classes would be replaced by singletons.

The usual way to define a global is just to do it on an assignment to a capitalized but undeclared identifier. The parser will then offer to declare the global for you. If you want to define a global programmatically, just execute Smalltalk at: #AGlobalName put: nil. To remove it, execute Smalltalk removeKey: #AGlobalName.

Class variables

Sometimes we need to share some data amongst all the instances of a class and the class itself. This is possible using *class variables*. The term class variable indicates that the lifetime of the variable is the same as that of the class. However, what the term does not convey is that these variables are shared amongst all the instances of a class as well as the class itself, as shown in Figure 5.5. Indeed, a better name would have been *shared variables* since this expresses more clearly their role, and also warns of the danger of using them, particularly if they are modified.

In Figure 5.5 we see that rgb and cachedDepth are instance variables of Color, hence only accessible to instances of Color. We also see that superclass, subclass, methodDict and so on are class instance variables, *i.e.*, instance variables only accessible to the Color class.

But we can also see something new: ColorNames and CachedColormaps are *class variables* defined for Color. The capitalization of these variables gives us a hint that they are shared. In fact, not only may all instances of Color access these shared variables, but also the Color class itself, *and any of its subclasses*. Both instance methods and class methods can access these shared variables.

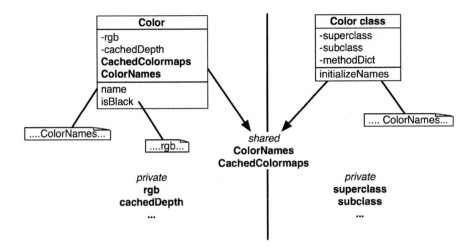

Figure 5.5: Instance and class methods accessing different variables.

A class variable is declared in the class definition template. For example, the class Color defines a large number of class variables to speed up color creation; its definition is shown below (class 5.20).

Class 5.20: *Color and its class variables*

```
Object subclass: #Color
    instanceVariableNames: 'rgb cachedDepth cachedBitPattern'
    classVariableNames: 'Black Blue BlueShift Brown CachedColormaps ColorChart
    ColorNames ComponentMask ComponentMax Cyan DarkGray Gray
    GrayToIndexMap Green GreenShift HalfComponentMask HighLightBitmaps
    IndexedColors LightBlue LightBrown LightCyan LightGray LightGreen LightMagenta
    LightOrange LightRed LightYellow Magenta MaskingMap Orange PaleBlue
    PaleBuff PaleGreen PaleMagenta PaleOrange PalePeach PaleRed PaleTan
    PaleYellow PureBlue PureCyan PureGreen PureMagenta PureRed PureYellow
    RandomStream Red RedShift TranslucentPatterns Transparent VeryDarkGray
    VeryLightGray VeryPaleRed VeryVeryDarkGray VeryVeryLightGray White Yellow'
    poolDictionaries: ''
    category: 'Graphics–Primitives'
```

The class variable ColorNames is an array containing the name of frequently-used colors. This array is shared by all the instances of Color and its subclass TranslucentColor. It is accessible from all the instance and class methods.

ColorNames is initialized once in Color class»initializeNames, but it is accessed from instances of Color. The method Color»name uses the variable to find the name of a color. Since most colors do not have names, it was thought inappropriate to add an instance variable name to every color.

Class initialization

The presence of class variables raises the question: how do we initialize them? One solution is lazy initialization. This can be done by introducing an accessor method which, when executed, initializes the variable if it has not yet been initialized. This implies that we must use the accessor all the time and never use the class variable directly. This furthermore imposes the cost of the accessor send and the initialization test. It also arguably defeats the point of using a class variable, since in fact it is no longer shared.

Method 5.21: *Color class»colorNames*

```
Color class»colorNames
    ColorNames ifNil: [self initializeNames].
    ↑ ColorNames
```

Another solution is to override the class method initialize.

Method 5.22: *Color class»initialize*

```
Color class»initialize
    ...
    self initializeNames
```

If you adopt this solution, you need to remember to invoke the initialize method after you define it, *e.g.*, by evaluating Color initialize. Although class side initialize methods are executed automatically when code is loaded into memory, they are *not* executed automatically when they are first typed into the browser and compiled, or when they are edited and re-compiled.

Pool variables

Pool variables are variables that are shared between several classes that may not be related by inheritance. Pool variables were originally stored in pool dictionaries; now they should be defined as class variables of dedicated classes (subclasses of SharedPool). Our advice is to avoid them; you will need them only in rare and specific circumstances. Our goal here is therefore to explain pool variables just enough so that you can understand them when you are reading code.

A class that accesses a pool variable must mention the pool in its class definition. For example, the class Text indicates that it is using the pool dictionary TextConstants, which contains all the text constants such as CR and LF. This dictionary has a key #CR that is bound to the value Character cr, *i.e.*, the carriage return character.

Class 5.23: *Pool dictionaries in the* Text *class*

```
ArrayedCollection subclass: #Text
    instanceVariableNames: 'string runs'
    classVariableNames: ''
    poolDictionaries: 'TextConstants'
    category: 'Collections–Text'
```

This allows methods of the class Text to access the keys of the dictionary in the method body *directly*, *i.e.*, by using variable syntax rather than an explicit dictionary lookup. For example, we can write the following method.

Method 5.24: *Text»testCR*

```
Text»testCR
    ↑ CR == Character cr
```

Once again, we recommend that you avoid the use of pool variables and pool dictionaries.

5.8 Chapter summary

The object model of Pharo is both simple and uniform. Everything is an object, and pretty much everything happens by sending messages.

- Everything is an object. Primitive entities like integers are objects, but also classes are first-class objects.

- Every object is an instance of a class. Classes define the structure of their instances via *private* instance variables and the behaviour of their instances via *public* methods. Each class is the unique instance of its metaclass. Class variables are private variables shared by the class and all the instances of the class. Classes cannot directly access instance variables of their instances, and instances cannot access instance variables of their class. Accessors must be defined if this is needed.

- Every class has a superclass. The root of the single inheritance hierarchy is ProtoObject. Classes you define, however, should normally inherit from Object or its subclasses. There is no syntax for defining abstract classes. An abstract class is simply a class with an abstract method — one whose implementation consists of the expression self subclassResponsibility. Although Pharo supports only single inheritance, it is easy to share implementations of methods by packaging them as *traits*.

- Everything happens by sending messages. We do not "call methods", we "send messages". The receiver then chooses its own method for responding to the message.

- Method lookup follows the inheritance chain; self sends are dynamic and start the method lookup again in the class of the receiver, whereas super sends are static, and start in the superclass of class in which the super send is written.

- There are three kinds of shared variables. Global variables are accessible everywhere in the system. Class variables are shared between a class, its subclasses and its instances. Pool variables are shared between a selected set of classes. You should avoid shared variables as much as possible.

Chapter 6

The Pharo programming environment

The goal of this chapter is to show you how to develop programs in the Pharo programming environment. You have already seen how to define methods and classes using the browser; this chapter will show you more of the features of the browser, and introduce you to some of the other browsers.

Of course, very occasionally you may find that your program does not work as you expect. Pharo has an excellent debugger, but like most powerful tools, it can be confusing on first use. We will walk you through a debugging session and demonstrate some of the features of the debugger.

One of the unique features of Smalltalk is that while you are programming, you are living in a world of live objects, not in a world of static program text. This makes it possible to get very rapid feedback while programming, which makes you more productive. There are two tools that let you look at, and indeed change, live objects: the *inspector* and the *explorer*.

The consequence of programming in a world of live objects rather than with files and a text editor is that you have to do something explicit to export your program from your Smalltalk image. The old way of doing this, also supported by all Smalltalk dialects, is by creating a *fileout* or a *change set*, which are essentially encoded text files that can be imported into another system. The new way of doing this in Pharo is to upload your code to a versioned repository on a server. This is done using a tool called Monticello, and is a much more powerful and effective way to work, especially when working in a team.

6.1   Overview

Smalltalk and modern graphical interfaces were developed together. Even before the first public release of Smalltalk in 1983, Smalltalk had a self-hosting graphical development environment, and all Smalltalk development was taking place in it. Let's start by looking at the main tools in Pharo.

- The `Browser` is the central development tool. You will use it to create, define, and organize your classes and methods. Using it you can also navigate through all the library classes: unlike other environments where the source code is stored in separate files, in Smalltalk all classes and methods are contained in the image.

- The `Message Names` tool is used to look at all of the methods with a particular selector, or with a selector containing a substring.

- The `Method Finder` tool will also let you find methods, but according to what they *do* as well as what they are called.

- The `Monticello Browser` is the starting point for loading code from, and saving code in, Monticello packages.

- The `Process Browser` provides a view on all of the processes (threads) executing in Smalltalk.

- The `Test Runner` lets you run and debug SUnit tests, and is described in Chapter 7.

- The `Transcript` is a window on the Transcript output stream, which is useful for writing log messages and has already been described in Section 1.5.

- The `Workspace` is a window into which you can type input. It can be used for any purpose, but is most often used for typing Smalltalk expressions and executing them as `do it`s. The use of the workspace was also illustrated in Section 1.5.

The `Debugger` has an obvious role, but you will discover that it has a more central place compared to debuggers for other programming languages, because in Smalltalk you can *program* in the debugger. The debugger is not launched from a menu; it is normally entered by running a failing test, by typing CMD–. to interrupt a running process, or by inserting a `self halt` expression in code.

6.2   The Browser

Many different class browsers have been developed over the years for Smalltalk. Pharo simplifies this story by offering a single browser that integrates various views. Figure 6.1 shows the browser as it appears when you first open it.[1]

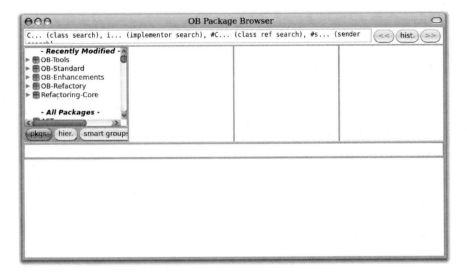

Figure 6.1: The Browser

The four small panes at the top of the browser represent a hierarchic view of the methods in the system, much in the same way as the NeXTstep *File Viewer* and the Mac OS X *Finder* in column mode provide a view of the files on the disk. The leftmost pane lists *packages* of classes; select one (say *Kernel*) and the pane immediately to the right will then show all of the classes in that package.

Similarly, if you select one of the classes in the second pane, say, Model (see Figure 6.2), the third pane will show all of the *protocols* defined for that class, as well as a virtual protocol *--all--*, which is selected by default. Protocols are a way of categorizing methods; they make it easier to find and think about the behaviour of a class by breaking it up into smaller, conceptually coherent pieces. The fourth pane shows the names of all of the methods defined in the selected protocol. If you then select a method name, the source code of the corresponding method appears in the large pane at the bottom of the browser, where you can view it, edit it, and save the edited version. If you select class

---

[1]Recall that if the browser you get does not look like the one shown in Figure 1.12, then you may need to change the default browser. See FAQ 5, p. 316.

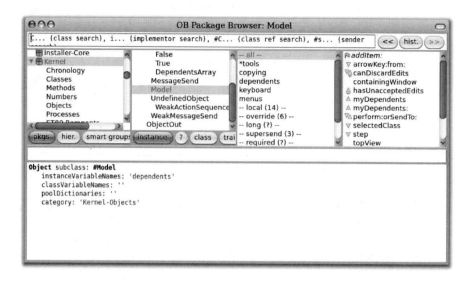

Figure 6.2: Browser with the class Model selected

Model, protocol *dependents* and the method myDependents, the browser should look like Figure 6.3.

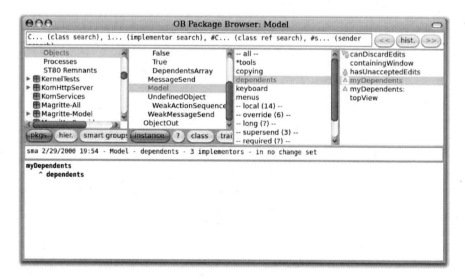

Figure 6.3: Browser showing the myDependents method in class Model

Unlike directories in the Mac OS X *Finder*, the four top panes of the browser are not quite equal. Whereas classes and methods are part of the

Smalltalk language, packages and protocols are not: they are a convenience introduced by the browser to limit the amount of information that needs to be shown in each pane. For example, if there were no protocols, the browser would have to show a list of all of the methods in the selected class; for many classes this list would be too large to navigate conveniently.

Because of this, the way that you create a new package or a new protocol is different from the way that you create a new class or a new method. To create a new package, action-click in the package pane and select new package; to create a new protocol, action-click in the protocol pane and select new protocol. Enter the name of the new thing in the dialog, and you are done: there is nothing more to a package or a protocol than its name and its contents.

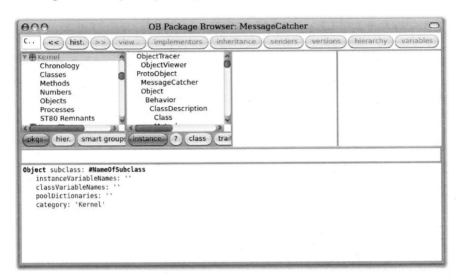

Figure 6.4: Browser showing the class-creation template

In contrast, to create a new class or a new method, you will actually have to write some Smalltalk code. If you click the currently selected package (in the left-most pane), the bottom browser pane will display a class creation template (Figure 6.4). You create a new class by editing this template: replace Object by the name of the existing class of which you wish to create a subclass, replace NameOfSubclass by the name that you would like to give to your new subclass, and fill in the instance variable names if you know them. The category for the new class is by default the category of the currently selected package[2], but you can change this too if you like. If you already have the browser focussed on the class that you wish to subclass, you can get the same template with slightly different initialization by action-clicking in the class

---

[2]Recall that packages and categories are not exactly the same thing. We will look at the precise relationship in Section 6.3

pane, and selecting class templates ... ▷ subclass template. You can also just edit the definition of an existing class, changing the class name to something new. In all cases, when you accept the new definition, the new class (the one whose name follows the #) is created (as is the corresponding metaclass). Creating a class also creates a global variable that references the class, which is why you can refer to all of the existing classes by using their names.

Can you see why the name of the new class has to appear as a Symbol (*i.e.,* prefixed with #) in the class creation template, but after the class is created, code can refer to the class by using the name as an identifier (*i.e.,* without the #)?

The process of creating a new method is similar. First select the class in which you want the method to live, and then select a protocol. The browser will display a method-creation template, as shown in Figure 6.5, which you can fill-in or edit.

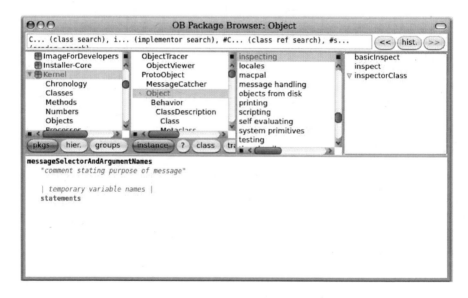

Figure 6.5: Browser showing the method-creation template

Navigating the code space

The browser provides several tools for exploring and analysing code. These tools can be accessed by action-clicking in the various contextual menus, or, in the case of the most frequently used tools, by means of keyboard shortcuts.

Opening a new browser window

Sometimes you want to open multiple browser windows. When you are writing code you will almost certainly need at least two: one for the method that you are typing, and another to browse around the system to see how things work. You can open a browser on a class named by any selected text using the CMD−b keyboard shortcut.

ⓘ *Try this: in a workspace window, type the name of a class (for instance* Morph*), select it, and then press* CMD−b. *This trick is often useful; it works in any text window.*

Senders and implementors of a message

Action-clicking browse ... ▷ senders (n) in the method pane will bring up a list of all methods that may use the selected method. With the browser open on Morph, click on the drawOn: method in the method pane; the body of drawOn: displays in the bottom part of the browser. If you now select senders (n) (Figure 6.6), a menu will appear with drawOn: as the topmost item, and below it, all the messages that drawOn: sends (Figure 6.7). Selecting an item in this menu will open a browser with the list of all methods in the image that send the selected message (Figure 6.8).

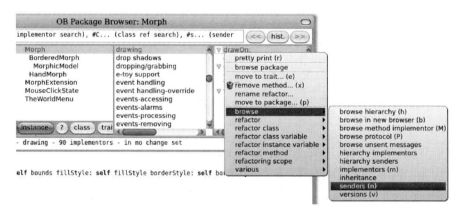

Figure 6.6: The senders (n) menu item.

The "n" in senders (n) tells you that the keyboard shortcut for finding the senders of a message is CMD−n. This will work in *any* text window.

ⓘ *Select the text "drawOn:" in the code pane and press* CMD−n *to immediately bring up the senders of* drawOn:.

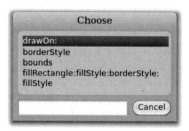

Figure 6.7: Choose senders of which message.

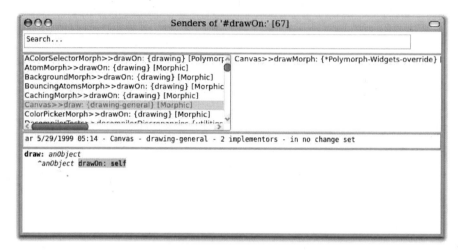

Figure 6.8: The Senders Browser showing that the Canvas»draw method sends the drawOn: message to its argument.

If you look at the senders of drawOn: in AtomMorph»drawOn:, you will see that it is a super send. So we know that the method that will be executed will be in AtomMorph's superclass. What class is that? Action-click browse ▷ hierarchy implementors and you will see that it is EllipseMorph.

Now look at the sixth sender in the list, Canvas»draw, shown in Figure 6.8. You can see that this method sends drawOn: to whatever object is passed to it as an argument, which could potentially be an instance of any class at all. Dataflow analysis can help figure out the class of the receiver of some messages, but in general, there is no simple way for the browser to know which message-sends might cause which methods to be executed. For this reason, the "senders" browser shows exactly what its name suggests: all of the senders of the message with the chosen selector. The senders browser is nevertheless extremely useful when you need to understand how you can

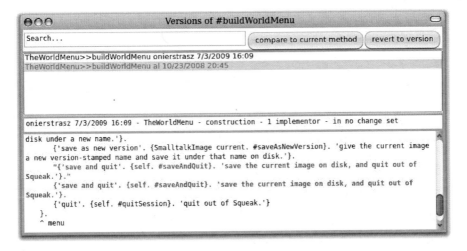

Figure 6.9: The versions browser showing two versions of the TheWorldMenu»
buildWorldMenu: method

use a method: it lets you navigate quickly through example uses. Since all of
the methods with the same selector ought to be used in the same way, all of
the uses of a given message ought to be similar.

The implementors browser works in a similar way, but instead of listing
the senders of a message, it lists all of the classes that implement a method
with the same selector. To see this, select drawOn: in the method pane and
select browse ▷ implementors (m) (or select the "drawOn:" text in the code pane
and press CMD−m). You should get a method list window showing a scrolling
list of the 90-odd classes that implement a drawOn: method. It shouldn't be all
that surprising that so many classes implement this method: drawOn: is the
message that is understood by every object that is capable of drawing itself
on the screen.

Versions of a method

When you save a new version of a method, the old one is not lost. Pharo
keeps all of the old versions, and allows you to compare different versions
and to go back ("revert") to an old version. The browse ▷ versions (v) menu
item gives access to the successive modifications made to the selected method.
In Figure 6.9 we can see two versions of the buildWorldMenu: method.

The top pane displays one line for each version of the method, listing the
initials of the programmer who wrote it, the date and time at which it was
saved, the names of the class and the method, and the protocol in which it
was defined. The current (active) version is at the top of the list; whichever

version is selected is displayed in the bottom pane. Buttons are also provided for displaying the differences between the selected method and the current version, and for reverting to the selected version.

The existence of the versions browser means that you never have to worry about preserving code that you think might no longer be needed: just delete it. If you find that you *do* need it, you can always revert to the old version, or copy the needed code fragment out of the old version and paste it into a another method. Get into the habit of using versions; "commenting out" code that is no longer needed is a bad practice because it makes the current code harder to read. Smalltalkers rate code readability extremely highly.

HINT | *What if you delete a method entirely, and then decide that you want it back? You can find the deletion in a change set, where you can ask to see versions by action-clicking. The change set browser is described in Section 6.8*

Method overridings

The inheritance browser displays all the methods overridden by the displayed method. To see how it works, select the ImageMorph»drawOn: method in the browser. Note the triangular icons next to the method name (Figure 6.10). The upward-pointing triangle tells you that ImageMorph»drawOn: overrides an inherited method (*i.e.*, Morph»drawOn:), and the downward-pointing triangle tells you that it is overridden by subclasses. (You can also click on the icons to navigate to these methods.) Now select browse ▷ inheritance . The inheritance browser shows you the hierarchy of overridden methods (see Figure 6.10).

The Hierarchy view

By default, the browser presents a list of packages in the leftmost pane. However it is possible to switch to a class hierarchy view. Simply select a particular class of interest, such as ImageMorph and then click on the hier. button. You will then see in the left-most pane a class hierarchy displaying all superclasses and subclasses of the selected class. The second pane lists the packages implementing methods of the selected class. In Figure 6.11, the hierarchy browser reveals that the direct superclass of ImageMorph is Morph.

Finding variable references

By action-clicking on a class in the class pane, and selecting browse ▷ chase variables , you can find out where an instance variable or a class variable is used. You will be presented with a *chasing browser* that will allow you to walk through the accessors of all instance variables and class variables, and, in turn, methods that send these accessors, and so on

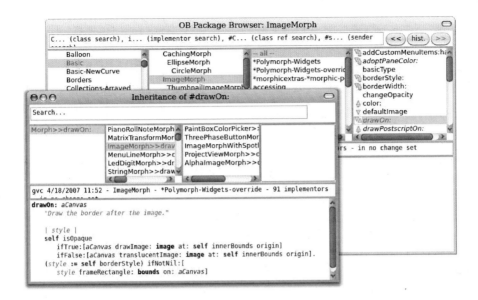

Figure 6.10: ImageMorph»drawOn: and the methods that it overrides. The siblings of the selected methods are shown in the scrolling lists.

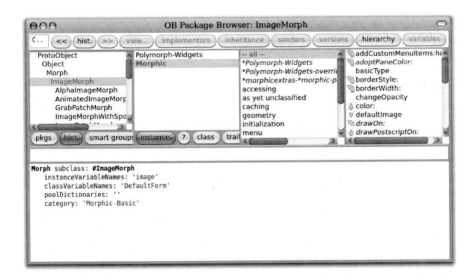

Figure 6.11: A hierarchy view of ImageMorph.

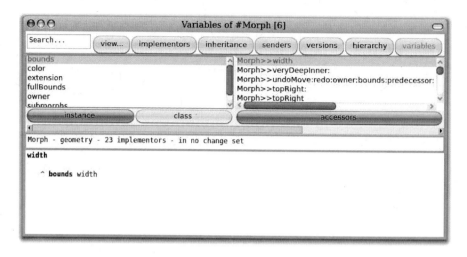

Figure 6.12: A chasing browser for Morph.

(Figure 6.12).

Source

The various ▷view... menu item available by action-clicking in the method pane brings up the "how to show" menu, which allows you to choose how the browser shows the selected method in the source pane. Options include the source code, prettyPrinted source code, byteCode and source code decompiled from the byte codes.

Note that selecting prettyPrint in the "how to show" menu is *not* the same as pretty printing a method before you save it[3]. The menu controls only how the browser displays, and has no effect on the code stored in the system. You can verify this by opening two browsers, and selecting prettyPrint in one and source in the other. In fact, focussing two browsers on the same method and selecting byteCode in one and decompile in another is a good way to learn about the Pharo virtual machine's byte-coded instruction set.

Refactoring

The contextual menus offer a large number of standard refactorings. Simply action-click in any of the four panes to see the currently available refactoring operations. See Figure 6.13.

---

[3] pretty print (r) is the first menu item in the method pane, or half-way down in the code pane.

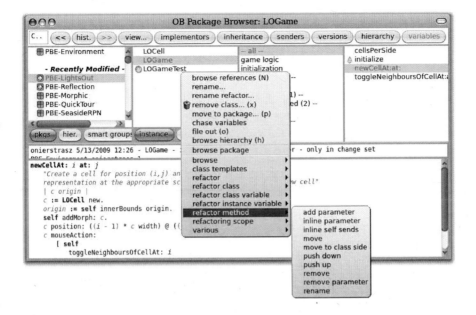

Figure 6.13: Refactoring operations.

Refactoring was formerly available only in a special browser called the refactoring browser, but it can now be accessed from any browser.

The browser menus

Many additional functions are available by action-clicking in the browser panes. Even if the labels on the menu items are the same, their *meaning* may be context dependent. For example, the package pane, the class pane, the protocol pane and the method pane all have a file out menu item. However, they do different things: the package pane's file out menu files out the whole package, the class pane's file out menu files-out the whole class, the protocol pane's file out menu files out the whole protocol, and the method pane's file out menu files-out just the displayed method. Although this may seem obvious, it can be a source of confusion for beginners.

Possibly the most useful menu item is find class... (f) in the package pane. Although the categories are useful for the code that we are actively developing, most of us do not know the categorization of the whole system, and it is much faster to type CMD−f followed by the first few characters of the name of a class than to guess which package it might be in. recent classes... can also help you quickly go back to a class that you have browsed recently, even if you have forgotten its name.

You can also search for a specific class or method by typing the name into the query box at the top left of the browse. When you enter return, a query will be posed on the system, and the query results will be displayed. Note that by prefixing your query with #, you can search for references to a class or senders of a message. If you are searching for a particular method of the selected class, it is often quicker to browse the --all-- protocol (which is the default), place the mouse in the method pane, and type the first letter of the name of the method that you are looking for. This will usually scroll the pane so that the sought-for method name is visible.

(🖉)   *Try both ways of navigating to* OrderedCollection»removeAt:

There are many other options available in the menus. It pays to spend a few minutes working with the browser and seeing what is there.

(🖉)   *Compare the result of* Browse Protocol, Browse Hierarchy, *and* Show Hierarchy *in the class pane menu.*

Browsing programmatically

The class SystemNavigation provides a number of utility methods that are useful for navigating around the system. Many of the functions offered by the classic browser are implemented by SystemNavigation.

(🖉)   *Open a workspace and evaluate the following code to browse the senders of* drawOn::

```
SystemNavigation default browseAllCallsOn: #drawOn:
```

To restrict the search for senders to the methods of a specific class:

```
SystemNavigation default browseAllCallsOn: #drawOn: from: ImageMorph
```

Because the development tools are objects, they are completely accessible from programs and you can develop your own tools or adapt the existing tools to your needs.

The programmatic equivalent to the implementors menu item is:

```
SystemNavigation default browseAllImplementorsOf: #drawOn:
```

To learn more about what is available, explore the class SystemNavigation with the browser. Further navigation examples can be found in the FAQ (Appendix A).

6.3 Monticello

We gave you a quick overview of Monticello, Pharo's packaging tool, in Section 2.9. However, Monticello has many more features than were discussed there. Because Monticello manages *packages*, before telling you more about Monticello, it's important that we first explain exactly what a package is.

Packages: declarative categorization of Pharo code

We have pointed out earlier, in Section 2.3 that packages are more or less equivalent to categories. Now we will see exactly what the relationship is. The package system is a simple, lightweight way of organizing Smalltalk source code that exploits a simple naming convention for categories and protocols.

Let's explain this using an example. Suppose that you are developing a framework named to facilitate the use of relational databases from Pharo. You have decided to call your framework PharoLink, and have created a series of categories to contain all of the classes that you have written, *e.g.*, category 'PharoLink–Connections' contains OracleConnection MySQLConnection PostgresConnection and category 'PharoLink–Model' contains DBTable DBRow DBQuery, and so on. However, not all of your code will reside in these classes. For example, you may also have a series of methods to convert objects into an SQL-friendly format:

```
Object»asSQL
String»asSQL
Date»asSQL
```

These methods belong in the same package as the classes in the categories PharoLink–Connections and PharoLink–Model. But clearly the whole of class Object does not belong in your package! So you need a way of putting certain *methods* in a package, even though the rest of the class is in another package.

The way that you do this is by placing those methods in a protocol (of Object, String, Date, and so on) named *PharoLink (note the initial asterisk). The combination of the PharoLink-... categories and the *PharoLink protocols form a package named PharoLink. To be precise, the rules for what goes in a package are as follows.

A package named Foo contains:

1. all *class definitions* of classes in the category *Foo*, or in categories with names starting with *Foo-*, and

2. all *methods* in *any class* in protocols named *Foo or *foo[4], or whose name

---

[4]When performing this comparison, the case of the letters in the names is ignored.

starts with *Foo-* or *foo-*, and

3. all *methods* in classes in the category *Foo,* or in a category whose name starts with *Foo-, except* for those methods in protocols whose names start with *.

A consequence of these rules is that each class definition and each method belongs to exactly one package. The *except* in the last rule has to be there because those methods must belong to other packages. The reason for ignoring case in rule 2 is that, by convention, protocol names are typically (but not necessarily) lower case (and may include spaces), while category names use CamelCase (and don't include spaces).

The class PackageInfo implements these rules, and one way to get a feel for them is to experiment with this class.

(!) *Evalute the following expression in a workspace:*

```
mc := PackageInfo named: 'Monticello'
```

It is now possible to introspect on this package. For example, printing mc classes in the workspace pane will return the long list of classes that make up the Monticello package. mc coreMethods will return a list of MethodReferences for all of the methods in those classes. mc extensionMethods is perhaps one of the most interesting queries: it will return a list of all methods contained in the Monticello package but not contained within a Monticello class.

Packages are a relatively new addition to Pharo, but since the package naming conventions were based on those already in use, it is possible to use PackageInfo to analyze older code that has not been explicitly adapted to work with it.

(!) *Print* (PackageInfo named: 'Collections') externalSubclasses; *this expression will answer a list of all subclasses of* Collection *that are* not *in the* Collections *package.*

Basic Monticello

Monticello is named after the mountaintop home of Thomas Jefferson, third president of the United States and author of the Statute of Virginia for Religious Freedom. The name means "little mountain" in Italian, and so it is always pronounced with an Italian "c", which sounds like the "ch" in chair: Mont-y'-che-llo.

When you open the Monticello browser, you will see two list panes and a row of buttons, as shown in Figure 6.14. The left-hand pane lists all of the packages that have been loaded into the image that you are running; the particular version of the package is shown in parentheses after the name.

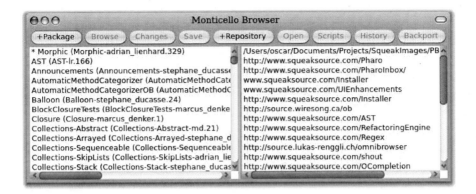

Figure 6.14: The Monticello browser.

The right-hand pane lists all of the source-code repositories that Monticello knows about, usually because it has loaded code from them. If you select a package in the left pane, the right pane is filtered to show only those repositories that contain versions of the selected package.

One of the repositories is a directory named *package-cache*, which is a subdirectory of the directory in which your image is running. When you load code from or write code to a remote repository, a copy is also saved in the package cache. This can be useful if the network is not available and you need to access a package. Also, if you are given a Monticello (.mcz) file directly, for example as an email attachment, the most convenient way to access it is to place it in the package-cache directory.

To add a new repository to the list, click the +Repository, and choose the kind of repository from the pop-up menu. Let's add an HTTP repository.

Open Monticello, click on +Repository, and select HTTP. Edit the dialog to read:

```
MCHttpRepository
    location: 'http://squeaksource.com/PharoByExample'
    user: ''
    password: ''
```

Then click on Open to open a repository browser on this repository. You should see something like Figure 6.15. On the left is a list of all of the packages in the repository; if you select one, then the pane on the right will show all of the versions of the selected package in this repository.

If you select one of the versions, you can Browse it (without loading it into your image), Load it, or look at the Changes that will be made to your image

Figure 6.15: A Repository browser.

by loading the selected version. You can also make a ⬚Copy⬚ of a version of a package, which you can then write to another repository.

As you can see, the names of versions contain the name of the package, the initials of the author of the version, and a version number. The version name is also the name of the file in the repository. Never change these names; correct operation of Monticello depends on them! Monticello version files are just zip archives, and if you are curious you can unpack them with a zip tool, but the best way to look at their contents is using Monticello itself.

To create a package with Monticello, you have to do two things: write some code, and tell Monticello about it.

🖲 *Create a package called* PBE-Monticello, *and put a couple of classes in it, as shown in Figure 6.16. Also, create a method in an existing class, such as* Object, *and put it in the same package as your classes, using the rules from page 117 — see Figure 6.17.*

To tell Monticello about your package, click on ⬚+Package⬚, and type the name of the package, in this case "PBE". Monticello will add PBE to its list of packages; the package entry will be marked with an asterisk to show that the version in the image has not yet been written to any repository. Note that you now should have two packages in Monticello, one called PBE and another called PBE–Monticello. That's alright because PBE will contain PBE–Monticello, and any other packages starting with PBE–.

Initially, the only repository associated with this package will be your package cache, as shown in Figure 6.18. That's OK: you can still save the code,

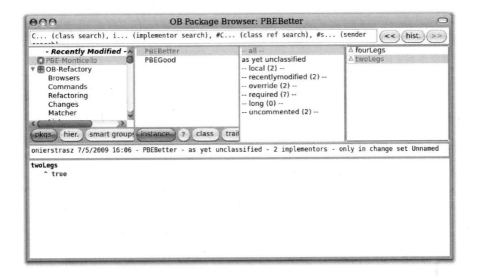

Figure 6.16: Two classes in the "PBE" package.

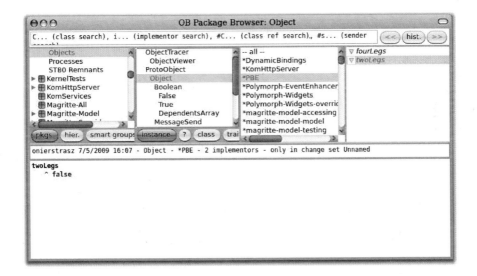

Figure 6.17: An extension method that will also be in the "PBE" package.

which will cause it to be written to the package cache. Just click $\boxed{\text{Save}}$ and you will be invited to provide a log message for the version of the package that you are about to save, as shown in Figure 6.19; when you accept the message, Monticello will save your package. To indicate this, the asterisk

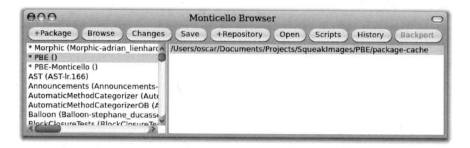

Figure 6.18: The as-yet-unsaved PBE package in Monticello.

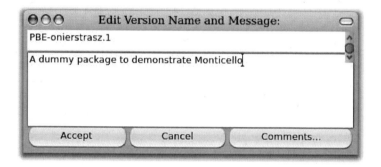

Figure 6.19: Providing a log message for a new version of a package.

decorating the name in Monticello's package pane will be removed, and the version number added.

If you then make a change to the package — say by adding a method to one of the classes — the asterisk will re-appear, showing that you have unsaved changes. If you open a repository browser on the package cache, you can select the saved version, and use Changes and the other buttons. You can of course save the new version to the repository too; once you Refresh the repository view, it should look like Figure 6.20.

To save the new package to a repository other than the package cache, you need to first make sure that Monticello knows about the repository, adding it if necessary. Then you can use the Copy in the package-cache repository browser, and select the repository to which the package should be copied. You can also associate the desired repository with the package by action-clicking on the repository and selecting add to package ... , as shown in Figure 6.21. Once the package knows about a repository, you can save a new version by selecting the repository and the package in the Monticello Browser, and clicking Save. Of course, you must have permission to write to a repository.

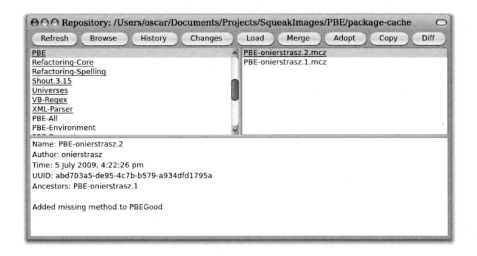

Figure 6.20: Two versions of our package are now in the package cache.

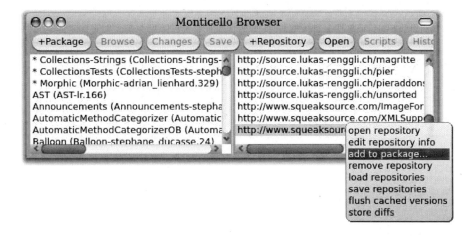

Figure 6.21: Adding a repository to the set of repositories associated with a package.

The PharoByExample repository on *SqueakSource* is world readable but not world writable, so if you try and save there, you will see an error message. However, you can create your own repository on SqueakSource by using the web interface at http://www.squeaksource.com, and use this to save your work. This is especially useful as a mechanism to share your code with friends, or if you use multiple computers.

If you do try and save to a repository where you don't have write permis-

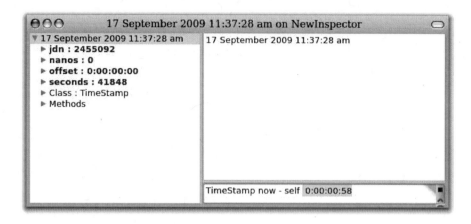

Figure 6.22: Inspecting TimeStamp now

sion, a version will nevertheless be written to the package-cache. So you can recover by editing the repository information (action-click in the Monticello Browser) or choosing a different repository, and then using Copy from the package-cache browser.

6.4   The Inspector and the Explorer

One of the things that makes Smalltalk so different from many other programming environments is that it is provides you with a window onto a world of live objects, not a world of static code. Any of those objects can be examined by the programmer, and even changed — although some care is necessary when changing the basic objects that support the system. By all means experiment, but save your image first!

The Inspector

ⓘ   *As an illustration of what you can do with an inspector, type* TimeStamp now *in a workspace, and then action-click and choose* inspect it.

(It's not necessary to select the text before using the menu; if no text is selected, the menu operations work on the whole of the current line. You can also type CMD–i for inspect it.)

A window like that shown in Figure 6.22 will appear. This is an inspector, and can be thought of as a window onto the internals of a particular object — in this case, the particular instance of TimeStamp that was created when you evaluated the expression TimeStamp now. The title bar of the window shows the printable representation of the object that is being inspected. If you select self at the top of the left pane, the right pane will show the printstring of the object. The left pane shows a tree view of the object, with self at the root. Instance variables can be explored by expanding the triangles next to their names.

The horizontal pane at the bottom of the inspector is a small workspace window. It is useful because in this window, the pseudo-variable self is bound to the object that you have selected in the left pane. So, if you inspect it on

self – TimeStamp today

in the workspace pane, the result will be a Duration object that represents the time interval between midnight today and the instant at which you evaluated TimeStamp now and created the TimeStamp object that you are inspecting. You can also try evaluating TimeStamp now – self; this will tell you how long you have spent reading this section of this book!

In addition to self, all the instance variables of the object are in scope in the workspace pane, so you can use them in expressions or even assign to them. For example, if you select the root object in the left pane and evaluate jdn := jdn – 1 in the workspace pane, you will see that the value of the jdn instance variable will indeed change, and the value of TimeStamp now – self will increase by one day.

There are special variants of the inspector for Dictionaries, OrderedCollections, CompiledMethods and a few other classes that make it easier to examine the contents of these special objects.

The Object Explorer

The *object explorer* is conceptually similar to the inspector, but presents its information in a different way. To see the difference, we'll *explore* the same object that we were just inspecting.

🥐 *Select* self *in the inspector's left-hand pane, then action-click and choose* explore (I).

The explorer window looks like Figure 6.23. If you click on the small triangle next to root, the view will change to Figure 6.24, which shows the instance variables of object that you are exploring. Click on the triangle next to offset, and you will see *its* instance variables. The explorer is really useful when you need to explore a complex hierarchic structure—hence the name.

The workspace pane of the object explorer works slightly differently from that of the inspector. self is not bound to the root object, but rather to the

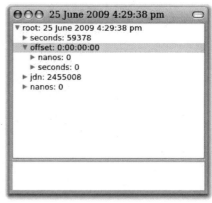

Figure 6.23: Exploring TimeStamp now

Figure 6.24: Exploring the instance variables

object that is currently selected; the instance variables of the selected object are also in scope.

To see the value of the explorer, let's use it to explore a deeply-nested structure of objects.

⓵ *Evaluate* Object explore *in a workspace.*

This is the object that represents the class Object in Pharo. Note that you can navigate directly to the objects representing the method dictionary and even the compiles methods of this class (see Figure 6.25).

6.5   The Debugger

The debugger is arguably the most powerful tool in the Pharo tool suite. It is used not just for debugging, but also for writing new code. To demonstrate the debugger, let's start by creating a bug!

⓵ *Using the browser, add the following method to the class* String:

Method 6.1: *A buggy method*

```
suffix
    "assumes that I'm a file name, and answers my suffix, the part after the last dot"
    | dot dotPosition |
    dot := FileDirectory dot.
    dotPosition := (self size to: 1 by: –1) detect: [ :i | (self at: i) = dot ].
    ↑ self copyFrom: dotPosition to: self size
```

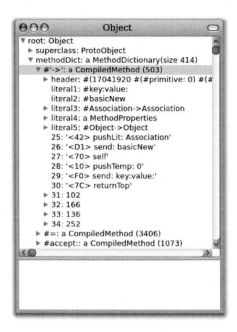

Figure 6.25: Exploring a ExploreObject

Figure 6.26: A PreDebugWindow notifies us of a bug.

Of course, we are sure that such a trivial method will work, so instead of writing an SUnit test, we just type 'readme.txt' suffix in a workspace and print it (p). What a surprise! Instead of getting the expected answer 'txt', a PreDebugWindow pops up, as shown in Figure 6.26.

The PreDebugWindow has a title-bar that tells us what error occurred, and shows us a *stack trace* of the messages that led up to the error. Starting from the bottom of the trace, UndefinedObject»DoIt represents the code that was compiled

Figure 6.27: The debugger.

and run when we selected 'readme.txt' suffix in the workspace and asked Pharo to print it. This code, of course, sent the message suffix to a ByteString object ('readme.txt'). This caused the inherited suffix method in class String to execute; all this information is encoded in the next line of the stack trace, ByteString (String)»suffix. Working up the stack, we can see that suffix sent detect:... and eventually detect:ifNone sent errorNotFound.

To find out *why* the dot was not found, we need the debugger itself, so click on Debug.

The debugger is shown in Figure 6.27; it looks intimidating at first, but it is quite easy to use. The title-bar and the top pane are very similar to those that we saw in the PreDebugWindow. However, the debugger combines the stack trace with a method browser, so when you select a line in the stack trace, the corresponding method is shown in the pane below. It's important to realize that the execution that caused the error is still in your image, but in a suspended state. Each line of the stack trace represents a frame on the execution stack that contains all of the information necessary to continue the execution. This includes all of the objects involved in the computation, with their instance variables, and all of the temporary variables of the executing methods.

In Figure 6.27 we have selected the detect:ifNone: method in the top pane. The method body is displayed in the center pane; the blue highlight around the message value shows that the current method has sent the message value and is waiting for an answer.

The four panes at the bottom of the debugger are really two mini-inspectors (without workspace panes). The inspector on the left shows the current object, that is, the object named self in the center pane. As you select different stack frames, the identity of self may change, and so will the contents of the self-inspector. If you click on self in the bottom-left pane, you will see that self is the interval (10 to: 1 by –1), which is what we expect. The workspace panes are not needed in the debugger's mini-inspectors because all of the variables are also in scope in the method pane; you should feel free to type or select expressions in this pane and evaluate them. You can always cancel (l) your changes using the menu or CMD–*l*.

The inspector on the right shows the temporary variables of the current context. In Figure 6.27, value was sent to the parameter exceptionBlock.

As we can see one method lower in the stack trace, the exceptionBlock is [self errorNotFound: ...], so, it is not surprising that we see the corresponding error message.

Incidentally, if you want to open a full inspector or explorer on one of the variables shown in the mini-inspectors, just double-click on the name of the variable, or select the name of the variable and action-click to choose inspect (i) or explore (l). This can be useful if you want to watch how a variable changes while you execute other code.

Looking back at the method window, we see that we expected the penultimate line of the method to find dot in the string 'readme.txt', and that execution should never have reached the final line. Pharo does not let us run an execution backwards, but it does let us start a method again, which works very well in code such as this that does not mutate objects, but instead creates new ones.

⟳ Click Restart, *and you will see that the locus of execution returns to the first statement of the current method. The blue highlight shows that the next message to be sent will be do: (see Figure 6.28).*

The Into and Over buttons give us two different ways to step through the execution. If you click Over, Pharo executes the current message-send (in this case the do:) in one step, unless there is an error. So Over will take us to the next message-send in the current method, which is value — this is exactly

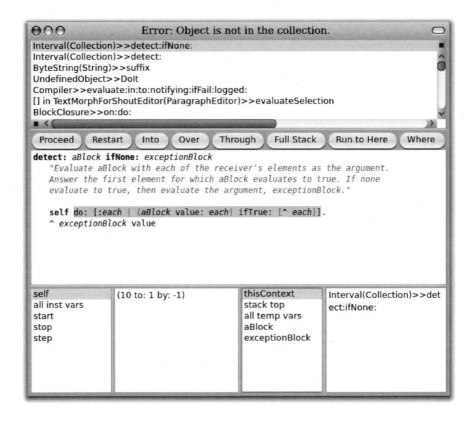

Figure 6.28: The debugger after restarting the detect: ifNone: method

where we started, and not much help. What we need to do is to find out why the do: is not finding the character that we are looking for.

🛈 *After clicking* |Over|, *click* |Restart| *to get back to the situation shown in Figure 6.28.*

🛈 *Click* |Into|; *Pharo will go into the method corresponding to the highlighted message-send, in this case,* Collection»do:.

However, it turns out that this is not much help either: we can be fairly confident that Collection»do: is not broken. The bug is much more likely to be in *what* we asked Pharo to do. |Through| is the appropriate button to use in this case: we want to ignore the details of the do: itself and focus on the execution of the argument block.

🛈 *Select the* detect:ifNone: *method again and* |Restart| *to get back to the state shown in Figure 6.28. Now click on* |Through| *a few times. Select* each *in the context window*

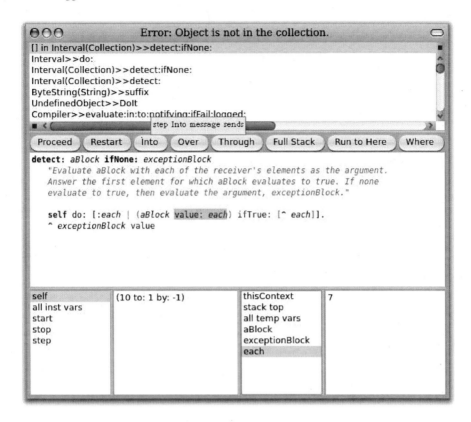

Figure 6.29: The debugger after stepping Through the do: method several times.

as you do so. You should see each *count down from* 10 *as the* do: *method executes.*

When each is 7 we expect the ifTrue: block to be executed, but it isn't. To see what is going wrong, go Into the execution of value: as illustrated in Figure 6.29.

After clicking Into, we find ourselves in the position shown in Figure 6.30. It looks at first that we have gone *back* to the suffix method, but this is because we are now executing the block that suffix provided as argument to detect:. If you select dot in the context inspector, you will see that its value is '.'. And now you see why they are not equal: the seventh character of 'readme.txt' is of course a Character, while dot is a String.

Now that we see the bug, the fix is obvious: we have to convert dot to a character before starting to search for it.

ⓘ *Change the code right in the debugger so that the assignment reads* dot := FileDirectory dot first *and* accept *the change.*

Figure 6.30: The debugger showing why 'readme.txt' at: 7 is not equal to dot

Because we are executing code inside a block that is inside a detect:, several stack frames will have to be abandoned in order to make this change. Pharo asks us if this is what we want (see Figure 6.31), and, assuming that we click yes, will save (and compile) the new method.

The evaluation of the expression 'readme.txt' suffix will complete, and print the answer '.txt'.

Is the answer correct? Unfortunately, we can't say for sure. Should the suffix be .txt or txt? The method comment in suffix is not very precise. The way to avoid this sort of problem is to write an SUnit test that defines the answer.

Method 6.2: *A simple test for the* suffix *method*

```
testSuffixFound
    self assert: 'readme.txt' suffix = 'txt'
```

The effort required to do that was little more than to run the same test in the workspace, but using SUnit saves the test as executable documentation,

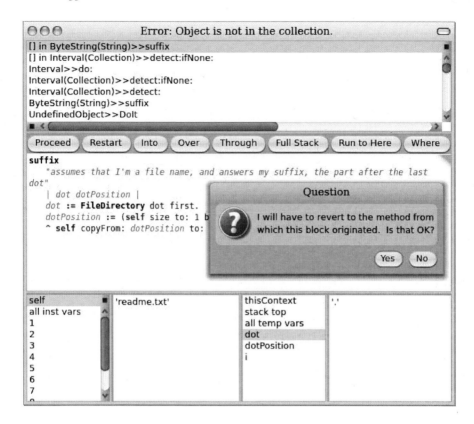

Figure 6.31: Changing the suffix method in the debugger: asking for confirmation of the exit from an inner block

and makes it easy for others to run. Moreover, if you add method 6.2 to the class StringTest and run that test suite with SUnit, you can very quickly get back to debugging the error. SUnit opens the debugger on the failing assertion, but you need only go back down the stack one frame, Restart the test and go Into the suffix method, and you can correct the error, as we are doing in Figure 6.32. It is then only a second of work to click on the Run Failures button in the SUnit Test Runner, and confirm that the test now passes.

Here is a better test:

Method 6.3: *A better test for the* suffix *method*

```
testSuffixFound
    self assert: 'readme.txt' suffix = 'txt'.
    self assert: 'read.me.txt' suffix = 'txt'
```

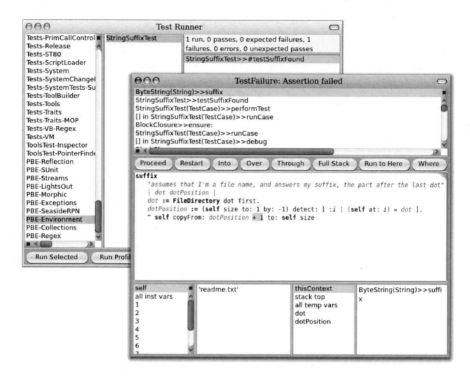

Figure 6.32: Changing the suffix method in the debugger: fixing the off-by-one error after an SUnit assertion failure

Why is this test better? Because it tells the reader what the method should do if there is more than one dot in the target String.

There are a few other ways to get into the debugger in addition to catching errors and assertion failures. If you execute code that goes into an infinite loop, you can interrupt it and open a debugger on the computation by typing CMD−. (that's a full stop or a period, depending on where you learned English).[5] You can also just edit the suspect code to insert self halt. So, for example, we might edit the suffix method to read as follows:

Method 6.4: *Inserting a halt into the suffix method.*

```
suffix
    "assumes that I'm a file name, and answers my suffix, the part after the last dot"
    | dot dotPosition |
    dot := FileDirectory dot first.
    dotPosition := (self size to: 1 by: −1) detect: [ :i | (self at: i) = dot ].
    self halt.
```

---

[5]It is also useful to know that you can bring up an emergency debugger at any time by typing CMD−SHIFT−.

```
↑ self copyFrom: dotPosition to: self size
```

When we run this method, the execution of the self halt will bring up the pre-debugger, from where we can proceed, or go into the debugger and look at variables, step the computation, and edit the code.

That's all there is to the debugger, but it's not all there is to the suffix method. The initial bug should have made you realize that if there is no dot in the target string, the suffix method will raise an error. This isn't the behaviour that we want, so let's add a second test to specify what should happen in this case.

Method 6.5: *A second test for the* suffix *method: the target has no suffix*

```
testSuffixNotFound
    self assert: 'readme' suffix = ''
```

(?) *Add method 6.5 to the test suite in class* StringTest, *and watch the test raise an error. Enter the debugger by selecting the erroneous test in SUnit, and edit the code so that the test passes. The easiest and clearest way to do this is to replace the* detect: *message by* detect: ifNone:, *where the second argument is a block that simply returns the string size.*

We will learn more about SUnit in Chapter 7.

6.6 The Process Browser

Smalltalk is a multi-threaded system: there are many lightweight processes (also known as threads) running concurrently in your image. In the future the Pharo virtual machine may take advantage of multiprocessors when they are available, but at present concurrency is implemented by time-slicing.

The process browser is a cousin of the debugger that lets you look at the various processes running inside Pharo. Figure 6.33 shows a screenshot. The top-left pane lists all of the processes in Pharo, in priority order, from the timer interrupt watcher at priority 80 to the idle process at priority 10. Of course, on a uniprocessor, the only process that can be running when you look is the UI process; all others will be waiting for some kind of event. By default, the display of processes is static; it can be updated by action-clicking and selecting turn on auto-update (a)

If you select a process in the top-left pane, its stack trace is displayed in the top-right pane, just as with the debugger. If you select a stack frame, the corresponding method is displayed in the bottom pane. The process browser is not equipped with mini-inspectors for self and thisContext, but action-clicking on the stack frames provide equivalent functionality.

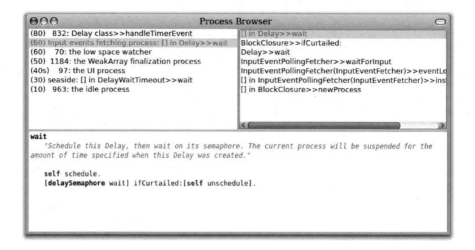

Figure 6.33: The Process Browser

6.7 Finding methods

There are two tools in Pharo to help you find messages. They differ in both interface and functionality.

The *method finder* was described at some length in Section 1.9; you can use it to find methods by name or by functionality. However, to look at the body of a method, the method finder opens a new browser. This can quickly become overwhelming.

The *message names* browser has more limited search functionality: you type a fragment of a message selector in the search box, and the browser lists all methods that contain that fragment in their names, as shown in Figure 6.34. However, it is a full-fledged browser: if you select one of the names in the left pane, all of the methods with that name are listed in the right pane, and can be browsed in the bottom pane. As with the browser, the message names browser has a button bar that can be used to open other browsers on the selected method or its class.

6.8 Change sets and the Change Sorter

Whenever you are working in Pharo, any changes that you make to methods and classes are recorded in a change set. This includes creating new classes, re-naming classes, changing categories, adding methods to existing classes — just about everything of significance. However, arbitrary *doits* are

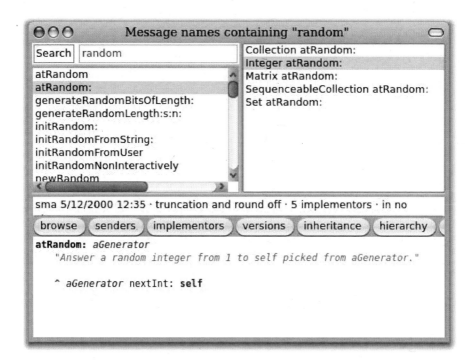

Figure 6.34: The message names browser showing all methods containing the substring random in their selectors.

not included, so if, for example, you create a new global variable by assigning to it in a workspace, the variable creation will not make it into a change set.

At any time, many change sets exist, but only one of them — ChangeSet current — is collecting the changes that are being made to the image. You can see which change set is current and can examine all of the change sets using the change sorter, available by selecting World ▷ Tools ... ▷ Change Sorter.

Figure 6.35 shows this browser. The title bar shows which change set is current, and this change set is selected when the change sorter opens.

Other change sets can be selected in the top-left pane; the action-click menu allows you to make a different change set current, or to create a new change set. The next pane lists all of the classes affected by the selected change set (with their categories). Selecting one of the classes displays the names of those of its methods that are also in the change set (*not* all of the methods in the class) in the left central pane, and selecting a method name displays the method definition in the bottom pane. Note that the change sorter does *not* show you whether the creation of the class itself is part of the change set, although this information is stored in the object structure that is

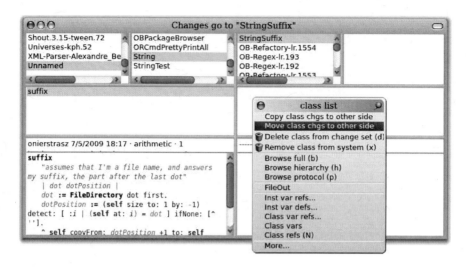

Figure 6.35: The Change Sorter

used to represent the change set.

The change sorter also lets you delete classes and methods from the change set using the action-click menu on the corresponding items.

The change sorter allows you to simultaneously view two change sets, one on the left hand side and the other on the right. This layout supports the change sorter's main feature, which is the ability to move or copy changes from one change set to another, as shown by the action-click menu in Figure 6.35. It is also possible to copy individual methods from one side to the other.

You may be wondering why you should care about the composition of a change set. the answer is that change sets provide a simple mechanism for exporting code from Pharo to the file system, from where it can be imported into another Pharo image, or into another non-Pharo Smalltalk. Change set export is known as "filing-out", and can be accomplished using the action-click menu on any change set, class or method in either browser. Repeated file outs create new versions of the file, but change sets are not a versioning tool like Monticello: they do not keep track of dependencies.

Before the advent of Monticello, change sets were the main means for exchanging code between Pharoers. They have the advantage of simplicity (the file out is just a text file, although we *don't* recommend that you try to edit them with a text editor), and a degree of portability.

The main drawback of change sets, compared to Monticello packages, is that they do not support the notion of dependencies. A filed-out change set is a set of *actions* that change any image into which it is loaded. To successfully load a change set requires that the image be in an appropriate state. For example, the change set might contain an action to add a method to a class; this can only be accomplished if the class is already defined in the image. Similarly, the change set might rename or re-categorize a class, which obviously will only work if the class is present in the image; methods may use instance variables that were declared when they were filed out, but which do not exist in the image into which they are imported. The problem is that change sets do not explicitly describe the conditions under which they can be filed in: the file in process just hopes for the best, usually resulting in a cryptic error message and a stack trace when things go wrong. Even if the file in works, one change set might silently undo a change made by another change set.

In contrast, Monticello packages represent code in a declarative fashion: they describe the state of the image should be in after they have been loaded. This permits Monticello to warn you about conflicts (when two packages require contradictory final states) and to offer to load a series of packages in dependency order.

In spite of these shortcomings, change sets still have their uses; in particular, you may find change sets on the Internet that you want to look at and perhaps use. So, having filed out a change set using the change sorter, we will now tell you how to file one in. This requires the use of another tool, the file list browser.

6.9 The File List Browser

The file list browser is in fact a general-purpose tool for browsing the file system (and also FTP servers) from Pharo. You can open it from the World ▷ Tools . . . ▷ File Browser menu. What you see of course depends on the contents of your local file system, but a typical view is shown in Figure 6.36.

When you first open a file list browser it will be focussed on the current directory, that is, the one from which you started Pharo. The title bar shows the path to this directory. The larger pane on the left-hand side can be used to navigate the file system in the conventional way. When a directory is selected, the files that it contains (but not the directories) are displayed on the right. This list of files can be filtered by entering a Unix-style pattern in the small box at the top-left of the window. Initially, this pattern is *, which matches all file names, but you can type a different string there and accept it, changing the pattern. (Note that a * is implicitly prepended and appended to the pattern that you type.) The sort order of the files can be changes using the name , date and size buttons. The rest of the buttons depend on the name of the file selected in the browser. In Figure 6.36, the file name has the suffix

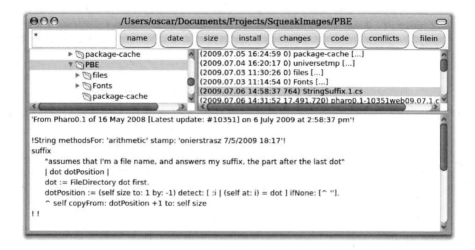

Figure 6.36: A file list browser

.cs, so the browser assumes that it is a change set, and provides buttons to install it (which *files it in* to a new change set whose name is derived from the name of the file), to browse the changes in the file, to examine the code in the file, and to filein the code into the *current* change set. You might think that the conflicts button would tell you about changes in the change set that conflicted with existing code in the image, but it doesn't. Instead it just checks for potential problems in the file that might indicate that the file cannot properly be loaded (such as the presence of linefeeds).

Because the choice of buttons to display depends on the file's *name*, and not on its contents, sometimes the button that you want won't be on the screen. However, the full set of options is always available from the action-click more ... menu, so you can easily work around this problem.

The code button is perhaps the most useful for working with change sets; it opens a browser on the contents of the change set file; an example is shown in Figure 6.37. The file contents browser is similar to the browser except that it does not show categories, just classes, protocols and methods. For each class, the browser will tell you whether the class already exists in the system and whether it is defined in the file (but *not* whether the definitions are identical). It will show the methods in each class, and (as shown in Figure 6.37) will show you the differences between the current version and the version in the file. Contextual menu items in each of the top four panes will also let you file in the whole of the change set, or the corresponding class, protocol or method.

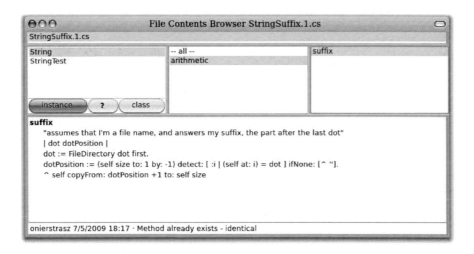

Figure 6.37: A File Contents Browser

6.10 In Smalltalk, you can't lose code

It is quite possible to crash Pharo: as an experimental system, Pharo lets you change anything, including things that are vital to make Pharo work!

To maliciously crash Pharo, try Object become: nil.

The good news is that you need never lose any work, even if you crash and go back to the last saved version of your image, which might be hours old. This is because all of the code that you executed is saved in the *.changes* file. All of it! This includes one liners that you evaluate in a workspace, as well as code that you add to a class while programming.

So here are the instructions on how to get your code back. There is no need to read this until you need it. However, when you do need it, you'll find it here waiting for you.

In the worst case, you can use a text editor on the *.changes* file, but since it is many megabytes in size, this can be slow and is not recommended. Pharo offers you better ways.

How to get your code back

Restart Pharo from the most recent snapshot, and select World ▷ Tools ... ▷ Recover lost changes .

This will give the opportunity to decide how far back in history you wish to browse. Normally, it's sufficient to browse changes as far back as the last snapshot. (You can get much the same effect by editing ChangeList browseRecent: 2000 so that the number 2000 becomes something else, using trial and error.)

One you have a *recent changes* browser, showing, say, changes back as far as your last snapshot, you will have a list of everything that you have done to Pharo during that time. You can delete items from this list using the action-click menu. When you are satisfied, you can file-in what is left, thus incorporating the changes into your new image. It's a good idea to start a new change set, using the ordinary change set browser, before you do the file in, so that all of your recovered code will be in a new change set. You can then file out this change set.

One useful thing to do in the *recent changes* browser is to remove doIts . Usually, you won't want to file in (and thus re-execute) doIts. However, there is an exception. Creating a class shows up as a doIt . *Before you can file in the methods for a class, the class must exist.* So, if you have created any new classes, *first* file-in the class creation doIts, then remove doIts and file in the methods.

When I am finished with the recovery, I like to file out my new change set, quit Pharo without saving the image, restart, and make sure that the new change set files back in cleanly.

6.11   Chapter summary

In order to develop effectively with Pharo, it is important to invest some effort into learning the tools available in the environment.

- The standard *browser* is your main interface for browsing existing categories, classes, method protocols and methods, and for defining new ones. The browser offers several useful buttons to directly jump to senders or implementors of a message, versions of a method, and so on.

- There exist several different browsers (such as the OmniBrowser and the Refactoring Browser), and several specialized browsers (such as the hierarchy browser) which provide different views of classes and methods.

- From any of the tools, you can highlight the name of a class or a method and immediately jump to a browser by using the keyboard shortcut CMD−b.

- You can also browse the Smalltalk system programmatically by sending messages to SystemNavigation default.

- *Monticello* is a tool for exporting, importing, versioning and sharing packages of classes and methods. A Monticello package consists of a category, subcategories, and related methods protocols in other categories.

- The *inspector* and the *explorer* are two tools that are useful for exploring and interacting with live objects in your image. You can even inspect tools by meta-clicking to bring up their morphic halo and selecting the debug handle Ⓐ.

- The *debugger* is a tool that not only lets you inspect the run-time stack of your program when an error is raised, but it also enables you to interact with all of the objects of your application, including the source code. In many cases you can modify your source code from the debugger and continue executing. The debugger is especially effective as a tool to support test-first development in tandem with SUnit (Chapter 7).

- The *process browser* lets you monitor, query and interact with the processes current running in your image.

- The *method finder* and the *message names browser* are two tools for locating methods. The first is more useful when you are not sure of the name, but you know the expected behaviour. The second offers a more advanced browsing interface when you know at least a fragment of the name.

- *Change sets* are automatically generated logs of all changes to the source code of your image. They have largely been superseded by Monticello as a means to store and exchange versions of your source code, but are still useful, especially for recovering from catastrophic failures, however rare these may be.

- The *file list browser* is a tool for browsing the file system. It also allows you to filein source code from the file system.

- In case your image crashes before you could save it or backup your source code with Monticello, you can always recover your most recent changes using a *change list browser*. You can then select the changes you want to replay and file them into the most recent copy of your image.

Chapter 7

SUnit

7.1 Introduction

SUnit is a minimal yet powerful framework that supports the creation and deployment of tests. As might be guessed from its name, the design of SUnit focussed on *Unit Tests*, but in fact it can be used for integration tests and functional tests as well. SUnit was originally developed by Kent Beck and subsequently extended by Joseph Pelrine and others to incorporate the notion of a resource, which we will describe in Section 7.6.

The interest in testing and Test Driven Development is not limited to Pharo or Smalltalk. Automated testing has become a hallmark of the Agile software development movement, and any software developer concerned with improving software quality would do well to adopt it. Indeed, developers in many languages have come to appreciate the power of unit testing, and versions of xUnit now exist for many languages, including Java, Python, Perl, .Net and Oracle. This chapter describes SUnit 3.3 (the current version as of this writing); the official web site of SUnit is sunit.sourceforge.net, where updates can be found.

Neither testing, nor the building of test suites, is new: everybody knows that tests are a good way to catch errors. eXtreme Programming, by making testing a core practice and by emphasizing *automated* tests, has helped to make testing productive and fun, rather than a chore that programmers dislike. The Smalltalk community has a long tradition of testing because of the incremental style of development supported by its programming environment. In traditional Smalltalk development, the programmer would write tests in a workspace as soon as a method was finished. Sometimes a test would be incorporated as a comment at the head of the method that it exercised, or tests that needed some set up would be included as example methods in the class. The problem with these practices is that tests in a workspace are not available to other programmers who modify the code; comments and example methods are better in this respect, but there is still no easy way to keep track of them and to run them automatically. Tests that are not run do not help you to find bugs! Moreover, an example method does not inform the reader of the expected result: you can run the example and see the — perhaps surprising — result, but you will not know if the observed behaviour is correct.

SUnit is valuable because it allows us to write tests that are self-checking: the test itself defines what the correct result should be. It also helps us to organize tests into groups, to describe the context in which the tests must run, and to run a group of tests automatically. In less than two minutes you can write tests using SUnit, so instead of writing small code snippets in a workspace, we encourage you to use SUnit and get all the advantages of stored and automatically executable tests.

In this chapter we start by discussing why we test, and what makes a good test. We then present a series of small examples showing how to use SUnit. Finally, we look at the implementation of SUnit, so that you can understand how Smalltalk uses the power of reflection in supporting its tools.

7.2   Why testing is important

Unfortunately, many developers believe that tests are a waste of their time. After all, *they* do not write bugs — only *other* programmers do that. Most of us have said, at some time or other: "I would write tests if I had more time." If you never write a bug, and if your code will never be changed in the future, then indeed tests are a waste of your time. However, this most likely also means that your application is trivial, or that it is not used by you or anyone else. Think of tests as an investment for the future: having a suite of tests will be quite useful now, but it will be *extremely* useful when your application, or the environment in which it executes, changes in the future.

Tests play several roles. First, they provide documentation of the functionality that they cover. Moreover, the documentation is active: watching the tests pass tells you that the documentation is up-to-date. Second, tests help developers to confirm that some changes that they have just made to a package have not broken anything else in the system — and to find the parts that break when that confidence turns out to be misplaced. Finally, writing tests at the same time as — or even before — programming forces you to think about the functionality that you want to design, *and how it should appear to the client*, rather than about how to implement it. By writing the tests first — before the code — you are compelled to state the context in which your functionality will run, the way it will interact with the client code, and the expected results. Your code will improve: try it.

We cannot test all aspects of any realistic application. Covering a complete application is simply impossible and should not be the goal of testing. Even with a good test suite some bugs will still creep into the application, where they can lay dormant waiting for an opportunity to damage your system. If you find that this has happened, take advantage of it! As soon as you uncover the bug, write a test that exposes it, run the test, and watch it fail. Now you can start to fix the bug: the test will tell you when you are done.

7.3   What makes a good test?

Writing good tests is a skill that can be learned most easily by practicing. Let us look at the properties that tests should have to get a maximum benefit.

1. Tests should be repeatable. You should be able to run a test as often as you want, and always get the same answer.

2. Tests should run without human intervention. You should even be able to run them during the night.

3. Tests should tell a story. Each test should cover one aspect of a piece of code. A test should act as a scenario that you or someone else can read to understand a piece of functionality.

4. Tests should have a change frequency lower than that of the functionality they cover: you do not want to have to change all your tests every time you modify your application. One way to achieve this is to write tests based on the public interfaces of the class that you are testing. It is OK to write a test for a private "helper" method if you feel that the method is complicated enough to need the test, but you should be aware that such a test may have to be changed, or thrown away entirely, when you think of a better implementation.

A consequence of property (3) is that the number of tests should be somewhat proportional to the number of functions to be tested: changing one aspect of the system should not break all the tests but only a limited number. This is important because having 100 tests fail should send a much stronger message than having 10 tests fail. However, it is not always possible to achieve this ideal: in particular, if a change breaks the initialization of an object, or the set-up of a test, it is likely to cause all of the tests to fail.

   eXtreme Programming advocates writing tests before writing code. This may seem to go against our deep instincts as software developers. All we can say is: go ahead and try it. We have found that writing the tests before the code helps us to know what we want to code, helps us know when we are done, and helps us conceptualize the functionality of a class and to design its interface. Moreover, test-first development gives us the courage to go fast, because we are not afraid that we will forget something important.

7.4   SUnit by example

Before going into the details of SUnit, we will show a step by step example. We use an example that tests the class Set. Try entering the code as we go along.

Step 1: create the test class

First you should create a new subclass of TestCase *called* ExampleSetTest. *Add two instance variables so that your new class looks like this:*

Class 7.1: *An Example Set Test class*

```
TestCase subclass: #ExampleSetTest
    instanceVariableNames: 'full empty'
    classVariableNames: ''
    poolDictionaries: ''
    category: 'MySetTest'
```

We will use the class ExampleSetTest to group all the tests related to the class Set. It defines the context in which the tests will run. Here the context is described by the two instance variables full and empty that we will use to represent a full and an empty set.

The name of the class is not critical, but by convention it should end in Test. If you define a class called Pattern and call the corresponding test class PatternTest, the two classes will be alphabetized together in the browser (assuming that they are in the same category). It *is* critical that your class be a subclass of TestCase.

Step 2: initialize the test context

The method setUp defines the context in which the tests will run, a bit like an initialize method. setUp is invoked before the execution of each test method defined in the test class.

Define the setUp *method as follows, to initialize the* empty *variable to refer to an empty set and the* full *variable to refer to a set containing two elements.*

Method 7.2: *Setting up a fixture*

```
ExampleSetTest»setUp
    empty := Set new.
    full := Set with: 5 with: 6
```

In testing jargon the context is called the *fixture* for the test.

Step 3: write some test methods

Let's create some tests by defining some methods in the class ExampleSetTest. Each method represents one test; the name of the method should start with the string 'test' so that SUnit will collect them into test suites. Test methods take no arguments.

② *Define the following test methods.*

The first test, named testIncludes, tests the includes: method of Set. The test says that sending the message includes: 5 to a set containing 5 should return true. Clearly, this test relies on the fact that the setUp method has already run.

Method 7.3: *Testing set membership*

```
ExampleSetTest»testIncludes
    self assert: (full includes: 5).
    self assert: (full includes: 6)
```

The second test, named testOccurrences, verifies that the number of occurrences of 5 in full set is equal to one, even if we add another element 5 to the set.

Method 7.4: *Testing occurrences*

```
ExampleSetTest»testOccurrences
    self assert: (empty occurrencesOf: 0) = 0.
    self assert: (full occurrencesOf: 5) = 1.
    full add: 5.
    self assert: (full occurrencesOf: 5) = 1
```

Finally, we test that the set no longer contains the element 5 after we have removed it.

Method 7.5: *Testing removal*

```
ExampleSetTest»testRemove
    full remove: 5.
    self assert: (full includes: 6).
    self deny: (full includes: 5)
```

Note the use of the method deny: to assert something that should not be true. aTest deny: anExpression is equivalent to aTest assert: anExpression not, but is much more readable.

Step 4: run the tests

The easiest way to run the tests is directly from the browser. Simply action-click on the package, class name, or on an individual test method, and select run the tests (t). The test methods will be flagged red or green, depending on whether they pass or not, and the class will be flagged fully or partially green or red depending on whether all, some or none of the tests pass.

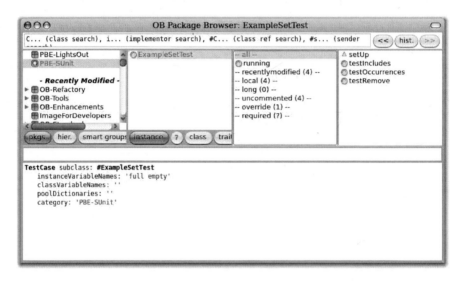

Figure 7.1: Running SUnit tests from the browser

You can also select sets of test suites to run, and obtain a more detailed log of the results using the SUnit *Test Runner*, which you can open by selecting World ▷ Test Runner. The *TestRunner*, shown in Figure 7.2, is designed to make it easy to execute groups of tests. The left-most pane lists all of the categories that contain test classes (*i.e.*, subclasses of TestCase); when some of these categories are selected, the test classes that they contain appear in the pane to the right. Abstract classes are italicized, and the test class hierarchy is shown by indentation, so subclasses of ClassTestCase are indented more than subclasses of TestCase.

✐ *Open a Test Runner, select the category* MyTest*, and click the* Run Selected *button.*

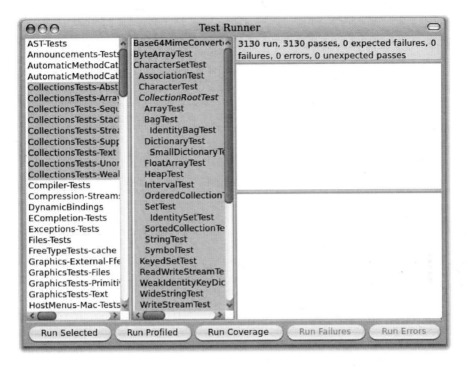

Figure 7.2: The Pharo SUnit Test Runner

(!) *Introduce a bug in* ExampleSetTest»testRemove *and run the tests again. For example, change* 5 *to* 4.

The tests that did not pass (if any) are listed in the right-hand panes of the *Test Runner*; if you want to debug one, to see why it failed, just click on the name.

Step 5: interpret the results

The method assert: , which is defined in the class TestCase, expects a boolean argument, usually the value of a tested expression. When the argument is true, the test passes; when the argument is false, the test fails.

There are actually three possible outcomes of a test. The outcome that we hope for is that all of the assertions in the test are true, in which case the test passes. In the test runner, when all of the tests pass, the bar at the top turns green. However, there are also two kinds of thing that can go wrong when you run a test. Most obviously, one of the assertions can be false, causing the test to *fail*. However, it is also possible that some kind of error occurs during the execution of the test, such as a *message not understood* error or an *index out of bounds* error. If an error occurs, the assertions in the test method may not have been executed at all, so we can't say that the test has failed; nevertheless, something is clearly wrong! In the test runner, failing tests cause the bar at the top to turn yellow, and are listed in the middle pane on the right, whereas erroneous tests cause the bar to turn red, and are listed in the bottom pane on the right.

(2)   *Modify your tests to provoke both errors and failures.*

7.5   The SUnit cook book

This section will give you more details on how to use SUnit. If you have used another testing framework such as JUnit[1], much of this will be familiar, since all these frameworks have their roots in SUnit. Normally you will use SUnit's GUI to run tests, but there are situations where you may not want to use it.

Other assertions

In addition to assert: and deny:, there are several other methods that can be used to make assertions.

First, assert:description: and deny:description: take a second argument which is a message string that can be used to describe the reason for the failure, if it is not obvious from the test itself. These methods are described in Section 7.7.

Next, SUnit provides two additional methods, should:raise: and shouldnt:raise: for testing exception propagation. For example, you would use (self should: aBlock raise: anException) to test that a particular exception is raised during the execution of aBlock. Method 7.6 illustrates the use of should:raise:.

(2)   *Try running this test.*

Note that the first argument of the should: and shouldnt: methods is a *block* that *contains* the expression to be evaluated.

Method 7.6: *Testing error raising*

```
ExampleSetTest»testIllegal
    self should: [empty at: 5] raise: Error.
    self should: [empty at: 5 put: #zork] raise: Error
```

SUnit is portable: it can be used from all dialects of Smalltalk. To make SUnit portable, its developers factored-out the dialect-dependent aspects. The class method TestResult class»error answers the system's error class in a

---

[1] http://junit.org

dialect-independent fashion. You can take advantage of this: if you want to write tests that will work in any dialect of Smalltalk, instead of method 7.6 you would write:

Method 7.7: *Portable error handling*

```
ExampleSetTest»testIllegal
    self should: [empty at: 5] raise: TestResult error.
    self should: [empty at: 5 put: #zork] raise: TestResult error
```

🕭 *Give it a try.*

Running a single test

Normally, you will run your tests using the Test Runner. If you don't want to launch the Test Runner from the open... menu, you can execute TestRunner open as a print it .

You can run a single test as follows.

```
ExampleSetTest run: #testRemove    ⟶    1 run, 1 passed, 0 failed, 0 errors
```

Running all the tests in a test class

Any subclass of TestCase responds to the message suite, which will build a test suite that contains all the methods in the class whose names start with the string "test". To run the tests in the suite, send it the message run. For example:

```
ExampleSetTest suite run    ⟶    5 run, 5 passed, 0 failed, 0 errors
```

Must I subclass TestCase?

In JUnit you can build a TestSuite from an arbitrary class containing test* methods. In Smalltalk you can do the same but you will then have to create a suite by hand and your class will have to implement all the essential TestCase methods like assert:. We recommend that you not try to do this. The framework is there: use it.

7.6   The SUnit framework

SUnit consists of four main classes: TestCase, TestSuite, TestResult, and TestResource, as shown in Figure 7.3. The notion of a *test resource* was introduced in SUnit 3.1 to represent a resource that is expensive to set-up but which can be used by a whole series of tests. A TestResource specifies a setUp method that is executed just once before a suite of tests; this is in distinction to the TestCase»setUp method, which is executed before each test.

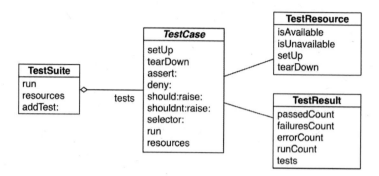

Figure 7.3: The four classes representing the core of SUnit

TestCase

TestCase is an abstract class that is designed to be subclassed; each of its subclasses represents a group of tests that share a common context (that is, a test suite). Each test is run by creating a new instance of a subclass of TestCase, running setUp, running the test method itself, and then running tearDown.

The context is specified by instance variables of the subclass and by the specialization of the method setUp, which initializes those instance variables. Subclasses of TestCase can also override method tearDown, which is invoked after the execution of each test, and can be used to release any objects allocated during setUp.

TestSuite

Instances of the class TestSuite contain a collection of test cases. An instance of TestSuite contains tests, and other test suites. That is, a test suite contains sub-instances of TestCase and TestSuite. Both individual TestCases and TestSuites understand the same protocol, so they can be treated in the same way; for example, both can be run. This is in fact an application of the composite pattern in which TestSuite is the composite and the TestCases are the leaves — see *Design Patterns* for more information on this pattern[2].

---

[2] Erich Gamma et al., *Design Patterns: Elements of Reusable Object-Oriented Software*. Reading, Mass.: Addison Wesley, 1995, ISBN 0–201–63361–2–(3).

TestResult

The class TestResult represents the results of a TestSuite execution. It records the number of tests passed, the number of tests failed, and the number of errors signalled.

TestResource

One of the important features of a suite of tests is that they should be independent of each other: the failure of one test should not cause an avalanche of failures of other tests that depend upon it, nor should the order in which the tests are run matter. Performing setUp before each test and tearDown afterwards helps to reinforce this independence.

However, there are occasions where setting up the necessary context is just too time-consuming for it to be practical to do once before the execution of each test. Moreover, if it is known that the test cases do not disrupt the resources used by the tests, then it is wasteful to set them up afresh for each test; it is sufficient to set them up once for each suite of tests. Suppose, for example, that a suite of tests needs to query a database, or do some analysis on some compiled code. In such cases, it may make sense to set up the database and open a connection to it, or to compile some source code, before any of the tests start to run.

Where should we cache these resources, so that they can be shared by a suite of tests? The instance variables of a particular TestCase sub-instance won't do, because such an instance persists only for the duration of a single test. A global variable would work, but using too many global variables pollutes the name space, and the binding between the global and the tests that depend on it will not be explicit. A better solution is to put the necessary resources in a singleton object of some class. The class TestResource exists to be subclassed by such resource classes. Each subclass of TestResource understands the message current, which will answer a singleton instance of that subclass. Methods setUp and tearDown should be overridden in the subclass to ensure that the resource is initialized and finalized.

One thing remains: somehow, SUnit has to be told which resources are associated with which test suite. A resource is associated with a particular subclass of TestCase by overriding the *class* method resources. By default, the resources of a TestSuite are the union of the resources of the TestCases that it contains.

Here is an example. We define a subclass of TestResource called MyTestResource and we associate it with MyTestCase by specializing the class method resources to return an array of the test classes that it will use.

Class 7.8: *An example of a TestResource subclass*

```
TestResource subclass: #MyTestResource
   instanceVariableNames: "

MyTestCase class»resources
   "associate the resource with this class of test cases"
   ↑{ MyTestResource }
```

7.7   Advanced features of SUnit

In addition to TestResource, the current version of SUnit contains assertion description strings, logging support, and resumable test failures.

Assertion description strings

The TestCase assertion protocol includes a number of methods that allow the programmer to supply a description of the assertion. The description is a String; if the test case fails, this string will be displayed by the test runner. Of course, this string can be constructed dynamically.

```
| e |
e := 42.
self assert: e = 23
   description: 'expected 23, got ', e printString
```

The relevant methods in TestCase are:

```
#assert:description:
#deny:description:
#should:description:
#shouldnt:description:
```

Logging support

The description strings described above may also be logged to a Stream such as the Transcript, or a file stream. You can choose whether to log by overriding TestCase»isLogging in your test class; you must also choose where to log by overriding TestCase»failureLog to answer an appropriate stream.

Continuing after a failure

SUnit also allows us to specify whether or not a test should continue after a failure. This is a really powerful feature that uses the exception mechanisms offered by Smalltalk. To see what this can be used for, let's look at an example. Consider the following test expression:

```
aCollection do: [ :each | self assert: each even]
```

In this case, as soon as the test finds the first element of the collection that isn't even, the test stops. However, we would usually like to continue, and see both how many elements, and which elements, aren't even, and maybe also log this information. You can do this as follows:

```
aCollection do:
    [:each |
    self
        assert: each even
        description: each printString , ' is not even'
        resumable: true]
```

This will print out a message on your logging stream for each element that fails. It doesn't accumulate failures, *i.e.*, if the assertion fails 10 times in your test method, you'll still only see one failure. All the other assertion methods that we have seen are not resumable; assert: p description: s is equivalent to assert: p description: s resumable: false.

7.8   The implementation of SUnit

The implementation of SUnit makes an interesting case study of a Smalltalk framework. Let's look at some key aspects of the implementation by following the execution of a test.

Running one test

To execute one test, we evaluate the expression (aTestClass selector: aSymbol) run.

The method TestCase»run creates an instance of TestResult that will accumulate the results of the tests, then it sends itself the message run:. (See Figure 7.4.)

Method 7.9: *Running a test case*

```
TestCase»run
    | result |
    result := TestResult new.
    self run: result.
    ↑result
```

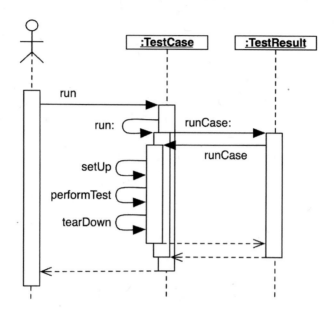

Figure 7.4: Running one test

The method TestCase»run: sends the message runCase: to the test result:

Method 7.10: *Passing the test case to the test result*

```
TestCase»run: aResult
  aResult runCase: self
```

The method TestResult»runCase: sends the message runCase to an individual test, to execute the test. TestResult»runCase deals with any exceptions that may be raised during the execution of a test, runs a TestCase by sending it the message runCase, and counts the errors, failures and passes.

Method 7.11: *Catching test case errors and failures*

```
TestResult»runCase: aTestCase
  | testCasePassed |
  testCasePassed := true.
  [[aTestCase runCase]
      on: self class failure
      do:
          [:signal |
          failures add: aTestCase.
          testCasePassed := false.
          signal return: false]]
              on: self class error
              do:
```

```
                [:signal |
                errors add: aTestCase.
                testCasePassed := false.
                signal return: false].
    testCasePassed ifTrue: [passed add: aTestCase]
```

The method TestCase»runCase sends the messages setUp and tearDown as shown below.

Method 7.12: *Test case template method*

```
TestCase»runCase
    [self setUp.
    self performTest] ensure: [self tearDown]
```

Running a TestSuite

To run more than one test, we send the message run to a TestSuite that contains the relevant tests. TestCase class provides some functionality to build a test suite from its methods. The expression MyTestCase buildSuiteFromSelectors returns a suite containing all the tests defined in the MyTestCase class. The core of this process is

Method 7.13: *Auto-building the test suite*

```
TestCase class»testSelectors
    ↑self selectors asSortedCollection asOrderedCollection select: [:each |
        ('test*' match: each) and: [each numArgs isZero]]
```

The method TestSuite»run creates an instance of TestResult, verifies that all the resources are available, and then sends itself the message run:, which runs all the tests in the suite. All the resources are then released.

Method 7.14: *Running a test suite*

```
TestSuite»run
    | result |
    result := TestResult new.
    self resources do: [ :res |
        res isAvailable ifFalse: [↑res signalInitializationError]].
    [self run: result] ensure: [self resources do: [:each | each reset]].
    ↑result
```

Method 7.15: *Passing the test result to the test suite*

```
TestSuite»run: aResult
    self tests do: [:each |
        self changed: each.
        each run: aResult].
```

The class TestResource and its subclasses keep track of their currently created instances (one per class) that can be accessed and created using the class method current. This instance is cleared when the tests have finished running and the resources are reset.

The resource availability check makes it possible for the resource to be re-created if needed, as shown in the class method TestResource class»isAvailable. During the TestResource instance creation, it is initialized and the method setUp is invoked.

Method 7.16: *Test resource availability*

```
TestResource class»isAvailable
  ↑self current notNil and: [self current isAvailable]
```

Method 7.17: *Test resource creation*

```
TestResource class»current
  current isNil ifTrue: [current := self new].
  ↑current
```

Method 7.18: *Test resource initialization*

```
TestResource»initialize
  super initialize.
  self setUp
```

7.9   Some advice on testing

While the mechanics of testing are easy, writing good tests is not. Here is some advice on how to design tests.

Feathers' Rules for Unit tests. Michael Feathers, an agile process consultant and author, writes:[3]

> *A test is not a unit test if:*
> - *it talks to the database,*
> - *it communicates across the network,*
> - *it touches the file system,*
> - *it can't run at the same time as any of your other unit tests, or*
> - *you have to do special things to your environment (such as editing config files) to run it.*

---

[3]See http://www.artima.com/weblogs/viewpost.jsp?thread=126923. 9 September 2005

> *Tests that do these things aren't bad. Often they are worth writing, and they can be written in a unit test harness. However, it is important to be able to separate them from true unit tests so that we can keep a set of tests that we can run fast whenever we make our changes.*

Never get yourself into a situation where you don't want to run your unit test suite because it takes too long.

Unit Tests *vs*. Acceptance Tests. Unit tests capture one piece of functionality, and as such make it easier to identify bugs in that functionality. As far as possible try to have unit tests for each method that could possibly fail, and group them per class. However, for certain deeply recursive or complex setup situations, it is easier to write tests that represent a scenario in the larger application; these are called acceptance tests or functional tests. Tests that break Feathers' rules may make good acceptance tests. Group acceptance tests according to the functionality that they test. For example, if you are writing a compiler, you might write acceptance tests that make assertions about the code generated for each possible source language statement. Such tests might exercise many classes, and might take a long time to run because they touch the file system. You can write them using SUnit, but you won't want to run them each time you make a small change, so they should be separated from the true unit tests.

Black's Rule of Testing. For every test in the system, you should be able to identify some property for which the test increases your confidence. It's obvious that there should be no important property that you are not testing. This rule states the less obvious fact that there should be no test that does not add value to the system by increasing your confidence that a useful property holds. For example, several tests of the same property do no good. In fact, they do harm in two ways. First, they make it harder to infer the behaviour of the class by reading the tests. Second, because one bug in the code might then break many tests, they make it harder to estimate how many bugs remain in the code. So, have a property in mind when you write a test.

7.10 Chapter summary

This chapter explained why tests are an important investment in the future of your code. We explained in a step-by-step fashion how to define a few tests for the class Set. Then we gave an overview of the core of the SUnit framework by presenting the classes TestCase, TestResult, TestSuite and TestResources. Finally we looked deep inside SUnit by following the execution of a test and a test suite.

- To maximize their potential, unit tests should be fast, repeatable, independent of any direct human interaction and cover a single unit of functionality.

- Tests for a class called MyClass belong in a class classed MyClassTest, which should be introduced as a subclass of TestCase.

- Initialize your test data in a setUp method.

- Each test method should start with the word "test".

- Use the TestCase methods assert:, deny: and others to make assertions.

- Run tests using the SUnit test runner tool (in the tool bar).

Chapter 8

Basic Classes

Most of the magic of Smalltalk is not in the language but in the class libraries. To program effectively with Smalltalk, you need to learn how the class libraries support the language and environment. The class libraries are entirely written in Smalltalk and can easily be extended since a package may add new functionality to a class even if it does not define this class.

Our goal here is not to present in tedious detail the whole of the Pharo class library, but rather to point out the key classes and methods that you will need to use or override to program effectively. In this chapter we cover the basic classes that you will need for nearly every application: Object, Number and its subclasses, Character, String, Symbol and Boolean.

8.1 Object

For all intents and purposes, Object is the root of the inheritance hierarchy. Actually, in Pharo the true root of the hierarchy is ProtoObject, which is used to define minimal entities that masquerade as objects, but we can ignore this point for the time being.

Object can be found in the *Kernel-Objects* category. Astonishingly, there are some 400 methods to be found here (including extensions). In other words, every class that you define will automatically provide these 400 methods, whether you know what they do or not. Note that some of the methods should be removed and new versions of Pharo may remove some of the superfluous methods.

The class comment for the Object states:

*Object is the root class for almost all of the other classes in the class
hierarchy. The exceptions are* ProtoObject *(the superclass of* Object*) and
its subclasses. Class* Object *provides default behaviour common to all
normal objects, such as access, copying, comparison, error handling,
message sending, and reflection. Also utility messages that all objects
should respond to are defined here.* Object *has no instance variables,
nor should any be added. This is due to several classes of objects that
inherit from* Object *that have special implementations (*SmallInteger *and*
UndefinedObject *for example) or the VM knows about and depends on
the structure and layout of certain standard classes.*

If we begin to browse the method categories on the instance side of Object
we start to see some of the key behaviour it provides.

Printing

Every object in Smalltalk can return a printed form of itself. You can select
any expression in a workspace and select the print it menu: this executes the
expression and asks the returned object to print itself. In fact this sends the
message printString to the returned object. The method printString, which is a
template method, at its core sends the message printOn: to its receiver. The
message printOn: is a hook that can be specialized.

Object»printOn: is very likely one of the methods that you will most frequently override. This method takes as its argument a Stream on which a
String representation of the object will be written. The default implementation
simply writes the class name preceded by "a" or "an". Object»printString returns
the String that is written.

For example, the class Browser does not redefine the method printOn: and
sending the message printString to an instance executes the methods defined
in Object.

Browser new printString $\longrightarrow$ 'a Browser'

The class Color shows an example of printOn: specialization. It prints the
name of the class followed the name of the class method used to generate
that color.

Method 8.1: *printOn: redefinition.*

```
Color»printOn: aStream
   | name |
   (name := self name) ifNotNil:
     [ ↑ aStream
        nextPutAll: 'Color ';
        nextPutAll: name ].
   self storeOn: aStream
```

```
Color red printString  ⟶  'Color red'
```

Note that the message printOn: is not the same as storeOn:. The message storeOn: puts on its argument stream an expression that can be used to recreate the receiver. This expression is evaluated when the stream is read using the message readFrom:. printOn: just returns a textual version of the receiver. Of course, it may happen that this textual representation may represent the receiver as a self-evaluating expression.

A word about representation and self-evaluating representation.   In functional programming, expressions return values when executed. In Smalltalk, messages (expressions) return objects (values). Some objects have the nice properties that their value is themselves. For example, the value of the object true is itself *i.e.*, the object true. We call such objects *self-evaluating objects*. You can see a *printed* version of an object value when you print the object in a workspace. Here are some examples of such self-evaluating expressions.

```
true        ⟶    true
3@4         ⟶    3@4
$a          ⟶    $a
#(1 2 3)    ⟶    #(1 2 3)
Color red   ⟶    Color red
```

Note that some objects such as arrays are self-evaluating or not depending on the objects they contain. For example, an array of booleans is self-evaluating whereas an array of persons is not. The following example shows that a dynamic array is self-evaluating only if its elements are:

```
{10@10 . 100@100}        ⟶    {10@10 . 100@100}
{Browser new . 100@100}  ⟶    an Array(a Browser 100@100)
```

Remember that literal arrays can only contain literals. Hence the following array does not contain two points but rather six literal elements.

```
#(10@10 100@100)   ⟶    #(10 #@ 10 100 #@ 100)
```

Lots of printOn: method specializations implement self-evaluating behavior. The implementations of Point»printOn: and Interval»printOn: are self-evaluating.

Method 8.2: *Self-evaluation of* Point

```
Point»printOn: aStream
    "The receiver prints on aStream in terms of infix notation."
    x printOn: aStream.
    aStream nextPut: $@.
    y printOn: aStream
```

Method 8.3: *Self-evaluation of* Interval

```
Interval»printOn: aStream
   aStream nextPut: $(;
      print: start;
      nextPutAll: ' to: ';
      print: stop.
   step ~= 1 ifTrue: [aStream nextPutAll: ' by: '; print: step].
   aStream nextPut: $)
```

1 to: 10   ⟶   (1 to: 10)   *"intervals are self–evaluating"*

Identity and equality

In Smalltalk, the message = tests object *equality* (*i.e.,* whether two objects represent the same value) whereas == tests object *identity* (*i.e.,* whether two expressions represent the same object).

The default implementation of object equality is to test for object identity:

Method 8.4: *Object equality*

```
Object»= anObject
   "Answer whether the receiver and the argument represent the same object.
   If = is redefined in any subclass, consider also redefining the message hash."
   ↑ self == anObject
```

This is a method that you will frequently want to override. Consider the case of Complex numbers:

(1 + 2 i) = (1 + 2 i)   ⟶   true   *"same value"*
(1 + 2 i) == (1 + 2 i)   ⟶   false   *"but different objects"*

This works because Complex overrides = as follows:

Method 8.5: *Equality for complex numbers*

```
Complex»= anObject
   anObject isComplex
      ifTrue: [↑ (real = anObject real) & (imaginary = anObject imaginary)]
      ifFalse: [↑ anObject adaptToComplex: self andSend: #=]
```

The default implementation of Object»~= simply negates Object»=, and should not normally need to be changed.

(1 + 2 i) ~= (1 + 4 i)   ⟶   true

If you override =, you should consider overriding hash. If instances of your class are ever used as keys in a Dictionary, then you should make sure that instances that are considered to be equal have the same hash value:

Method 8.6: *Hash must be reimplemented for complex numbers*

```
Complex»hash
    "Hash is reimplemented because = is implemented."
    ↑ real hash bitXor: imaginary hash.
```

Although you should override = and hash together, you should *never* override ==. (The semantics of object identity is the same for all classes.) == is a primitive method of ProtoObject.

Note that Pharo has some strange behaviour compared to other Smalltalks: for example a symbol and a string can be equal. (We consider this be a bug, not a feature.)

```
#'lulu' = 'lulu'    ⟶    true
'lulu' = #'lulu'    ⟶    true
```

Class membership

Several methods allow you to query the class of an object.

class. You can ask any object about its class using the message class.

```
1 class    ⟶    SmallInteger
```

Conversely, you can ask if an object is an instance of a specific class:

```
1 isMemberOf: SmallInteger    ⟶    true    "must be precisely this class"
1 isMemberOf: Integer         ⟶    false
1 isMemberOf: Number          ⟶    false
1 isMemberOf: Object          ⟶    false
```

Since Smalltalk is written in itself, you can really navigate through its structure using the right combination of superclass and class messages (see Chapter 13).

isKindOf: Object»isKindOf: answers whether the receiver's class is either the same as, or a subclass of the argument class.

```
1 isKindOf: SmallInteger    ⟶    true
1 isKindOf: Integer         ⟶    true
1 isKindOf: Number          ⟶    true
1 isKindOf: Object          ⟶    true
1 isKindOf: String          ⟶    false

1/3 isKindOf: Number        ⟶    true
1/3 isKindOf: Integer       ⟶    false
```

1/3 which is a Fraction is a kind of Number, since the class Number is a super-class of the class Fraction, but 1/3 is not a Integer.

respondsTo: Object»respondsTo: answers whether the receiver understands the message selector given as an argument.

```
1 respondsTo: #,   ⟶   false
```

Normally it is a bad idea to query an object for its class, or to ask it which messages it understands. Instead of making decisions based on the class of object, you should simply send a message to the object and let it decide (*i.e.*, on the basis of its class) how it should behave.

Copying

Copying objects introduces some subtle issues. Since instance variables are accessed by reference, a *shallow copy* of an object would share its references to instance variables with the original object:

```
a1 := { { 'harry' } }.
a1    ⟶    #(#('harry'))
a2 := a1 shallowCopy.
a2    ⟶    #(#('harry'))
(a1 at: 1) at: 1 put: 'sally'.
a1    ⟶    #(#('sally'))
a2    ⟶    #(#('sally'))    "the subarray is shared"
```

Object»shallowCopy is a primitive method that creates a shallow copy of an object. Since a2 is only a shallow copy of a1, the two arrays share a reference to the nested Array that they contain.

Object»shallowCopy is the "public interface" to Object»copy and should be overridden if instances are unique. This is the case, for example, with the classes Boolean, Character, SmallInteger, Symbol and UndefinedObject.

Object»copyTwoLevel does the obvious thing when a simple shallow copy does not suffice:

```
a1 := { { 'harry' } } .
a2 := a1 copyTwoLevel.
(a1 at: 1) at: 1 put: 'sally'.
a1    ⟶    #(#('sally'))
a2    ⟶    #(#('harry'))    "fully independent state"
```

Object»deepCopy makes an arbitrarily deep copy of an object.

```
a1 := { { { 'harry' } } } .
a2 := a1 deepCopy.
```

```
(a1 at: 1) at: 1 put: 'sally'.
a1    ⟶    #(#('sally'))
a2    ⟶    #(#(#('harry')))
```

The problem with deepCopy is that it will not terminate when applied to a mutually recursive structure:

```
a1 := { 'harry' }.
a2 := { a1 }.
a1 at: 1 put: a2.
a1 deepCopy    ⟶    ... does not terminate!
```

Although it is possible to override deepCopy to do the right thing, Object» copy offers a better solution:

Method 8.7: *Copying objects as a template method*

```
Object»copy
    "Answer another instance just like the receiver.
    Subclasses typically override postCopy;
    they typically do not override shallowCopy."
    ↑self shallowCopy postCopy
```

You should override postCopy to copy any instance variables that should not be shared. postCopy should always do a super postCopy.

Debugging

The most important method here is halt. In order to set a breakpoint in a method, simply insert the message send self halt at some point in the body of the method. When this message is sent, execution will be interrupted and a debugger will open to this point in your program. (See Chapter 6 for more details about the debugger.)

The next most important message is assert:, which takes a block as its argument. If the block returns true, execution continues. Otherwise an AssertionFailure exception will be raised. If this exception is not otherwise caught, the debugger will open to this point in the execution. assert: is especially useful to support *design by contract*. The most typical usage is to check non-trivial pre-conditions to public methods of objects. Stack»pop could easily have been implemented as follows:

Method 8.8: *Checking a pre-condition*

```
Stack»pop
    "Return the first element and remove it from the stack."
    self assert: [ self isEmpty not ].
    ↑self linkedList removeFirst element
```

Do not confuse Object»assert: with TestCase»assert:, which occurs in the SUnit testing framework (see Chapter 7). While the former expects a block as its argument[1], the latter expects a Boolean. Although both are useful for debugging, they each serve a very different intent.

Error handling

This protocol contains several methods useful for signaling run-time errors.

Sending self deprecated: *anExplanationString* signals that the current method should no longer be used, if deprecation has been turned on in the *debug* protocol of the preference browser. The String argument should offer an alternative.

```
1 doIfNotNil: [ :arg | arg printString, ' is not nil' ]
     ⟶     SmallInteger(Object)»doIfNotNil: has been deprecated. use ifNotNilDo:
```

doesNotUnderstand: is sent whenever message lookup fails. The default implementation, *i.e.*, Object»doesNotUnderstand: will trigger the debugger at this point. It may be useful to override doesNotUnderstand: to provide some other behaviour.

Object»error and Object»error: are generic methods that can be used to raise exceptions. (Generally it is better to raise your own custom exceptions, so you can distinguish errors arising from your code from those coming from kernel classes.)

Abstract methods in Smalltalk are implemented by convention with the body self subclassResponsibility. Should an abstract class be instantiated by accident, then calls to abstract methods will result in Object»subclassResponsibility being evaluated.

Method 8.9: *Signaling that a method is abstract*

```
Object»subclassResponsibility
    "This message sets up a framework for the behavior of the class' subclasses.
    Announce that the subclass should have implemented this message."
    self error: 'My subclass should have overridden ', thisContext sender selector
        printString
```

Magnitude, Number and Boolean are classical examples of abstract classes that we shall see shortly in this chapter.

```
Number new + 1     ⟶     Error: My subclass should have overridden #+
```

self shouldNotImplement is sent by convention to signal that an inherited method is not appropriate for this subclass. This is generally a sign that

---

[1] Actually, it will take any argument that understands value, including a Boolean.

something is not quite right with the design of the class hierarchy. Due to the limitations of single inheritance, however, sometimes it is very hard to avoid such workarounds.

A typical example is Collection»remove: which is inherited by Dictionary but flagged as not implemented. (A Dictionary provides removeKey: instead.)

Testing

The *testing* methods have nothing to do with SUnit testing! A testing method is one that lets you ask a question about the state of the receiver and returns a Boolean.

Numerous testing methods are provided by Object. We have already seen isComplex. Others include isArray, isBoolean, isBlock, isCollection and so on. Generally such methods are to be avoided since querying an object for its class is a form of violation of encapsulation. Instead of testing an object for its class, one should simply send a request and let the object decide how to handle it.

Nevertheless some of these testing methods are undeniably useful. The most useful are probably ProtoObject»isNil and Object»notNil (though the Null Object[2] design pattern can obviate the need for even these methods).

Initialize release

A final key method that occurs not in Object but in ProtoObject is initialize.

Method 8.10: initialize *as an empty hook method*

```
ProtoObject»initialize
    "Subclasses should redefine this method to perform initializations on instance creation"
```

The reason this is important is that in Pharo, the default new method defined for every class in the system will send initialize to newly created instances.

Method 8.11: new *as a class-side template method*

```
Behavior»new
    "Answer a new initialized instance of the receiver (which is a class) with no indexable
    variables. Fail if the class is indexable."
    ↑ self basicNew initialize
```

This means that simply by overriding the initialize hook method, new instances of your class will automatically be initialized. The initialize method

---

[2]Bobby Woolf, Null Object. In Robert Martin, Dirk Riehle and Frank Buschmann, editors, Pattern Languages of Program Design 3. Addison Wesley, 1998.

should normally perform a super initialize to establish the class invariant for any inherited instance variables. (Note that this is *not* the standard behaviour of other Smalltalks.)

8.2 Numbers

Remarkably, numbers in Smalltalk are not primitive data values but true objects. Of course numbers are implemented efficiently in the virtual machine, but the Number hierarchy is as perfectly accessible and extensible as any other portion of the Smalltalk class hierarchy.

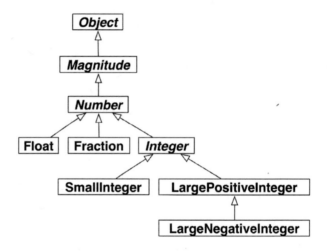

Figure 8.1: The Number Hierarchy

Numbers are found in the *Kernel-Numbers* category. The abstract root of this hierarchy is Magnitude, which represents all kinds of classes supporting comparision operators. Number adds various arithmetic and other operators as mostly abstract methods. Float and Fraction represent, respectively, floating point numbers and fractional values. Integer is also abstract, thus distinguishing between subclasses SmallInteger, LargePositiveInteger and LargeNegativeInteger. For the most part users do not need to be aware of the difference between the three Integer classes, as values are automatically converted as needed.

Magnitude

Magnitude is the parent not only of the Number classes, but also of other classes supporting comparison operations, such as Character, Duration and Timespan. (Complex numbers are not comparable, and so do not inherit from Number.)

Methods < and = are abstract. The remaining operators are generically defined. For example:

Method 8.12: *Abstract comparison methods*

```
Magnitude» < aMagnitude
    "Answer whether the receiver is less than the argument."
    ↑self subclassResponsibility

Magnitude» > aMagnitude
    "Answer whether the receiver is greater than the argument."
    ↑aMagnitude < self
```

Number

Similarly, Number defines +, –, * and / to be abstract, but all other arithmetic operators are generically defined.

All Number objects support various *converting* operators, such as asFloat and asInteger. There are also numerous *shortcut constructor methods*, such as i, which converts a Number to an instance of Complex with a zero real component, and others which generate Durations, such as hour, day and week.

Numbers directly support common *math functions* such as sin, log, raiseTo:, squared, sqrt and so on.

Number»printOn: is implemented in terms of the abstract method Number» printOn:base:. (The default base is 10.)

Testing methods include even, odd, positive and negative. Unsurprisingly Number overrides isNumber. More interesting, isInfinite is defined to return false.

Truncation methods include floor, ceiling, integerPart, fractionPart and so on.

```
1 + 2.5     ⟶    3.5        "Addition of two numbers"
3.4 * 5     ⟶    17.0       "Multiplication of two numbers"
8 / 2       ⟶    4          "Division of two numbers"
10 – 8.3    ⟶    1.7        "Subtraction of two numbers"
12 = 11     ⟶    false      "Equality between two numbers"
12 ~= 11    ⟶    true       "Test if two numbers are different"
12 > 9      ⟶    true       "Greater than"
12 >= 10    ⟶    true       "Greater or equal  than"
12 < 10     ⟶    false      "Smaller than"
100@10      ⟶    100@10     "Point creation"
```

The following example works surprisingly well in Smalltalk:

```
1000 factorial / 999 factorial    ⟶    1000
```

Note that 1000 factorial is really calculated which in many other languages can be quite difficult to compute. This is an excellent example of automatic coercion and exact handling of a number.

🕮   *Try to display the result of* 1000 factorial. *It takes more time to display it than to calculate it!*

Float

Float implements the abstract Number methods for floating point numbers.

More interestingly, Float class (*i.e.*, the class-side of Float) provides methods to return the following *constants*: e, infinity, nan and pi.

Float pi	⟶	3.141592653589793
Float infinity	⟶	Infinity
Float infinity isInfinite	⟶	true

Fraction

Fractions are represented by instance variables for the numerator and denominator, which should be Integers. Fractions are normally created by Integer division (rather than using the constructor method Fraction»numerator:denominator:):

6/8	⟶	(3/4)
(6/8) class	⟶	Fraction

Multiplying a Fraction by an Integer or another Fraction may yield an Integer:

6/8 * 4	⟶	3

Integer

Integer is the abstract parent of three concrete integer implementations. In addition to providing concrete implementations of many abstract Number methods, it also adds a few methods specific to integers, such as factorial, atRandom, isPrime, gcd: and many others.

SmallInteger is special in that its instances are represented compactly — instead of being stored as a reference, a SmallInteger is represented directly using the bits that would otherwise be used to hold a reference. The first bit of an object reference indicates whether the object is a SmallInteger or not.

The class methods minVal and maxVal tell us the range of a SmallInteger:

```
SmallInteger maxVal = ((2 raisedTo: 30) – 1)      ⟶    true
SmallInteger minVal = (2 raisedTo: 30) negated    ⟶    true
```

When a SmallInteger goes out of this range, it is automatically converted to a LargePositiveInteger or a LargeNegativeInteger, as needed:

```
(SmallInteger maxVal + 1) class   ⟶    LargePositiveInteger
(SmallInteger minVal – 1) class   ⟶    LargeNegativeInteger
```

Large integers are similarly converted back to small integers when appropriate.

As in most programming languages, integers can be useful for specifying iterative behaviour. There is a dedicated method timesRepeat: for evaluating a block repeatedly. We have already seen a similar example in Chapter 3:

```
n := 2.
3 timesRepeat: [ n := n*n ].
n    ⟶    256
```

8.3   Characters

Character is defined in the *Collections-Strings* category as a subclass of Magnitude. Printable characters are represented in Pharo as $\langle char \rangle$. For example:

```
$a < $b   ⟶    true
```

Non-printing characters can be generated by various class methods. Character class»value: takes the Unicode (or ASCII) integer value as argument and returns the corresponding character. The protocol *accessing untypeable characters* contains a number of convenience constructor methods such as backspace, cr, escape, euro, space, tab, and so on.

```
Character space = (Character value: Character space asciiValue)   ⟶    true
```

The printOn: method is clever enough to know which of the three ways to generate characters offers the most appropriate representation:

```
Character value: 1    ⟶    Character home
Character value: 2    ⟶    Character value: 2
Character value: 32   ⟶    Character space
Character value: 97   ⟶    $a
```

Various convenient *testing* methods are built in: isAlphaNumeric, isCharacter, isDigit, isLowercase, isVowel, and so on.

To convert a Character to the string containing just that character, send asString. In this case asString and printString yield different results:

```
$a asString      ⟶    'a'
$a               ⟶    $a
$a printString   ⟶    '$a'
```

Every ascii Character is a unique instance, stored in the class variable CharacterTable:

```
(Character value: 97) == $a   ⟶    true
```

Characters outside the range 0 to 255 are not unique, however:

```
Character characterTable size                          ⟶    256
(Character value: 500) == (Character value: 500)       ⟶    false
```

8.4 Strings

The String class is also defined in the category *Collections-Strings*. A String is an indexed Collection that holds only Characters.

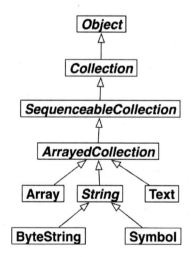

Figure 8.2: The String Hierarchy

In fact, String is abstract and Pharo Strings are actually instances of the concrete class ByteString.

```
'hello world' class   ⟶    ByteString
```

The other important subclass of String is Symbol. The key difference is that there is only ever a single instance of Symbol with a given value. (This is sometimes called "the unique instance property"). In contrast, two separately constructed Strings that happen to contain the same sequence of characters will often be different objects.

```
'hel','lo' == 'hello'   ⟶   false
```

```
('hel','lo') asSymbol == #hello   ⟶   true
```

Another important difference is that a String is mutable, whereas a Symbol is immutable.

```
'hello' at: 2 put: $u; yourself   ⟶   'hullo'
```

```
#hello at: 2 put: $u   ⟶   error
```

It is easy to forget that since strings are collections, they understand the same messages that other collections do:

```
#hello indexOf: $o   ⟶   5
```

Although String does not inherit from Magnitude, it does support the usual *comparing* methods, <, = and so on. In addition, String»match: is useful for some basic glob-style pattern-matching:

```
'*or*' match: 'zorro'   ⟶   true
```

Should you need more advanced support for regular expressions, have a look at the *Regex* package by Vassili Bykov.

Strings support rather a large number of conversion methods. Many of these are shortcut constructor methods for other classes, such as asDate, asFileName and so on. There are also a number of useful methods for converting a string to another string, such as capitalized and translateToLowercase.

For more on strings and collections, see Chapter 9.

8.5 Booleans

The class Boolean offers a fascinating insight into how much of the Smalltalk language has been pushed into the class library. Boolean is the abstract superclass of the Singleton classes True and False.

Most of the behaviour of Booleans can be understood by considering the method ifTrue:ifFalse:, which takes two Blocks as arguments.

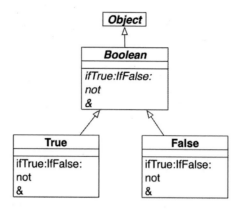

Figure 8.3: The Boolean Hierarchy

(4 factorial > 20) ifTrue: ['bigger'] ifFalse: ['smaller']   ⟶   'bigger'

The method is abstract in Boolean. The implementations in its concrete subclasses are both trivial:

Method 8.13: *Implementations of* ifTrue:ifFalse:

True»ifTrue: trueAlternativeBlock ifFalse: falseAlternativeBlock
    ↑trueAlternativeBlock value

False»ifTrue: trueAlternativeBlock ifFalse: falseAlternativeBlock
    ↑falseAlternativeBlock value

In fact, this is the essence of OOP: when a message is sent to an object, the object itself determines which method will be used to respond. In this case an instance of True simply evaluates the *true* alternative, while an instance of False evaluates the *false* alternative. All the abstract Boolean methods are implemented in this way for True and False. For example:

Method 8.14: *Implementing negation*

True»not
    "Negation---answer false since the receiver is true."
    ↑false

Booleans offer several useful convenience methods, such as ifTrue:, ifFalse:, ifFalse:ifTrue. You also have the choice between eager and lazy conjunctions and disjunctions.

(1>2) & (3<4)   ⟶   false   "must evaluate both sides"
(1>2) and: [3<4]   ⟶   false   "only evaluate receiver"

(1>2) and: [(1/0) > 0] $\longrightarrow$ false *"argument block is never evaluated, so no exception"*

In the first example, both Boolean subexpressions are evaluated, since & takes a Boolean argument. In the second and third examples, only the first is evaluated, since and: expects a Block as its argument. The Block is evaluated only if the first argument is true.

Try to imagine how and: *and* or: *are implemented. Check the implementations in* Boolean, True *and* False.

8.6 Chapter summary

- If you override = then you should override hash as well.

- Override postCopy to correctly implement copying for your objects.

- Send self halt to set a breakpoint.

- Return self subclassResponsibility to make a method abstract.

- To give an object a String representation you should override printOn:.

- Override the hook method initialize to properly initialize instances.

- Number methods automatically convert between Floats, Fractions and Integers.

- Fractions truly represent rational numbers rather than floats.

- Characters are unique instances.

- Strings are mutable; Symbols are not. Take care not to mutate string literals, however!

- Symbols are unique; Strings are not.

- Strings and Symbols are Collections and therefore support the usual Collection methods.

Chapter 9

Collections

9.1 Introduction

The collection classes form a loosely-defined group of general-purpose subclasses of Collection and Stream. The group of classes that appears in the "Blue Book"[1] contains 17 subclasses of Collection and 9 subclasses of Stream, for a total of 28 classes, and had already been redesigned several times before the Smalltalk-80 system was released. This group of classes is often considered to be a paradigmatic example of object-oriented design.

In Pharo, the abstract class Collection has 101 subclasses, and the abstract class Stream has 50 subclasses, but many of these (like Bitmap, FileStream and CompiledMethod) are special-purpose classes crafted for use in other parts of the system or in applications, and hence not categorized as "Collections" by the system organization. For the purposes of this chapter, we use the term "Collection Hierarchy" to mean Collection and its 47 subclasses that are *also* in the categories labelled *Collections-**. We use the term "Stream Hierarchy" to mean Stream and its 9 subclasses that are *also* in the *Collections-Streams* categories. These 56 classes respond to 982 messages and define a total of 1609 methods!

In this chapter we focus mainly on the subset of collection classes shown in Figure 9.1. Streams will be discussed separately in Chapter 10.

---

[1] Adele Goldberg and David Robson, *Smalltalk 80: the Language and its Implementation*. Reading, Mass.: Addison Wesley, May 1983, ISBN 0–201–13688–0.

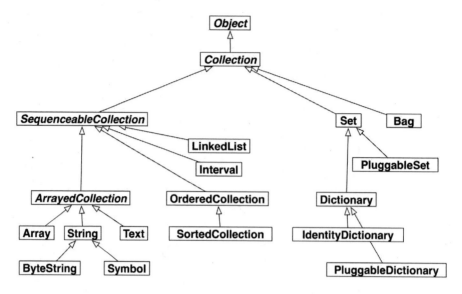

Figure 9.1: Some of the key collection classes in Pharo.

9.2   The varieties of collections

To make good use of the collection classes, the reader needs at least a superficial knowledge of the wide variety of collections that they implement, and their commonalities and differences.

Programming with collections rather than individual elements is an important way to raise the level of abstraction of a program. The Lisp function map, which applies an argument function to every element of a list and returns a new list containing the results is an early example of this style, but Smalltalk-80 adopted collection-based programming as a central tenet. Modern functional programming languages such as ML and Haskell have followed Smalltalk's lead.

Why is this a good idea? Suppose you have a data structure containing a collection of student records, and wish to perform some action on all of the students that meet some criterion. Programmers raised to use an imperative language will immediately reach for a loop. But the Smalltalk programmer will write:

```
students select: [ :each | each gpa < threshold ]
```

which evaluates to a new collection containing precisely those elements of students for which the bracketed function returns true[2]. The Smalltalk code

---

[2]The expression in brackets can be thought of as a λ-expression defining an anonymous

Protocol	Methods
accessing	size, capacity, at: *anIndex*, at: *anIndex* put: *anElement*
testing	isEmpty, includes: *anElement*, contains: *aBlock*, occurrencesOf: *anElement*
adding	add: *anElement*, addAll: *aCollection*
removing	remove: *anElement*, remove: *anElement* ifAbsent: *aBlock*, removeAll: *aCollection*
enumerating	do: *aBlock*, collect: *aBlock*, select: *aBlock*, reject: *aBlock*, detect: *aBlock*, detect: *aBlock* ifNone: *aNoneBlock*, inject: *aValue* into: *aBinaryBlock*
converting	asBag, asSet, asOrderedCollection, asSortedCollection, asArray, asSortedCollection: *aBlock*
creation	with: *anElement*, with:with:, with:with:with:, with:with:with:with:, withAll: *aCollection*

Figure 9.2: Standard Collection protocols

has the simplicity and elegance of a domain-specific query language.

The message select: is understood by *all* collections in Smalltalk. There is no need to find out if the student data structure is an array or a linked list: the select: message is understood by both. Note that this is quite different from using a loop, where one must know whether students is an array or a linked list before the loop can be set up.

In Smalltalk, when one speaks of a collection without being more specific about the kind of collection, one means an object that supports well-defined protocols for testing membership and enumerating the elements. *All* collections understand the *testing* messages includes:, isEmpty and occurrencesOf:. *All* collections understand the *enumeration* messages do:, select:, reject: (which is the opposite of select:), collect: (which is like lisp's map), detect:ifNone:, inject:into: (which performs a left fold) and many more. It is the ubiquity of this protocol, as well as its variety, that makes it so powerful.

Figure 9.2 summarizes the standard protocols supported by most of the classes in the collection hierarchy. These methods are defined, redefined, optimized or occasionally even forbidden by subclasses of Collection.

Beyond this basic uniformity, there are many different kinds of collection either supporting different protocols, or providing different behaviour for the same requests. Let us briefly survey some of the key differences:

- **Sequenceable:** Instances of all subclasses of SequenceableCollection start from a first element and proceed in a well-defined order to a last ele-

---

function $\lambda x.x$ gpa $<$ threshold.

ment. Instances of Set, Bag and Dictionary, on the other hand, are not sequenceable.

- **Sortable:** A SortedCollection maintains its elements in sort order.

- **Indexable:** Most sequenceable collections are also indexable, that is, elements can be retrieved with at:. Array is the familiar indexable data structure with a fixed size; anArray at: n retrieves the nth element of anArray, and anArray at: n put: v changes the nth element to v. LinkedLists and SkipList s are sequenceable but not indexable, that is, they understand first and last, but not at:.

- **Keyed:** Instances of Dictionary and its subclasses are accessed by keys instead of indices.

- **Mutable:** Most collections are mutable, but Intervals and Symbols are not. An Interval is an immutable collection representing a range of Integers. For example, 5 to: 16 by: 2 is an interval that contains the elements 5, 7, 9, 11, 13 and 15. It is indexable with at:, but cannot be changed with at:put:.

- **Growable:** Instances of Interval and Array are always of a fixed size. Other kinds of collections (sorted collections, ordered collections, and linked lists) can grow after creation.

  The class OrderedCollection is more general than Array; the size of an OrderedCollection grows on demand, and it has methods for addFirst: and addLast: as well as at: and at:put:.

- **Accepts duplicates:** A Set will filter out duplicates, but a Bag will not. Dictionary, Set and Bag use the = method provided by the elements; the Identity variants of these classes use the == method, which tests whether the arguments are the same object, and the Pluggable variants use an arbitrary equivalence relation supplied by the creator of the collection.

- **Heterogeneous:** Most collections will hold any kind of element. A String , CharacterArray or Symbol, however, only holds Characters. An Array will hold any mix of objects, but a ByteArray only holds Bytes, an IntegerArray only holds Integers and a FloatArray only holds Floats. A LinkedList is constrained to hold elements that conform to the *Link ▷ accessing* protocol.

9.3   Implementations of collections

These categorizations by functionality are not our only concern; we must also consider how the collection classes are implemented. As shown in Figure 9.3, five main implementation techniques are employed.

Arrayed Implementation	Ordered Implementation	Hashed Implementation	Linked Implementation	Interval Implementation
Array String Symbol	OrderedCollection SortedCollection Text Heap	Set IdentitySet PluggableSet Bag IdentityBag Dictionary IdentityDictionary PluggableDictionary	LinkedList SkipList	Interval

Figure 9.3: Some collection classes categorized by implementation technique.

1. Arrays store their elements in the (indexable) instance variables of the collection object itself; as a consequence, arrays must be of a fixed size, but can be created with a single memory allocation.

2. OrderedCollections and SortedCollections store their elements in an array that is referenced by one of the instance variables of the collection. Consequently, the internal array can be replaced with a larger one if the collection grows beyond its storage capacity.

3. The various kinds of set and dictionary also reference a subsidiary array for storage, but use the array as a hash table. Bags use a subsidiary Dictionary, with the elements of the bag as keys and the number of occurrences as values.

4. LinkedLists use a standard singly-linked representation.

5. Intervals are represented by three integers that record the two endpoints and the step size.

In addition to these classes, there are also "weak" variants of Array, Set and of the various kinds of dictionary. These collections hold onto their elements weakly, *i.e.*, in a way that does not prevent the elements from being garbage collected. The Pharo virtual machine is aware of these classes and handles them specially.

Readers interested in learning more about the Smalltalk collections are referred to LaLonde and Pugh's excellent book[3].

---

[3] Wilf LaLonde and John Pugh, *Inside Smalltalk: Volume 1*. Prentice Hall, 1990, ISBN 0–13–468414–1.

9.4 Examples of key classes

We present now the most common or important collection classes using simple code examples. The main protocols of collections are: at:, at:put: — to access an element, add:, remove: — to add or remove an element, size, isEmpty, include: — to get some information about the collection, do:, collect:, select: — to iterate over the collection. Each collection may implement or not such protocols, and when they do, they interpret them to fit with their semantics. We suggest you browse the classes themselves to identify specific and more advanced protocols.

We will focus on the most common collection classes: OrderedCollection, Set, SortedCollection, Dictionary, Interval, and Array.

Common creation protocol. There are several ways to create instances of collections. The most generic ones use the methods new: and with:. new: anInteger creates a collection of size anInteger whose elements will all be nil. with: anObject creates a collection and adds anObject to the created collection. Different collections will realize this behaviour differently.

You can create collections with initial elements using the methods with:, with:with: etc. for up to six elements.

```
Array with: 1     ⟶   #(1)
Array with: 1 with: 2     ⟶    #(1 2)
Array with: 1 with: 2 with: 3     ⟶   #(1 2 3)
Array with: 1 with: 2 with: 3 with: 4     ⟶    #(1 2 3 4)
Array with: 1 with: 2 with: 3 with: 4 with: 5     ⟶   #(1 2 3 4 5)
Array with: 1 with: 2 with: 3 with: 4 with: 5 with: 6     ⟶    #(1 2 3 4 5 6)
```

You can also use addAll: to add all elements of one kind of collection to another kind:

```
(1 to: 5) asOrderedCollection addAll: '678'; yourself     ⟶     an OrderedCollection(1 2 3
    4 5 $6 $7 $8)
```

Take care that addAll: also returns its argument, and not the receiver!

You can also create many collections with withAll: or newFrom:

```
Array withAll: #(7 3 1 3)             ⟶    #(7 3 1 3)
OrderedCollection withAll: #(7 3 1 3)     ⟶    an OrderedCollection(7 3 1 3)
SortedCollection withAll: #(7 3 1 3)      ⟶    a SortedCollection(1 3 3 7)
Set withAll: #(7 3 1 3)                   ⟶    a Set(7 1 3)
Bag withAll: #(7 3 1 3)                   ⟶    a Bag(7 1 3 3)
Dictionary withAll: #(7 3 1 3)            ⟶    a Dictionary(1->7 2->3 3->1 4->3 )
```

```
Array newFrom: #(7 3 1 3)                              ⟶    #(7 3 1 3)
OrderedCollection newFrom: #(7 3 1 3)                  ⟶    an OrderedCollection(7 3 1
    3)
SortedCollection newFrom: #(7 3 1 3)                   ⟶    a SortedCollection(1 3 3 7)
Set newFrom: #(7 3 1 3)                                ⟶    a Set(7 1 3)
Bag newFrom: #(7 3 1 3)                                ⟶    a Bag(7 1 3 3)
Dictionary newFrom: {1 –> 7. 2 –> 3. 3 –> 1. 4 –> 3}   ⟶    a Dictionary(1–>7 2–>3 3–
    >1 4–>3 )
```

Note that these two methods are not identical. In particular, Dictionary class
»withAll: interprets its argument as a collection of values, whereas Dictionary
class»newFrom: expects a collection of associations.

Array

An Array is a fixed-sized collection of elements accessed by integer indices.
Contrary to the C convention, the first element of a Smalltalk array is at
position 1 and not 0. The main protocol to access array elements is the
method at: and at:put:. at: anInteger returns the element at index anInteger. at:
anInteger put: anObject puts anObject at index anInteger. Arrays are fixed-size
collections therefore we cannot add or remove elements at the end of an
array. The following code creates an array of size 5, puts values in the first 3
locations and returns the first element.

```
anArray := Array new: 5.
anArray at: 1 put: 4.
anArray at: 2 put: 3/2.
anArray at: 3 put: 'ssss'.
anArray at: 1     ⟶    4
```

There are several ways to create instances of the class Array. We can use
new:, with:, and the constructs #( ) and { }.

Creation with new: new: anInteger creates an array of size anInteger. Array new:
5 creates an array of size 5.

Creation with with: with: methods allows one to specify the value of the
elements. The following code creates an array of three elements consisting of
the number 4, the fraction 3/2 and the string 'lulu'.

```
Array with: 4 with: 3/2 with: 'lulu'     ⟶    {4 . (3/2) . 'lulu'}
```

Literal creation with #().　#() creates literal arrays with static (or "literal") elements that have to be known when the expression is compiled, and not when it is executed. The following code creates an array of size 2 where the first element is the (literal) number 1 and the second the (literal) string 'here'.

```
#(1 'here') size   ⟶   2
```

Now, if you evaluate #(1+2), you do not get an array with a single element 3 but instead you get the array #(1 #+ 2) *i.e.*, with three elements: 1, the symbol #+ and the number 2.

```
#(1+2)   ⟶   #(1 #+ 2)
```

This occurs because the construct #() causes the compiler to interpret literally the expressions contained in the array. The expression is scanned and the resulting elements are fed to a new array. Literal arrays contain numbers, nil, true, false, symbols and strings.

Dynamic creation with { }.　Finally, you can create a dynamic array using the construct {}. { a . b } is equivalent to Array with: a with: b. This means in particular that the expressions enclosed by { and } are executed.

```
{ 1 + 2 }   ⟶   #(3)
{(1/2) asFloat} at: 1   ⟶   0.5
{10 atRandom . 1/3} at: 2   ⟶   (1/3)
```

Element Access.　Elements of all sequenceable collections can be accessed with at: and at:put:.

```
anArray := #(1 2 3 4 5 6) copy.
anArray at: 3   ⟶   3
anArray at: 3 put: 33.
anArray at: 3   ⟶   33
```

Be careful with code that modifies literal arrays! The compiler tries to allocate space just once for literal arrays. Unless you copy the array, the second time you evaluate the code your "literal" array may not have the value you expect. (Without cloning, the second time around, the literal #(1 2 3 4 5 6) will actually be #(1 2 33 4 5 6)!) Dynamic arrays do not have this problem.

OrderedCollection

OrderedCollection is one of the collections that can grow, and to which elements can be added sequentially. It offers a variety of methods such as add:, addFirst:, addLast:, and addAll:.

```
ordCol := OrderedCollection new.
ordCol add: 'Seaside'; add: 'SqueakSource'; addFirst: 'Monticello'.
ordCol   ⟶   an OrderedCollection('Monticello' 'Seaside' 'SqueakSource')
```

Removing Elements.   The method remove: anObject removes the first occurrence of an object from the collection. If the collection does not include such an object, it raises an error.

```
ordCol add: 'Monticello'.
ordCol remove: 'Monticello'.
ordCol   ⟶   an OrderedCollection('Seaside' 'SqueakSource' 'Monticello')
```

There is a variant of remove: named remove:ifAbsent: that allows one to specify as second argument a block that is executed in case the element to be removed is not in the collection.

```
res := ordCol remove: 'zork' ifAbsent: [33].
res   ⟶   33
```

Conversion.   It is possible to get an OrderedCollection from an Array (or any other collection) by sending the message asOrderedCollection:

```
#(1 2 3) asOrderedCollection      ⟶   an OrderedCollection(1 2 3)
'hello' asOrderedCollection   ⟶   an OrderedCollection($h $e $l $l $o)
```

Interval

The class Interval represents ranges of numbers. For example, the interval of numbers from 1 to 100 is defined as follows:

```
Interval from: 1 to: 100   ⟶   (1 to: 100)
```

The printString of this interval reveals that the class Number provides us with a convenience method called to: to generate intervals:

```
(Interval from: 1 to: 100) = (1 to: 100)   ⟶   true
```

We can use Interval class»from:to:by: or Number»to:by: to specify the step between two numbers as follow:

```
(Interval from: 1 to: 100 by: 0.5) size   ⟶   199
(1 to: 100 by: 0.5) at: 198   ⟶   99.5
(1/2 to: 54/7 by: 1/3) last   ⟶   (15/2)
```

Dictionary

Dictionaries are important collections whose elements are accessed using keys. Among the most commonly used messages of dictionary you will find at:, at:put:, at:ifAbsent:, keys and values.

```
colors := Dictionary new.
colors at: #yellow put: Color yellow.
colors at: #blue put: Color blue.
colors at: #red put: Color red.
colors at: #yellow     ⟶     Color yellow
colors keys            ⟶     a Set(#blue #yellow #red)
colors values          ⟶     {Color blue . Color yellow . Color red}
```

Dictionaries compare keys by equality. Two keys are considered to be the same if they return true when compared using =. A common and difficult to spot bug is to use as key an object whose = method has been redefined but not its hash method. Both methods are used in the implementation of dictionary and when comparing objects.

The class Dictionary clearly illustrates that the collection hierarchy is based on subclassing and not subtyping. Even though Dictionary is a subclass of Set, we would normally not want to use a Dictionary where a Set is expected. In its implementation, however, a Dictionary can clearly be seen as consisting of a set of associations (key value) created using the message –>. We can create a Dictionary from a collection of associations, or we may convert a dictionary to an array of associations.

```
colors := Dictionary newFrom: { #blue–>Color blue. #red–>Color red. #yellow–>Color
     yellow }.
colors removeKey: #blue.
colors associations     ⟶     {#yellow–>Color yellow . #red–>Color red}
```

IdentityDictionary. While a dictionary uses the result of the messages = and hash to determine if two keys are the same, the class IdentityDictionary uses the identity (message ==) of the key instead of its values, *i.e.*, it considers two keys to be equal *only* if they are the same object.

Often Symbols are used as keys, in which case it is natural to use an IdentityDictionary, since a Symbol is guaranteed to be globally unique. If, on the other hand, your keys are Strings, it is better to use a plain Dictionary, or you may get into trouble:

```
a := 'foobar'.
b := a copy.
trouble := IdentityDictionary new.
trouble at: a put: 'a'; at: b put: 'b'.
trouble at: a          ⟶     'a'
```

```
trouble at: b          ⟶    'b'
trouble at: 'foobar'   ⟶    'a'
```

Since a and b are different objects, they are treated as different objects. Interestingly, the literal 'foobar' is allocated just once, so is really the same object as a. You don't want your code to depend on behaviour like this! A plain Dictionary would give the same value for any key equal to 'foobar'.

Use only globally unique objects (like Symbols or SmallIntegers) as keys for a IdentityDictionary, and Strings (or other objects) as keys for a plain Dictionary.

Note that the global Smalltalk is an instance of SystemDictionary, a subclass of IdentityDictionary, hence all its keys are Symbols (actually, ByteSymbols, which contain only 8-bit characters).

```
Smalltalk keys collect: [ :each | each class ]   ⟶    a Set(ByteSymbol)
```

Sending keys or values to a Dictionary results in a Set, which we look at next.

Set

The class Set is a collection which behaves as a mathematical set, *i.e.*, as a collection with no duplicate elements and without any order. In a Set elements are added using the message add: and they cannot be accessed using the message at:. Objects put in a set should implement the methods hash and =.

```
s := Set new.
s add: 4/2; add: 4; add:2.
s size   ⟶    2
```

You can also create sets using Set class»newFrom: or the conversion message Collection»asSet:

```
(Set newFrom: #( 1 2 3 1 4 )) = #(1 2 3 4 3 2 1) asSet   ⟶    true
```

asSet offers us a convenient way to eliminate duplicates from a collection:

```
{ Color black. Color white. (Color red + Color blue + Color green) } asSet size   ⟶   2
```

Note that red + blue + green = white.

A Bag is much like a Set except that it does allow duplicates:

```
{ Color black. Color white. (Color red + Color blue + Color green) } asBag size   ⟶   3
```

The set operations *union, intersection* and *membership test* are implemented by the Collection messages union:, intersection: and includes:. The receiver is first converted to a Set, so these operations work for all kinds of collections!

```
(1 to: 6) union: (4 to: 10)        ⟶    a Set(1 2 3 4 5 6 7 8 9 10)
'hello' intersection: 'there'      ⟶    'he'
#Smalltalk includes: $k            ⟶    true
```

As we explain below, elements of a set are accessed using iterators (see Section 9.5).

SortedCollection

In contrast to an OrderedCollection, a SortedCollection maintains its elements in sort order. By default, a sorted collection uses the message <= to establish sort order, so it can sort instances of subclasses of the abstract class Magnitude, which defines the protocol of comparable objects (<, =, >, >=, between:and:...). (See Chapter 8.)

You can create a SortedCollection by creating a new instance and adding elements to it:

```
SortedCollection new add: 5; add: 2; add: 50; add: –10; yourself.    ⟶    a
    SortedCollection(–10 2 5 50)
```

More usually, though, one will send the conversion message asSortedCollection to an existing collection:

```
#(5 2 50 –10) asSortedCollection    ⟶    a SortedCollection(–10 2 5 50)
```

This example answers the following FAQ:

> FAQ: How do you sort a collection?
> ANSWER: Send the message asSortedCollection to it.

```
'hello' asSortedCollection    ⟶    a SortedCollection($e $h $l $l $o)
```

How do you get a String back from this result? asString unfortunately returns the printString representation, which is not what we want:

```
'hello' asSortedCollection asString    ⟶    'a SortedCollection($e $h $l $l $o)'
```

The correct answer is to either use String class»newFrom:, String class»withAll: or Object»as::

```
'hello' asSortedCollection as: String           ⟶    'ehllo'
String newFrom: ('hello' asSortedCollection)    ⟶    'ehllo'
String withAll: ('hello' asSortedCollection)    ⟶    'ehllo'
```

It is possible to have different kinds of elements in a SortedCollection as long as they are all comparable. For example we can mix different kinds of numbers such as integers, floats and fractions:

```
{ 5. 2/–3. 5.21 } asSortedCollection    ⟶    a SortedCollection((–2/3) 5 5.21)
```

Imagine that you want to sort objects that do not define the method <= or that you would like to have a different sorting criterion. You can do this by supplying a two argument block, called a sortblock, to the sorted collection. For example, the class Color is not a Magnitude and it does not implement the method <=, but we can specify a block stating that the colors should be sorted according to their luminance (a measure of brightness).

```
col := SortedCollection sortBlock: [:c1 :c2 | c1 luminance <= c2 luminance].
col addAll: { Color red. Color yellow. Color white. Color black }.
col    ⟶    a SortedCollection(Color black Color red Color yellow Color white)
```

String

A Smalltalk String represents a collection of Characters. It is sequenceable, indexable, mutable and homogeneous, containing only Character instances. Like Arrays, Strings have a dedicated syntax, and are normally created by directly specifying a String literal within single quotes, but the usual collection creation methods will work as well.

```
'Hello'                              ⟶    'Hello'
String with: $A                      ⟶    'A'
String with: $h with: $i with: $!    ⟶    'hi!'
String newFrom: #($h $e $l $l $o)    ⟶    'hello'
```

In actual fact, String is abstract. When we instantiate a String we actually get either an 8-bit ByteString or a 32-bit WideString. To keep things simple, we usually ignore the difference and just talk about instances of String.

Two instances of String can be concatenated with a comma.

```
s := 'no', ' ', 'worries'.
s    ⟶    'no worries'
```

Since a string is a mutable collection we can also change it using the method at:put:.

```
s at: 4 put: $h; at: 5 put: $u.
s    ⟶    'no hurries'
```

Note that the comma method is defined by Collection, so it will work for any kind of collection!

```
(1 to: 3) , '45'   ⟶   #(1 2 3 $4 $5)
```

We can also modify an existing string using replaceAll:with: or replaceFrom:to:with: as shown below. Note that the number of characters and the interval should have the same size.

```
s replaceAll: $n with: $N.
s    ⟶    'No hurries'
s replaceFrom: 4 to: 5 with: 'wo'.
s    ⟶    'No worries'
```

In contrast to the methods described above, the method copyReplaceAll: creates a new string. (Curiously, here the arguments are substrings rather than individual characters, and their sizes do not have to match.)

```
s copyReplaceAll: 'rries' with: 'mbats'   ⟶   'No wombats'
```

A quick look at the implementation of these methods reveals that they are defined not only for Strings, but for any kind of SequenceableCollection, so the following also works:

```
(1 to: 6) copyReplaceAll: (3 to: 5) with: { 'three'. 'etc.' }   ⟶   #(1 2 'three' 'etc.' 6)
```

String matching. It is possible to ask whether a pattern matches a string by sending the match: message. The pattern can specify * to match an arbitrary series of characters and # to match a single character. Note that match: is sent to the pattern and not the string to be matched.

```
'Linux *' match: 'Linux mag'                ⟶    true
'GNU/Linux #ag' match: 'GNU/Linux tag'   ⟶    true
```

Another useful method is findString:.

```
'GNU/Linux mag' findString: 'Linux'                                        ⟶   5
'GNU/Linux mag' findString: 'linux' startingAt: 1 caseSensitive: false   ⟶   5
```

More advanced pattern matching facilities offering the capabilities of Perl are also available in the *Regex* package.

Some tests on strings. The following examples illustrate the use of isEmpty, includes: and anySatisfy: which are further messages defined not only on Strings but more generally on collections.

```
'Hello' isEmpty   ⟶    false
'Hello' includes: $a   ⟶    false
'JOE' anySatisfy: [:c | c isLowercase]   ⟶    false
'Joe' anySatisfy: [:c | c isLowercase]   ⟶    true
```

String templating. There are three messages that are useful to manage string templating: format:, expandMacros and expandMacrosWith:.

```
'{1} is {2}' format: {'Pharo' . 'cool'}     ⟶     'Pharo is cool'
```

The messages of the expandMacros family offer variable substitution, using <n> for carriage return, <t> for tabulation, <1s>, <2s>, <3s> for arguments (<1p>, <2p>, surrounds the string with single quotes), and <1?value1:value2> for conditional.

```
'look-<t>-here' expandMacros                                    ⟶     'look- -here'
'<1s> is <2s>' expandMacrosWith: 'Pharo' with: 'cool'           ⟶     'Pharo is cool'
'<2s> is <1s>' expandMacrosWith: 'Pharo' with: 'cool'           ⟶     'cool is Pharo'
'<1p> or <1s>' expandMacrosWith: 'Pharo' with: 'cool'           ⟶     '"Pharo" or Pharo'
'<1?Quentin:Thibaut> plays' expandMacrosWith: true              ⟶     'Quentin plays'
'<1?Quentin:Thibaut> plays' expandMacrosWith: false             ⟶     'Thibaut plays'
```

Some other utility methods. The class String offers numerous other utilities including the messages asLowercase, asUppercase and capitalized.

```
'XYZ' asLowercase    ⟶    'xyz'
'xyz' asUppercase    ⟶    'XYZ'
'hilaire' capitalized    ⟶    'Hilaire'
'1.54' asNumber    ⟶    1.54
'this sentence is without a doubt far too long' contractTo: 20    ⟶    'this sent...too long'
```

Note that there is generally a difference between asking an object its string representation by sending the message printString and converting it to a string by sending the message asString. Here is an example of the difference.

```
#ASymbol printString    ⟶    '#ASymbol'
#ASymbol asString    ⟶    'ASymbol'
```

A symbol is similar to a string but is guaranteed to be globally unique. For this reason symbols are preferred to strings as keys for dictionaries, in particular for instances of IdentityDictionary. See also Chapter 8 for more about String and Symbol.

9.5   Collection iterators

In Smalltalk loops and conditionals are simply messages sent to collections or other objects such as integers or blocks (see also Chapter 3). In addition to low-level messages such as to:do: which evaluates a block with an argument ranging from an initial to a final number, the Smalltalk collection hierarchy offers various high-level iterators. Using such iterators will make your code more robust and compact.

Iterating (do:)

The method do: is the basic collection iterator. It applies its argument (a block taking a single argument) to each element of the receiver. The following example prints all the strings contained in the receiver to the transcript.

```
#('bob' 'joe' 'toto') do: [:each | Transcript show: each; cr].
```

Variants. There are a lot of variants of do:, such as do:without:, doWithIndex: and reverseDo:: For the indexed collections (Array, OrderedCollection, SortedCollection) the method doWithIndex: also gives access to the current index. This method is related to to:do: which is defined in class Number.

```
#('bob' 'joe' 'toto') doWithIndex: [:each :i | (each = 'joe') ifTrue: [ ↑ i ] ]     ⟶    2
```

For ordered collections, reverseDo: walks the collection in the reverse order.

The following code shows an interesting message: do:separatedBy: which executes the second block only in between two elements.

```
res := ''.
#('bob' 'joe' 'toto') do: [:e | res := res, e ] separatedBy: [res := res, '.'].
res     ⟶     'bob.joe.toto'
```

Note that this code is not especially efficient since it creates intermediate strings and it would be better to use a write stream to buffer the result (see Chapter 10):

```
String streamContents: [:stream | #('bob' 'joe' 'toto') asStringOn: stream delimiter: '.' ]
        ⟶     'bob.joe.toto'
```

Dictionaries. When the message do: is sent to a dictionary, the elements taken into account are the values, not the associations. The proper methods to use are keysDo:, valuesDo:, and associationsDo:, which iterate respectively on keys, values or associations.

```
colors := Dictionary newFrom: { #yellow -> Color yellow. #blue -> Color blue. #red ->
        Color red }.
colors keysDo: [:key | Transcript show: key; cr].              "displays the keys"
colors valuesDo: [:value | Transcript show: value;cr].         "displays the values"
colors associationsDo: [:value | Transcript show: value;cr].   "displays the associations"
```

Collecting results (collect:)

If you want to process the elements of a collection and produce a new collection as a result, rather than using do:, you are probably better off using collect:, or one of the other iterator methods. Most of these can be found in the *enumerating* protocol of Collection and its subclasses.

Imagine that we want a collection containing the doubles of the elements in another collection. Using the method do: we must write the following:

```
double := OrderedCollection new.
#(1 2 3 4 5 6) do: [:e | double add: 2 * e].
double    ⟶    an OrderedCollection(2 4 6 8 10 12)
```

The method collect: executes its argument block for each element and returns a new collection containing the results. Using collect: instead, the code is much simpler:

```
#(1 2 3 4 5 6) collect: [:e | 2 * e]    ⟶    #(2 4 6 8 10 12)
```

The advantages of collect: over do: are even more dramatic in the following example, where we take a collection of integers and generate as a result a collection of absolute values of these integers:

```
aCol := #( 2 -3 4 -35 4 -11).
result := aCol species new: aCol size.
1 to: aCol size do: [ :each | result at: each put: (aCol at: each) abs].
result    ⟶    #(2 3 4 35 4 11)
```

Contrast the above with the much simpler following expression:

```
#( 2 -3 4 -35 4 -11) collect: [:each | each abs ]    ⟶    #(2 3 4 35 4 11)
```

A further advantage of the second solution is that it will also work for sets and bags.

Generally you should avoid using do:, unless you want to send messages to each of the elements of a collection.

Note that sending the message collect: returns the same kind of collection as the receiver. For this reason the following code fails. (A String cannot hold integer values.)

```
'abc' collect: [:ea | ea asciiValue ]    "error!"
```

Instead we must first convert the string to an Array or an OrderedCollection:

```
'abc' asArray collect: [:ea | ea asciiValue ]    ⟶    #(97 98 99)
```

Actually collect: is not guaranteed to return a collection of exactly the same class as the receiver, but only the same *"species"*. In the case of an Interval, the species is actually an Array!

```
(1 to: 5) collect: [ :ea | ea * 2 ]    ⟶    #(2 4 6 8 10)
```

Selecting and rejecting elements

select: returns the elements of the receiver that satisfy a particular condition:

```
(2 to: 20) select: [:each | each isPrime]    ⟶    #(2 3 5 7 11 13 17 19)
```

reject: does the opposite:

```
(2 to: 20) reject: [:each | each isPrime]    ⟶    #(4 6 8 9 10 12 14 15 16 18 20)
```

Identifying an element with detect:

The method detect: returns the first element of the receiver that matches block argument.

```
'through' detect: [:each | each isVowel]    ⟶    $o
```

The method detect:ifNone: is a variant of the method detect:. Its second block is evaluated when there is no element matching the block.

```
Smalltalk allClasses detect: [:each | '*cobol*' match: each asString] ifNone: [ nil ]
    ⟶    nil
```

Accumulating results with inject:into:

Functional programming languages often provide a higher-order function called *fold* or *reduce* to accumulate a result by applying some binary operator iteratively over all elements of a collection. In Pharo this is done by Collection» inject:into:.

The first argument is an initial value, and the second argument is a two-argument block which is applied to the result this far, and each element in turn.

A trivial application of inject:into: is to produce the sum of a collection of numbers. Following Gauss, in Pharo we could write this expression to sum the first 100 integers:

```
(1 to: 100) inject: 0 into: [:sum :each | sum + each ]    ⟶    5050
```

Another example is the following one-argument block which computes factorials:

```
factorial := [:n | (1 to: n) inject: 1 into: [:product :each | product * each ] ].
factorial value: 10    ⟶    3628800
```

Other messages

count: The message count: returns the number of elements satisfying a condition. The condition is represented as a boolean block.

Smalltalk allClasses count: [:each | 'Collection*' match: each asString] $\longrightarrow$ 3

includes: The message includes: checks whether the argument is contained in the collection.

colors := {Color white . Color yellow. Color red . Color blue . Color orange}.
colors includes: Color blue. $\longrightarrow$ true

anySatisfy: The message anySatisfy: answers true if at least one element of the collection satisfies the condition represented by the argument.

colors anySatisfy: [:c | c red > 0.5] $\longrightarrow$ true

9.6   Some hints for using collections

A common mistake with add: The following error is one of the most frequent Smalltalk mistakes.

collection := OrderedCollection new add: 1; add: 2.
collection $\longrightarrow$ 2

Here the variable collection does not hold the newly created collection but rather the last number added. This is because the method add: returns the element added and not the receiver.

The following code yields the expected result:

collection := OrderedCollection new.
collection add: 1; add: 2.
collection $\longrightarrow$ an OrderedCollection(1 2)

You can also use the message yourself to return the receiver of a cascade of messages:

collection := OrderedCollection new add: 1; add: 2; yourself $\longrightarrow$ an
    OrderedCollection(1 2)

Removing an element of the collection you are iterating on.   Another mistake you may make is to remove an element from a collection you are currently iterating over. remove:

```
range := (2 to: 20) asOrderedCollection.
range do: [:aNumber | aNumber isPrime ifFalse: [ range remove: aNumber ] ].
range     ⟶    an OrderedCollection(2 3 5 7 9 11 13 15 17 19)
```

This result is clearly incorrect since 9 and 15 should have been filtered out!

The solution is to copy the collection before going over it.

```
range := (2 to: 20) asOrderedCollection.
range copy do: [:aNumber | aNumber isPrime ifFalse: [ range remove: aNumber ] ].
range     ⟶    an OrderedCollection(2 3 5 7 11 13 17 19)
```

Redefining both = and hash.   A difficult error to spot is when you redefine = but not hash. The symptoms are that you will lose elements that you put in sets or other strange behaviour. One solution proposed by Kent Beck is to use xor: to redefine hash. Suppose that we want two books to be considered equal if their titles and authors are the same. Then we would redefine not only = but also hash as follows:

Method 9.1: *Redefining* = *and* hash.

```
Book»= aBook
  self class = aBook class ifFalse: [↑ false].
  ↑ title = aBook title and: [ authors = aBook authors]

Book»hash
  ↑ title hash xor: authors hash
```

Another nasty problem arises if you use a mutable object, *i.e.*, an object that can change its hash value over time, as an element of a Set or as a key to a Dictionary. Don't do this unless you love debugging!

9.7   Chapter summary

The Smalltalk collection hierarchy provides a common vocabulary for uniformly manipulating a variety of different kinds of collections.

- A key distinction is between SequenceableCollections, which maintain their elements in a given order, Dictionary and its subclasses, which maintain key-to-value associations, and Sets and Bags, which are unordered.

- You can convert most collections to another kind of collection by sending them the messages asArray, asOrderedCollection etc..

- To sort a collection, send it the message asSortedCollection.

- Literal Arrays are created with the special syntax #(...). Dynamic Arrays are created with the syntax { ... }.

- A Dictionary compares keys by equality. It is most useful when keys are instances of String. An IdentityDictionary instead uses object identity to compare keys. It is more suitable when Symbols are used as keys, or when mapping object references to values.

- Strings also understand the usual collection messages. In addition, a String supports a simple form of pattern-matching. For more advanced application, look instead at the RegEx package.

- The basic iteration message is do:. It is useful for imperative code, such as modifying each element of a collection, or sending each element a message.

- Instead of using do:, it is more common to use collect:, select:, reject:, includes:, inject:into: and other higher-level messages to process collections in a uniform way.

- Never remove an element from a collection you are iterating over. If you must modify it, iterate over a copy instead.

- If you override =, remember to override hash as well!

Chapter 10

Streams

Streams are used to iterate over sequences of elements such as sequenced collections, files, and network streams. Streams may be either readable, or writeable, or both. Reading or writing is always relative to the current position in the stream. Streams can easily be converted to collections, and vice versa.

10.1 Two sequences of elements

A good metaphor to understand a stream is the following: A stream can be represented as two sequences of elements: a past element sequence and a future element sequence. The stream is positioned between the two sequences. Understanding this model is important since all stream operations in Smalltalk rely on it. For this reason, most of the Stream classes are sub-classes of PositionableStream. Figure 10.1 presents a stream which contains five characters. This stream is in its original position, *i.e.*, there is no element in the past. You can go back to this position using the message reset.

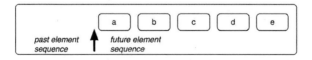

Figure 10.1: A stream positioned at its beginning.

Reading an element conceptually means removing the first element of the future element sequence and putting it after the last element in the past element sequence. After having read one element using the message next, the state of your stream is that shown in Figure 10.2.

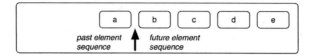

Figure 10.2: The same stream after the execution of the method next: the character a is "in the past" whereas b, c, d and e are "in the future".

Writing an element means replacing the first element of the future sequence by the new one and moving it to the past. Figure 10.3 shows the state of the same stream after having written an x using the message nextPut: anElement.

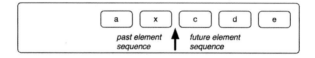

Figure 10.3: The same stream after having written an x.

10.2   Streams vs. collections

The collection protocol supports the storage, removal and enumeration of the elements of a collection, but does not allow these operations to be intermingled. For example, if the elements of an OrderedCollection are processed by a do: method, it is not possible to add or remove elements from inside the do: block. Nor does the collection protocol offer ways to iterate over two collections at the same time, choosing which collection goes forward and which does not. Procedures like these require that a traversal index or position reference is maintained outside of the collection itself: this is exactly the role of ReadStream, WriteStream and ReadWriteStream.

These three classes are defined to *stream over* some collection. For example, the following snippet creates a stream on an interval, then it reads two elements.

```
r := ReadStream on: (1 to: 1000).
r next.     ⟶    1
r next.     ⟶    2
r atEnd.    ⟶    false
```

WriteStreams can write data to the collection:

```
w := WriteStream on: (String new: 5).
w nextPut: $a.
w nextPut: $b.
w contents.     ⟶     'ab'
```

It is also possible to create ReadWriteStreams that support both the reading and writing protocols.

The main problem with WriteStream and ReadWriteStream is that they only support arrays and strings in Pharo. This is currently being changed by the development of a new library named Nile, but for now if you try to stream over another kind of collection, you will get an error:

```
w := WriteStream on: (OrderedCollection new: 20).
w nextPut: 12.     ⟶     raises an error
```

Streams are not only meant for collections, they can be used for files or sockets too. The following example creates a file named test.txt, writes two strings to it, separated by a carriage return, and closes the file.

```
StandardFileStream
  fileNamed: 'test.txt'
  do: [:str | str
          nextPutAll: '123';
          cr;
          nextPutAll: 'abcd'].
```

The following sections present the protocols in more depth.

10.3   Streaming over collections

Streams are really useful when dealing with collections of elements. They can be used for reading and writing elements in collections. We will now explore the stream features for the collections.

Reading collections

This section presents features used for reading collections. Using a stream to read a collection essentially provides you a pointer into the collection. That pointer will move forward on reading and you can place it wherever you want. The class ReadStream should be used to read elements from collections.

Methods next and next: are used to retrieve one or more elements from the collection.

```
stream := ReadStream on: #(1 (a b c) false).
stream next.    ⟶    1
stream next.    ⟶    #(#a #b #c)
stream next.    ⟶    false
```

```
stream := ReadStream on: 'abcdef'.
stream next: 0.    ⟶    ''
stream next: 1.    ⟶    'a'
stream next: 3.    ⟶    'bcd'
stream next: 2.    ⟶    'ef'
```

The message peek is used when you want to know what is the next element in the stream without going forward.

```
stream := ReadStream on: '–143'.
negative := (stream peek = $–).    "look at the first element without reading it"
negative.    ⟶    true
negative ifTrue: [stream next].    "ignores the minus character"
number := stream upToEnd.
number.    ⟶    '143'
```

This code sets the boolean variable negative according to the sign of the number in the stream and number to its absolute value. The method upToEnd returns everything from the current position to the end of the stream and sets the stream to its end. This code can be simplified using peekFor:, which moves forward if the following element equals the parameter and doesn't move otherwise.

```
stream := '–143' readStream.
(stream peekFor: $–)    ⟶    true
stream upToEnd    ⟶    '143'
```

peekFor: also returns a boolean indicating if the parameter equals the element.

You might have noticed a new way of constructing a stream in the above example: one can simply send readStream to a sequenceable collection to get a reading stream on that particular collection.

Positioning.   There are methods to position the stream pointer. If you have the index, you can go directly to it using position:. You can request the current position using position. Please remember that a stream is not positioned on an element, but between two elements. The index corresponding to the beginning of the stream is 0.

You can obtain the state of the stream depicted in Figure 10.4 with the following code:

```
stream := 'abcde' readStream.
stream position: 2.
stream peek    ⟶    $c
```

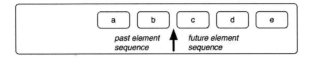

Figure 10.4: A stream at position 2

To position the stream at the beginning or the end, you can use reset or setToEnd. skip: and skipTo: are used to go forward to a location relative to the current position: skip: accepts a number as argument and skips that number of elements whereas skipTo: skips all elements in the stream until it finds an element equal to its parameter. Note that it positions the stream after the matched element.

```
stream := 'abcdef' readStream.
stream next.        ⟶    $a    "stream is now positioned just after the a"
stream skip: 3.                 "stream is now after the d"
stream position.    ⟶    4
stream skip: –2.                "stream is after the b"
stream position.    ⟶    2
stream reset.
stream position.    ⟶    0
stream skipTo: $e.              "stream is just after the e now"
stream next.        ⟶    $f
stream contents.    ⟶    'abcdef'
```

As you can see, the letter e has been skipped.

The method contents always returns a copy of the entire stream.

Testing. Some methods allow you to test the state of the current stream: atEnd returns true if and only if no more elements can be read whereas isEmpty returns true if and only if there is no element at all in the collection.

Here is a possible implementation of an algorithm using atEnd that takes two sorted collections as parameters and merges those collections into another sorted collection:

```
stream1 := #(1 4 9 11 12 13) readStream.
stream2 := #(1 2 3 4 5 10 13 14 15) readStream.

"The variable result will contain the sorted collection."
```

```
result := OrderedCollection new.
[stream1 atEnd not & stream2 atEnd not]
  whileTrue: [stream1 peek < stream2 peek
    "Remove the smallest element from either stream and add it to the result."
    ifTrue: [result add: stream1 next]
    ifFalse: [result add: stream2 next]].

"One of the two streams might not be at its end. Copy whatever remains."
result
  addAll: stream1 upToEnd;
  addAll: stream2 upToEnd.

result.    ⟶    an OrderedCollection(1 1 2 3 4 4 5 9 10 11 12 13 13 14 15)
```

Writing to collections

We have already seen how to read a collection by iterating over its elements using a ReadStream. We'll now learn how to create collections using WriteStreams.

WriteStreams are useful for appending a lot of data to a collection at various locations. They are often used to construct strings that are based on static and dynamic parts as in this example:

```
stream := String new writeStream.
stream
  nextPutAll: 'This Smalltalk image contains: ';
  print: Smalltalk allClasses size;
  nextPutAll: ' classes.';
  cr;
  nextPutAll: 'This is really a lot.'.

stream contents.    ⟶    'This Smalltalk image contains: 2322 classes.
This is really a lot.'
```

This technique is used in the different implementations of the method printOn: for example. There is a simpler and more efficient way of creating streams if you are only interested in the content of the stream:

```
string := String streamContents:
    [:stream |
      stream
        print: #(1 2 3);
        space;
        nextPutAll: 'size';
        space;
        nextPut: $=;
        space;
        print: 3.  ].
```

string.   ⟶   '#(1 2 3) size = 3'

The method streamContents: creates a collection and a stream on that collection for you. It then executes the block you gave passing the stream as a parameter. When the block ends, streamContents: returns the content of the collection.

The following WriteStream methods are especially useful in this context:

nextPut: adds the parameter to the stream;

nextPutAll: adds each element of the collection, passed as a parameter, to the stream;

print: adds the textual representation of the parameter to the stream.

There are also methods useful for printing different kinds of characters to the stream like space, tab and cr (carriage return). Another useful method is ensureASpace which ensures that the last character in the stream is a space; if the last character isn't a space it adds one.

About Concatenation.   Using nextPut: and nextPutAll: on a WriteStream is often the best way to concatenate characters. Using the comma concatenation operator (,) is far less efficient:

```
[| temp |
  temp := String new.
  (1 to: 100000)
    do: [:i | temp := temp, i asString, ' ']] timeToRun   ⟶   115176 "(milliseconds)"

[| temp |
  temp := WriteStream on: String new.
  (1 to: 100000)
    do: [:i | temp nextPutAll: i asString; space].
  temp contents] timeToRun   ⟶   1262 "(milliseconds)"
```

The reason that using a stream can be much more efficient is that comma creates a new string containing the concatenation of the receiver and the argument, so it must copy both of them. When you repeatedly concatenate onto the same receiver, it gets longer and longer each time, so that the number of characters that must be copied goes up exponentially. This also creates a lot of garbage, which must be collected. Using a stream instead of string concatenation is a well-known optimization. In fact, you can use streamContents: (mentioned on page 209) to help you do this:

```
String streamContents: [ :tempStream |
  (1 to: 100000)
    do: [:i | tempStream nextPutAll: i asString; space]]
```

Reading and writing at the same time

It's possible to use a stream to access a collection for reading and writing at the same time. Imagine you want to create an History class which will manage backward and forward buttons in a web browser. A history would react as in figures from 10.5 to 10.11.

Figure 10.5: A new history is empty. Nothing is displayed in the web browser.

Figure 10.6: The user opens to page 1.

Figure 10.7: The user clicks on a link to page 2.

Figure 10.8: The user clicks on a link to page 3.

This behaviour can be implemented using a ReadWriteStream.

Figure 10.9: The user clicks on the back button. He is now viewing page 2 again.

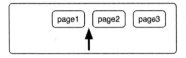

Figure 10.10: The user clicks again the back button. Page 1 is now displayed.

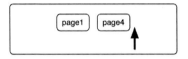

Figure 10.11: From page 1, the user clicks on a link to page 4. The history forgets pages 2 and 3.

```
Object subclass: #History
  instanceVariableNames: 'stream'
  classVariableNames: ''
  poolDictionaries: ''
  category: 'PBE-Streams'

History>>initialize
  super initialize.
  stream := ReadWriteStream on: Array new.
```

Nothing really difficult here, we define a new class which contains a stream. The stream is created during the initialize method.

We need methods to go backward and forward:

```
History>>goBackward
  self canGoBackward ifFalse: [self error: 'Already on the first element'].
  stream skip: -2.
  ↑ stream next.

History>>goForward
```

```
self canGoForward ifFalse: [self error: 'Already on the last element'].
↑ stream next
```

Until then, the code was pretty straightforward. Now, we have to deal with the goTo: method which should be activated when the user clicks on a link. A possible solution is:

```
History>>goTo: aPage
    stream nextPut: aPage.
```

This version is incomplete however. This is because when the user clicks on the link, there should be no more future pages to go to, *i.e.*, the forward button must be deactivated. To do this, the simplest solution is to write nil just after to indicate the history end:

```
History>>goTo: anObject
    stream nextPut: anObject.
    stream nextPut: nil.
    stream back.
```

Now, only methods canGoBackward and canGoForward have to be implemented.

A stream is always positioned between two elements. To go backward, there must be two pages before the current position: one page is the current page, and the other one is the page we want to go to.

```
History>>canGoBackward
    ↑ stream position > 1
```

```
History>>canGoForward
    ↑ stream atEnd not and: [stream peek notNil]
```

Let us add a method to peek at the contents of the stream:

```
History>>contents
    ↑ stream contents
```

And the history works as advertised:

```
History new
    goTo: #page1;
    goTo: #page2;
    goTo: #page3;
    goBackward;
    goBackward;
    goTo: #page4;
    contents      ⟶      #(#page1 #page4 nil nil)
```

10.4   Using streams for file access

You have already seen how to stream over collections of elements. It's also possible to stream over files on your hard disk. Once created, a stream on a file is really like a stream on a collection: you will be able to use the same protocol to read, write or position the stream. The main difference appears in the creation of the stream. There are several different ways to create file streams, as we shall now see.

Creating file streams

To create file streams, you will have to use one of the following instance creation methods offered by the class FileStream:

fileNamed: Open a file with the given name for reading and writing. If the file already exists, its prior contents may be modified or replaced, but the file will not be truncated on close. If the name has no directory part, then the file will be created in the default directory.

newFileNamed: Create a new file with the given name, and answer a stream opened for writing on that file. If the file already exists, ask the user what to do.

forceNewFileNamed: Create a new file with the given name, and answer a stream opened for writing on that file. If the file already exists, delete it without asking before creating the new file.

oldFileNamed: Open an existing file with the given name for reading and writing. If the file already exists, its prior contents may be modified or replaced, but the file will not be truncated on close. If the name has no directory part, then the file will be created in the default directory.

readOnlyFileNamed: Open an existing file with the given name for reading.

You have to remember that each time you open a stream on a file, you have to close it too. This is done through the close method.

```
stream := FileStream forceNewFileNamed: 'test.txt'.
stream
    nextPutAll: 'This text is written in a file named ';
    print: stream localName.
stream close.

stream := FileStream readOnlyFileNamed: 'test.txt'.
stream contents.    ⟶    'This text is written in a file named "test.txt"'
stream close.
```

The method localName answers the last component of the name of the file. You can also access the full path name using the method fullName.

You will soon notice that manually closing the file stream is painful and error-prone. That's why FileStream offers a message called forceNewFileNamed:do: to automatically close a new stream after evaluating a block that sets its contents.

```
FileStream
  forceNewFileNamed: 'test.txt'
  do: [:stream |
    stream
      nextPutAll: 'This text is written in a file named ';
      print: stream localName].
string := FileStream
      readOnlyFileNamed: 'test.txt'
      do: [:stream | stream contents].
string    ⟶    'This text is written in a file named "test.txt"'
```

The stream-creation methods that take a block as an argument first create a stream on a file, then execute the block with the stream as an argument, and finally close the stream. These methods return what is returned by the block, which is to say, the value of the last expression in the block. This is used in the previous example to get the content of the file and put it in the variable string.

Binary streams

By default, created streams are text-based which means you will read and write characters. If your stream must be binary, you have to send the message binary to your stream.

When your stream is in binary mode, you can only write numbers from 0 to 255 (1 Byte). If you want to use nextPutAll: to write more than one number at a time, you have to pass a ByteArray as argument.

```
FileStream
 forceNewFileNamed: 'test.bin'
 do: [:stream |
     stream
       binary;
       nextPutAll: #(145 250 139 98) asByteArray].

FileStream
 readOnlyFileNamed: 'test.bin'
 do: [:stream |
     stream binary.
     stream size.        ⟶    4
```

```
    stream next.        ⟶    145
    stream upToEnd.     ⟶    #[250 139 98]
  ].
```

Here is another example which creates a picture in a file named "test.pgm" (portable graymap file format). You can open this file with your favorite drawing program.

```
FileStream
  forceNewFileNamed: 'test.pgm'
  do: [:stream |
    stream
      nextPutAll: 'P5'; cr;
      nextPutAll: '4 4'; cr;
      nextPutAll: '255'; cr;
      binary;
      nextPutAll: #(255 0 255 0) asByteArray;
      nextPutAll: #(0 255 0 255) asByteArray;
      nextPutAll: #(255 0 255 0) asByteArray;
      nextPutAll: #(0 255 0 255) asByteArray
  ]
```

This creates a 4x4 checkerboard as shown in Figure 10.12.

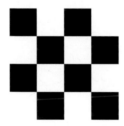

Figure 10.12: A 4x4 checkerboard you can draw using binary streams.

10.5 Chapter summary

Streams offer a better way than collections to incrementally read and write a sequence of elements. There are easy ways to convert back and forth between streams and collections.

- Streams may be either readable, writeable or both readable and writeable.

- To convert a collection to a stream, define a stream "on" a collection, *e.g.*, ReadStream on: (1 to: 1000), or send the messages readStream, etc. to the collection.

- To convert a stream to a collection, send the message contents.

- To concatenate large collections, instead of using the comma operator, it is more efficient to create a stream, append the collections to the stream with nextPutAll:, and extract the result by sending contents.

- File streams are by default character-based. Send binary to explicitly make them binary.

Chapter 11

Morphic

Morphic is the name given to Pharo's graphical interface. Morphic is written in Smalltalk, so it is fully portable between operating systems; as a consequence, Pharo looks exactly the same on Unix, MacOS and Windows. What distinguishes Morphic from most other user interface toolkits is that it does not have separate modes for "composing" and "running" the interface: all the graphical elements can be assembled and disassembled by the user, at any time.[1]

11.1   The history of Morphic

Morphic was developed by John Maloney and Randy Smith for the Self programming language, staring around 1993. Maloney later wrote a new version of Morphic for Squeak, but the basic ideas behind the Self version are still alive and well in Pharo Morphic: *directness* and *liveness*. Directness means that the shapes on the screen are objects that can be examined or changed directly, that is, by pointing at them using the mouse. Liveness means that the user interface is always able to respond to user actions: information on the screen is continuously updated as the world that it describes changes. A simple example of this is that you can detach a menu item and keep it as a button.

(?)   *Bring up the world menu. Meta-click once on the world menu to bring up its morphic halo[2], then meta-click again on the menu item you want to detach to bring up its halo. Now drag that item elsewhere on the screen by grabbing the black handle*

---

[1]We thank Hilaire Fernandes for permission to base this chapter on his original article in French.

[2]Recall that you should set halosEnabled in the Preferences browser. Alternatively, you can evaluate Preferences enable: #halosEnabled in a workspace.

, *as shown in Figure 11.1.*

Figure 11.1: Detaching a morph, here the `Workspace` menu item, to make it an independent button.

All of the objects that you see on the screen when you run Pharo are *Morphs*, that is, they are instances of subclasses of class `Morph`. `Morph` itself is a large class with many methods; this makes it possible for subclasses to implement interesting behaviour with little code. You can create a morph to represent any object, although how good a representation you get depends on the object!

To create a morph to represent a string object, execute the following code in a workspace.

```
'Morph' asMorph openInWorld
```

This creates a Morph to represent the string `'Morph'`, and then opens it (that is, displays it) in the "world", which is the name that Pharo gives to the screen. You should obtain a graphical element — a Morph — which you can manipulate by meta-clicking.

Of course, it is possible to define morphs that are more interesting graphical representations than the one that you have just seen. The method `asMorph` has a default implementation in class `Object` class that just creates a String-Morph. So, for example, `Color tan asMorph` returns a StringMorph labeled with the result of `Color tan printString`. Let's change this so that we get a coloured rectangle instead.

Open a browser on the `Color` *class and add the following method to it:*

Method 11.1: *Getting a morph for an instance of* Color.

Color»asMorph
   ↑ Morph new color: self

Now execute Color orange asMorph openInWorld in a workspace. Instead of the string-like morph, you get an orange rectangle!

11.2   Manipulating morphs

Morphs are objects, so we can manipulate them like any other object in Smalltalk: by sending messages, we can change their properties, create new subclasses of Morph, and so on.

Every morph, even if it is not currently open on the screen, has a position and a size. For convenience, all morphs are considered to occupy a rectangular region of the screen; if they are irregularly shaped, their position and size are those of the smallest rectangular "box" that surrounds them, which is known as the morph's bounding box, or just its "bounds". The position method returns a Point that describes the location of the morph's upper left corner (or the upper left corner of its bounding box). The origin of the coordinate system is the screen's upper left corner, with y coordinates increasing *down* the screen and x coordinates increasing to the right. The extent method also returns a point, but this point specifies the width and height of the morph rather than a location.

Type the following code into a workspace and do it*:*

```
joe := Morph new color: Color blue.
joe openInWorld.
bill := Morph new color: Color red .
bill openInWorld.
```

Then type joe position and print it. To move joe, execute joe position: (joe position + (10@3)) repeatedly.

It is possible to do a similar thing with size. joe extent answers joe's size; to have joe grow, execute joe extent: (joe extent ∗ 1.1). To change the color of a morph, send it the color: message with the desired Color object as argument, for instance, joe color: Color orange. To add transparency, try joe color: (Color orange alpha: 0.5).

To make bill follow joe, you can repeatedly execute this code:

```
bill position: (joe position + (100@0))
```

If you move joe using the mouse and then execute this code, bill will move so that it is 100 pixels to the right of joe. .

11.3 Composing morphs

One way of creating new graphical representations is by placing one morph inside another. This is called *composition*; morphs can be composed to any depth. You can place a morph inside another by sending the message addMorph: to the container morph.

🕑 *Try adding a morph to another one:*

```
star := StarMorph new color: Color yellow.
joe addMorph: star.
star position: joe position.
```

The last line positions the star at the same coordinates as joe. Notice that the coordinates of the contained morph are still relative to the screen, not to the containing morph. There are many methods available to position a morph; browse the *geometry* protocol of class Morph to see for yourself. For example, to center the star inside joe, execute star center: joe center.

Figure 11.2: The star is contained inside joe, the translucent blue morph.

If you now try to grab the star with the mouse, you will find that you actually grab joe, and the two morphs move together: the star is *embedded* inside joe. It is possible to embed more morphs inside joe. In addition to doing this programmatically, you can also embed morphs by direct manipulation.

11.4 Creating and drawing your own morphs

While it is possible to make many interesting and useful graphical representations by composing morphs, sometimes you will need to create something completely different. To do this you define a subclass of Morph and override the drawOn: method to change its appearance.

The morphic framework sends the message drawOn: to a morph when it needs to redisplay the morph on the screen. The parameter to drawOn: is a kind of Canvas; the expected behaviour is that the morph will draw itself on that canvas, inside its bounds. Let's use this knowledge to create a cross-shaped morph.

ⓘ *Using the browser, define a new class* CrossMorph *inheriting from* Morph:

Class 11.2: *Defining* CrossMorph

```
Morph subclass: #CrossMorph
    instanceVariableNames: ''
    classVariableNames: ''
    poolDictionaries: ''
    category: 'PBE-Morphic'
```

We can define the drawOn: method like this:

Method 11.3: *Drawing a* CrossMorph.

```
drawOn: aCanvas
    | crossHeight crossWidth horizontalBar verticalBar |
    crossHeight := self height / 3.0 .
    crossWidth := self width / 3.0 .
    horizontalBar := self bounds insetBy: 0 @ crossHeight.
    verticalBar := self bounds insetBy: crossWidth @ 0.
    aCanvas fillRectangle: horizontalBar color: self color.
    aCanvas fillRectangle: verticalBar color: self color
```

Cross

Figure 11.3: A CrossMorph with its halo; you can resize it as you wish.

Sending the bounds message to a morph answers its bounding box, which is an instance of Rectangle. Rectangles understand many messages that create other rectangles of related geometry; here we use the insetBy: message with a point as its argument to create first a rectangle with reduced height, and then another rectangle with reduced width.

🕮 *To test your new morph, execute* CrossMorph new openInWorld.

The result should look something like Figure 11.3. However, you will notice that the sensitive zone — where you can click to grab the morph — is still the whole bounding box. Let's fix this.

When the Morphic framework needs to find out which Morphs lie under the cursor, it sends the message containsPoint: to all the morphs whose bounding boxes lie under the mouse pointer. So, to limit the sensitive zone of the morph to the cross shape, we need to override the containsPoint: method.

🕮 *Define the following method in class* CrossMorph:

Method 11.4: *Shaping the sensitive zone of the* CrossMorph.

```
containsPoint: aPoint
  | crossHeight crossWidth horizontalBar verticalBar |
  crossHeight := self height / 3.0.
  crossWidth := self width / 3.0.
  horizontalBar := self bounds insetBy: 0 @ crossHeight.
  verticalBar := self bounds insetBy: crossWidth @ 0.
  ↑ (horizontalBar containsPoint: aPoint)
    or: [verticalBar containsPoint: aPoint]
```

This method uses the same logic as drawOn:, so we can be confident that the points for which containsPoint: answers true are the same ones that will be colored in by drawOn. Notice how we leverage the containsPoint: method in class Rectangle to do the hard work.

There are two problems with the code in methods 11.3 and 11.4. The most obvious is that we have duplicated code. This is a cardinal error: if we find that we need to change the way that horizonatalBar or verticalBar are calculated, we are quite likely to forget to change one of the two occurrences. The solution is to factor out these calculations into two new methods, which we put in the private protocol:

Method 11.5: horizontalBar.

```
horizontalBar
  | crossHeight |
  crossHeight := self height / 3.0.
  ↑ self bounds insetBy: 0 @ crossHeight
```

Method 11.6: verticalBar.

```
verticalBar
  | crossWidth |
  crossWidth := self width / 3.0.
  ↑ self bounds insetBy: crossWidth @ 0
```

We can then define both drawOn: and containsPoint: using these methods:

Figure 11.4: The center of the cross is filled twice with the colour.

Figure 11.5: The cross-shaped morph, showing a row of unfilled pixels.

Method 11.7: *Refactored* CrossMorph»drawOn:.

```
drawOn: aCanvas
    aCanvas fillRectangle: self horizontalBar color: self color.
    aCanvas fillRectangle: self verticalBar color: self color
```

Method 11.8: *Refactored* CrossMorph»containsPoint:.

```
containsPoint: aPoint
    ↑ (self horizontalBar containsPoint: aPoint)
        or: [self verticalBar containsPoint: aPoint]
```

This code is much simpler to understand, largely because we have given meaningful names to the private methods. In fact, it is so simple that you may have noticed the second problem: the area in the center of the cross, which is under both the horizontal and the vertical bars, is drawn twice. This doesn't matter when we fill the cross with an opaque colour, but the bug becomes apparent immediately if we draw a semi-transparent cross, as shown in Figure 11.4.

(!) *Execute the following code in a workspace, line by line:*

```
m := CrossMorph new bounds: (0@0 corner: 300@300).
m openInWorld.
m color: (Color blue alpha: 0.3).
```

The fix is to divide the vertical bar into three pieces, and to fill only the top and bottom. Once again we find a method in class Rectangle that does the hard work for us: r1 areasOutside: r2 answers an array of rectangles comprising the parts of r1 outside r2. Here is the revised code:

Method 11.9: *The revised* drawOn: *method, which fills the center of the cross once.*

```
drawOn: aCanvas
    | topAndBottom |
```

```
aCanvas fillRectangle: self horizontalBar color: self color.
topAndBottom := self verticalBar areasOutside: self horizontalBar.
topAndBottom do: [ :each | aCanvas fillRectangle: each color: self color]
```

This code seems to work, but if you try it on some crosses and resize them, you may notice that at some sizes, a one-pixel wide line separates the bottom of the cross from the remainder, as shown in Figure 11.5. This is due to rounding: when the size of the rectangle to be filled is not an integer, fillRectangle: color: seems to round inconsistently, leaving one row of pixels unfilled. We can work around this by rounding explicitly when we calculate the sizes of the bars.

Method 11.10: CrossMorph»horizontalBar *with explicit rounding.*

```
horizontalBar
   | crossHeight |
   crossHeight := (self height / 3.0) rounded.
   ↑ self bounds insetBy: 0 @ crossHeight
```

Method 11.11: CrossMorph»verticalBar *with explicit rounding.*

```
verticalBar
   | crossWidth |
   crossWidth := (self width / 3.0) rounded.
   ↑ self bounds insetBy: crossWidth @ 0
```

11.5   Interaction and animation

To build live user-interfaces using morphs, we need to be able to interact with them using the mouse and the keyboard. Moreover, the morphs need to be able respond to user input by changing their appearance and position — that is, by animating themselves.

Mouse events

When a mouse button is pressed, Morphic sends each morph under the mouse pointer the message handlesMouseDown:. If a morph answers true, then Morphic immediately sends it the mouseDown: message; it also sends the mouseUp: message when the user releases the mouse button. If all morphs answer false, then Morphic initiates a drag-and-drop operation. As we will discuss below, the mouseDown: and mouseUp: messages are sent with an argument — a MouseEvent object — that encodes the details of the mouse action.

Let's extend CrossMorph to handle mouse events. We start by ensuring that all crossMorphs answer true to the handlesMouseDown: message.

Ⓘ   *Add this method to* CrossMorph:

> Method 11.12: *Declaring that* CrossMorph *will react to mouse clicks.*

```
CrossMorph»handlesMouseDown: anEvent
    ↑true
```

Suppose that when we click on the cross, we want to change the color of the cross to red, and when we action-click on it, we want to change the color to yellow. This can be accomplished by method 11.13.

> Method 11.13: *Reacting to mouse clicks by changing the morph's color.*

```
CrossMorph»mouseDown: anEvent
    anEvent redButtonPressed "click"
        ifTrue: [self color: Color red].
    anEvent yellowButtonPressed "action–click"
        ifTrue: [self color: Color yellow].
    self changed
```

Notice that in addition to changing the color of the morph, this method also sends self changed. This makes sure that morphic sends drawOn: in a timely fashion. Note also that once the morph handles mouse events, you can no longer grab it with the mouse and move it. Instead you have to use the halo: meta-click on the morph to make the halo appear and grab either the brown move handle 🔳 or the black pickup handle 🔲 at the top of the morph.

The anEvent argument of mouseDown: is an instance of MouseEvent, which is a subclass of MorphicEvent. MouseEvent defines the redButtonPressed and yellowButtonPressed methods. Browse this class to see what other methods it provides to interrogate the mouse event.

Keyboard events

To catch keyboard events, we need to take three steps.

1. Give the "keyboard focus" to a specific morph: for instance we can give focus to our morph when the mouse is over it.

2. Handle the keyboard event itself with the handleKeystroke: method: this message is sent to the morph that has keyboard focus when the user presses a key.

3. Release the keyboard focus when the mouse is no longer over our morph.

Let's extend CrossMorph so that it reacts to keystrokes. First, we need to arrange to be notified when the mouse is over the morph. This will happen if our morph answers true to the handlesMouseOver: message

ⓖ *Declare that* CrossMorph *will react when it is under the mouse pointer.*

Method 11.14: *We want to handle "mouse over" events.*

```
CrossMorph»handlesMouseOver: anEvent
  ↑true
```

This message is the equivalent of handlesMouseDown: for the mouse position. When the mouse pointer enters or leaves the morph, the mouseEnter: and mouseLeave: messages are sent to it.

ⓖ *Define two methods so that* CrossMorph *catches and releases the keyboard focus, and a third method to actually handle the keystrokes.*

Method 11.15: *Getting the keyboard focus when the mouse enters the morph.*

```
CrossMorph»mouseEnter: anEvent
  anEvent hand newKeyboardFocus: self
```

Method 11.16: *Handing back the focus when the pointer goes away.*

```
CrossMorph»mouseLeave: anEvent
  anEvent hand newKeyboardFocus: nil
```

Method 11.17: *Receiving and handling keyboard events.*

```
CrossMorph»handleKeystroke: anEvent
  | keyValue |
  keyValue := anEvent keyValue.
  keyValue = 30    "up arrow"
    ifTrue: [self position: self position – (0 @ 1)].
  keyValue = 31    "down arrow"
    ifTrue: [self position: self position + (0 @ 1)].
  keyValue = 29    "right arrow"
    ifTrue: [self position: self position + (1 @ 0)].
  keyValue = 28    "left arrow"
    ifTrue: [self position: self position – (1 @ 0)]
```

We have written this method so that you can move the morph using the arrow keys. Note that when the mouse is no longer over the morph, the handleKeystroke: message is not sent, so the morph stops responding to keyboard commands. To discover the key values, you can open a Transcript window and add Transcript show: anEvent keyValue to method 11.17. The anEvent argument of handleKeystroke: is an instance of KeyboardEvent, another subclass of MorphicEvent. Browse this class to learn more about keyboard events.

Morphic animations

Morphic provides a simple animation system with two main methods: step is sent to a morph at regular intervals of time, while stepTime specifies the time in milliseconds between steps.[3] In addition, startStepping turns on the stepping mechanism, while stopStepping turns it off again; isStepping can be used to find out whether a morph is currently being stepped.

 Make CrossMorph *blink by defining these methods as follows:*

Method 11.18: *Defining the animation time interval.*

```
CrossMorph»stepTime
    ↑ 100
```

Method 11.19: *Making a step in the animation.*

```
CrossMorph»step
    (self color diff: Color black) < 0.1
        ifTrue: [self color: Color red]
        ifFalse: [self color: self color darker]
```

To start things off, you can open an inspector on a CrossMorph (using the debug handle ⊙ in the morphic halo), type self startStepping in the small workspace pane at the bottom, and do it. Alternatively, you can modify the handleKeystroke: method so that you can use the + and − keys to start and stop stepping.

 Add the following code to method 11.17:

```
keyValue = $+ asciiValue
    ifTrue: [self startStepping].
keyValue = $- asciiValue
    ifTrue: [self stopStepping].
```

11.6 Interactors

To prompt the user for input, the UIManager class provides a large number of ready-to-use dialog boxes. For instance, the request:initialAnswer: method returns the string entered by the user (Figure 11.6).

```
UIManager default request: 'What''s your name?' initialAnswer: 'no name'
```

---

[3]stepTime is actually the *minimum* time between steps. If you ask for a stepTime of 1 ms, don't be surprised if Pharo is too busy to step your morph that often.

Figure 11.6: An input dialog.

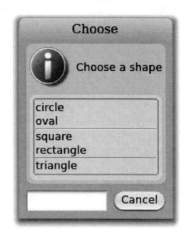

Figure 11.7: Pop-up menu.

To display a popup menu, use one of the various chooseFrom: methods
(Figure 11.7):

```
UIManager default
    chooseFrom: #('circle' 'oval' 'square' 'rectangle' 'triangle')
    lines: #(2 4) message: 'Choose a shape'
```

Browse the UIManager *class and try out some of the interaction methods offered.*

11.7   Drag-and-drop

Morphic also supports drag-and-drop. Let's examine a simple example with
two morphs, a receiver morph and a dropped morph. The receiver will
accept a morph only if the dropped morph matches a given condition: in
our example, the morph should be blue. If it is rejected, the dropped morph
decides what to do.

Let's first define the receiver morph:

Class 11.20: *Defining a morph on which we can drop other morphs*

```
Morph subclass: #ReceiverMorph
    instanceVariableNames: ''
    classVariableNames: ''
    poolDictionaries: ''
    category: 'PBE-Morphic'
```

(!) *Now define the initialization method in the usual way:*

Method 11.21: *Initializing* ReceiverMorph.

```
ReceiverMorph»initialize
    super initialize.
    color := Color red.
    bounds := 0 @ 0 extent: 200 @ 200
```

How do we decide if the receiver morph will accept or repel the dropped morph? In general, both of the morphs will have to agree to the interaction. The receiver does this by responding to wantsDroppedMorph:event:; the first argument is the dropped morph, and the second the mouse event, so that the receiver can, for example, see if any modifier keys were held down at the time of the drop. The dropped morph is also given the opportunity to check and see if it likes the morph onto which it is being dropped; it is sent the message wantsToBeDroppedInto:. The default implementation of this method (in class Morph) answers true.

Method 11.22: *Accept dropped morphs based on their color.*

```
ReceiverMorph»wantsDroppedMorph: aMorph event: anEvent
    ↑ aMorph color = Color blue
```

What happens to the dropped morph if the receiving morph doesn't want it? The default behaviour is for it to do nothing, that is, to sit on top of the receiving morph, but without interacting with it. A more intuitive behavior is for the dropped morph to go back to its original position. This can be achieved by the receiver answering true to the message repelsMorph:event: when it doesn't want the dropped morph:

Method 11.23: *Changing the behaviour of the dropped morph when it is rejected.*

```
ReceiverMorph»repelsMorph: aMorph event: ev
    ↑ (self wantsDroppedMorph: aMorph event: ev) not
```

That's all we need as far as the receiver is concerned.

(!) *Create instances of* ReceiverMorph *and* EllipseMorph *in a workspace:*

```
ReceiverMorph new openInWorld.
EllipseMorph new openInWorld.
```

Try to drag-and-drop the yellow EllipseMorph onto the receiver. It will be rejected and sent back to its initial position.

(!) *To change this behaviour, change the color of the ellipse morph to* Color blue *using an inspector. Blue morphs should be accepted by the* ReceiverMorph.

Let's create a specific subclass of Morph, named DroppedMorph, so we can experiment a bit more:

Class 11.24: *Defining a morph we can drag-and-drop onto* ReceiverMorph

```
Morph subclass: #DroppedMorph
    instanceVariableNames: ''
    classVariableNames: ''
    poolDictionaries: ''
    category: 'PBE-Morphic'
```

Method 11.25: *Initializing* DroppedMorph.

```
DroppedMorph»initialize
    super initialize.
    color := Color blue.
    self position: 250@100
```

Now we can specify what the dropped morph should do when it is rejected by the receiver; here it will stay attached to the mouse pointer:

Method 11.26: *Reacting when the morph was dropped but rejected.*

```
DroppedMorph»rejectDropMorphEvent: anEvent
    | h |
    h := anEvent hand.
    WorldState
        addDeferredUIMessage: [h grabMorph: self].
    anEvent wasHandled: true
```

Sending the hand message to an event answers the *hand*, an instance of HandMorph that represents the mouse pointer and whatever it holds. Here we tell the World that the hand should grab self, the rejected morph.

☺ *Create two instances of* DroppedMorph, *and then drag-and-drop them onto the receiver.*

```
ReceiverMorph new openInWorld.
(DroppedMorph new color: Color blue) openInWorld.
(DroppedMorph new color: Color green) openInWorld.
```

The green morph is rejected and therefore stays attached to the mouse pointer.

11.8 A complete example

Let's design a morph to roll a die[4]. Clicking on it will display the values of all sides of the die in a quick loop, and another click will stop the animation.

___
[4]NB: One die, two dice.

Die

Figure 11.8: The die in Morphic.

ⓘ *Define the die as a subclass of* BorderedMorph *instead of* Morph, *because we will make use of the border.*

Class 11.27: *Defining the die morph*

```
BorderedMorph subclass: #DieMorph
    instanceVariableNames: 'faces dieValue isStopped'
    classVariableNames: ''
    poolDictionaries: ''
    category: 'PBE-Morphic'
```

The instance variable faces records the number of faces on the die; we allow dice with up to 9 faces! dieValue records the value of the face that is currently displayed, and isStopped is true if the die animation has stopped running. To create a die instance, we define the faces: n method on the *class* side of DieMorph to create a new die with n faces.

Method 11.28: *Creating a new die with the number of faces we like.*

```
DieMorph class»faces: aNumber
    ↑ self new faces: aNumber
```

The initialize method is defined on the instance side in the usual way; remember that new sends initialize to the newly-created instance.

Method 11.29: *Initializing instances of* DieMorph.

```
DieMorph»initialize
    super initialize.
    self extent: 50 @ 50.
    self useGradientFill; borderWidth: 2; useRoundedCorners.
    self setBorderStyle: #complexRaised.
    self fillStyle direction: self extent.
    self color: Color green.
    dieValue := 1.
    faces := 6.
    isStopped := false
```

We use a few methods of BorderedMorph to give a nice appearance to the die: a thick border with a raised effect, rounded corners, and a color gradient

on the visible face. We define the instance method faces: to check for a valid
parameter as follows:

Method 11.30: *Setting the number of faces of the die.*

```
DieMorph»faces: aNumber
    "Set the number of faces"
    (aNumber isInteger
        and: [aNumber > 0]
        and: [aNumber <= 9])
      ifTrue: [faces := aNumber]
```

It may be good to review the order in which the messages are sent when a
die is created. For instance, if we start by evaluating DieMorph faces: 9:

1. The class method DieMorph class»faces: sends new to DieMorph class.

2. The method for new (inherited by DieMorph class from Behavior) creates
   the new instance and sends it the initialize message.

3. The initialize method in DieMorph sets faces to an initial value of 6.

4. DieMorph class»new returns to the class method DieMorph class»faces:,
   which then sends the message faces: 9 to the new instance.

5. The instance method DieMorph»faces: now executes, setting the faces
   instance variable to 9.

Before defining drawOn:, we need a few methods to place the dots on the
displayed face:

Methods 11.31: *Nine methods for placing points on the faces of the die.*

```
DieMorph»face1
    ↑{0.5@0.5}
DieMorph»face2
    ↑{0.25@0.25 . 0.75@0.75}
DieMorph»face3
    ↑{0.25@0.25 . 0.75@0.75 . 0.5@0.5}
DieMorph»face4
    ↑{0.25@0.25 . 0.75@0.25 . 0.75@0.75 . 0.25@0.75}
DieMorph»face5
    ↑{0.25@0.25 . 0.75@0.25 . 0.75@0.75 . 0.25@0.75 . 0.5@0.5}
DieMorph»face6
    ↑{0.25@0.25 . 0.75@0.25 . 0.75@0.75 . 0.25@0.75 . 0.25@0.5 . 0.75@0.5}
DieMorph»face7
    ↑{0.25@0.25 . 0.75@0.25 . 0.75@0.75 . 0.25@0.75 . 0.25@0.5 . 0.75@0.5 . 0.5@0.5}

DieMorph »face8
    ↑{0.25@0.25 . 0.75@0.25 . 0.75@0.75 . 0.25@0.75 . 0.25@0.5 . 0.75@0.5 . 0.5@0.5
       . 0.5@0.25}
```

```
DieMorph »face9
    ↑{0.25@0.25 . 0.75@0.25 . 0.75@0.75 . 0.25@0.75 . 0.25@0.5 . 0.75@0.5 . 0.5@0.5
        . 0.5@0.25 . 0.5@0.75}
```

These methods define collections of the coordinates of dots for each face. The coordinates are in a square of size 1×1; we will simply need to scale them to place the actual dots.

The drawOn: method does two things: it draws the die background with the super-send, and then draws the dots.

Method 11.32: *Drawing the die morph.*

```
DieMorph»drawOn: aCanvas
    super drawOn: aCanvas.
    (self perform: ('face' , dieValue asString) asSymbol)
        do: [:aPoint | self drawDotOn: aCanvas at: aPoint]
```

The second part of this method uses the reflective capacities of Smalltalk. Drawing the dots of a face is a simple matter of iterating over the collection given by the faceX method for that face, sending the drawDotOn:at: message for each coordinate. To call the correct faceX method, we use the perform: method which sends a message built from a string, here ('face', dieValue asString) asSymbol. You will encounter this use of perform: quite regularly.

Method 11.33: *Drawing a single dot on a face.*

```
DieMorph»drawDotOn: aCanvas at: aPoint
    aCanvas
        fillOval: (Rectangle
            center: self position + (self extent * aPoint)
            extent: self extent / 6)
        color: Color black
```

Since the coordinates are normalized to the [0:1] interval, we scale them to the dimensions of our die: self extent * aPoint.

ⓘ   *We can already create a die instance from a workspace:*

```
(DieMorph faces: 6) openInWorld.
```

To change the displayed face, we create an accessor that we can use as myDie dieValue: 4:

Method 11.34: *Setting the current value of the die.*

```
DieMorph»dieValue: aNumber
    (aNumber isInteger
        and: [aNumber > 0]
        and: [aNumber <= faces])
```

```
      ifTrue:
          [dieValue := aNumber.
          self changed]
```

Now we will use the animation system to show quickly all the faces:

Methods 11.35: *Animating the die.*

```
DieMorph»stepTime
    ↑ 100

DieMorph»step
    isStopped ifFalse: [self dieValue: (1 to: faces) atRandom]
```

Now the die is rolling!

To start or stop the animation by clicking, we will use what we learned previously about mouse events. First, activate the reception of mouse events:

Methods 11.36: *Handling mouse clicks to start and stop the animation.*

```
DieMorph»handlesMouseDown: anEvent
    ↑ true

DieMorph»mouseDown: anEvent
    anEvent redButtonPressed
        ifTrue: [isStopped := isStopped not]
```

Now the die will roll or stop rolling when we click on it.

11.9   More about the canvas

The drawOn: method has an instance of Canvas as its sole argument; the canvas is the area on which the morph draws itself. By using the graphics methods of the canvas you are free to give the appearance you want to a morph. If you browse the inheritance hierarchy of the Canvas class, you will see that it has several variants. The default variant of Canvas is FormCanvas; you will find the key graphics methods in Canvas and FormCanvas. These methods can draw points, lines, polygons, rectangles, ellipses, text, and images with rotation and scaling.

It is also possible to use other kinds of canvas, to obtain transparent morphs, more graphics methods, antialiasing, and so on. To use these features you will need an AlphaBlendingCanvas or a BalloonCanvas. But how can you obtain such a canvas in a drawOn: method, when drawOn: receives an instance of FormCanvas as its argument? Fortunately, you can transform one kind of canvas into another.

🛈 *To use a canvas with a 0.5 alpha-transparency in* DieMorph, *redefine* drawOn: *like this:*

Method 11.37: *Drawing a translucent die.*

```
DieMorph»drawOn: aCanvas
    | theCanvas |
    theCanvas := aCanvas asAlphaBlendingCanvas: 0.5.
    super drawOn: theCanvas.
    (self perform: ('face' , dieValue asString) asSymbol)
        do: [:aPoint | self drawDotOn: theCanvas at: aPoint]
```

That's all you need to do!

Figure 11.9: The die displayed with alpha-transparency.

11.10   Chapter summary

Morphic is a graphical framework in which graphical interface elements can be dynamically composed.

- You can convert an object into a morph and display that morph on the screen by sending it the messages asMorph openInWorld.

- You can manipulate a morph by meta-clicking on it and using the handles that appear. (Handles have help balloons that explain what they do.)

- You can compose morphs by embedding one onto another, either by drag and drop or by sending the message addMorph:.

- You can subclass an existing morph class and redefine key methods, like initialize and drawOn:.

- You can control how a morph reacts to mouse and keyboard events by redefining the methods handlesMouseDown:, handlesMouseOver:, etc.

- You can animate a morph by defining the methods step (what to do) and stepTime (the number of milliseconds between steps).

- Various pre-defined morphs, like PopUpMenu and FillInTheBlank, are available for interacting with users.

Chapter 12

Seaside by Example

Seaside is a framework for building web applications in Smalltalk. It was originally developed by Avi Bryant in 2002; once mastered, Seaside makes web applications almost as easy to write as desktop applications.

Two of the better known applications built with Seaside are SqueakSource[1] and Dabble DB[2]. Seaside is unusual in that it is thoroughly object-oriented: there are no XHTML templates, no complicated control flows through web pages, and no encoding of state in URLs. Instead, you just send messages to objects. What a nice idea!

12.1   Why do we need Seaside?

Modern web applications try to interact with the user in the same way as desktop applications: they ask the user questions and the user responds, usually by filling in a form or clicking a button. But the web works the other way around: the user's browser makes a request of the server, and the server responds with a new web page. So web application development frameworks have to cope with a host of problems, chief among them being the management of this "inverted" control flow. Because of this, many web applications try to forbid the use of the browser's "back" button due to the difficulty of keeping track of the state of a session. Expressing non-trivial control flows across multiple web pages is often cumbersome, and multiple control flows can be difficult or impossible to express.

Seaside is a component-based framework that makes web development easier in several ways. First, control flow can be expressed naturally using message sends. Seaside keeps track of which web page corresponds to which

---

[1] http://SqueakSource.com
[2] http://DabbleDB.com

point in the execution of the web application. This means that the browser's "back" button works correctly.

Second, state is managed for you. As the developer, you have the choice of enabling backtracking of state, so that navigation "back" in time will undo side-effects. Alternatively, you can use the transaction support built into Seaside to prevent users from undoing permanent side-effects when they use the back button. You do not have to encode state information in the URL — this too is managed automatically for you.

Third, web pages are built up from nested components, each of which can support its own, independent control flow. There are no XHTML templates — instead valid XHTML is generated programmatically using a simple Smalltalk protocol. Seaside supports Cascading Style Sheets (CSS), so content and layout are cleanly separated.

Finally, Seaside provides a convenient web-based development interface, making it easy to develop applications iteratively, debug applications interactively, and recompile and extend applications while the server is running.

12.2   Getting started

The easiest way to get started is to download the "Seaside One-Click Experience" from the Seaside web site[3]. This is a prepackaged version of Seaside 2.8 for Mac OSX, Linux and Windows. The same web site lists many pointers to additional resources, including documentation and tutorials. Be warned, however, that Seaside has evolved considerably over the years, and not all available material refers to the latest version of Seaside.

Seaside includes a web server; you can turn the server on, telling it to listen on port 8080, by evaluating WAKom startOn: 8080, and you can turn it off again by evaluating WAKom stop. In the default installation, the default administrator login is admin and the default password is seaside. To change them, evaluate: WADispatcherEditor initialize. This will prompt you for a new name and password.

(!) *Start the Seaside server and direct a web browser to* http://localhost:8080/ seaside/.

You should see a web page that looks like Figure 12.1.

(!) *Navigate to the* examples ▷ counter *page. (Figure 12.2)*

This page is a small Seaside application: it displays a counter that can be incremented or decremented by clicking on the ++ and −− links.

---
[3]http://seaside.st

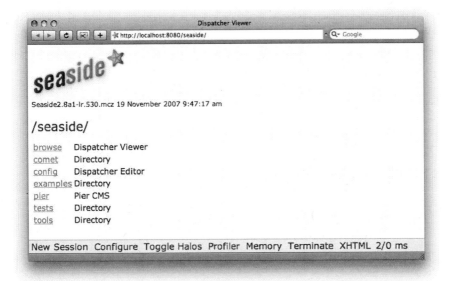

Figure 12.1: Starting up Seaside

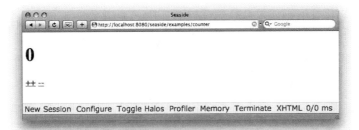

Figure 12.2: The counter.

Play with the counter by clicking on these links. Use your browser's "back"

button to go back to a previous state, and then click on ++ again. Notice how the counter is correctly incremented with respect to the currently displayed state, rather than the state that the counter was in when you started using the "back" button.

Notice the toolbar at the bottom of the web page in Figure 12.1. Seaside supports a notion of "sessions" to keep track of the state of the application for different users. New Session will start a new session on the counter application. Configure allows you to configure the settings of your application through a convenient web-interface. (To close the Configure view, click on the x in the top right corner.) Toggle Halos provides a way to explore the state of the application running on the Seaside server. Profiler and Memory provide detailed information about the run-time performance of the application. XHTML can be used to validate the generated web page, but works only when the web page is publicly accessible from the Internet, because it uses the W3C validation service.

Seaside applications are built up from pluggable "components". In fact, components are ordinary Smalltalk objects. The only thing that is special about them is that they should be instances of classes that inherit from the Seaside framework class WAComponent. We can explore components and their classes from the Pharo image, or directly from the web interface using halos.

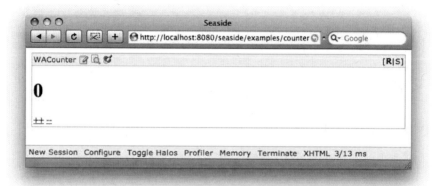

Figure 12.3: Halos

ⓘ   *Select* Toggle Halos. *You should see a web page like Figure 12.3. At the top left the text* WACounter *tells us the class of the Seaside component that implements the behavior of this web page. Next to this are three clickable icons. The first, with the pencil, activates a Seaside class browser on this class. The second, with the magnifying glass, opens an object inspector on the currently active* WACounter *instance. The third, with the coloured circles, displays the CSS style sheet for this component. At the top right, the* R *and* S *let you toggle between the rendered and source views of the web page. Experiment with all of these links. Note that the* ++ *and* – *links are also active in the source view. Contrast the nicely-formatted source view provided by the Halos with the unformatted source view offered by your browser.*

The Seaside class browser and object inspector can be very convenient when the server is running on another computer, especially when the server does not have a display, or if it is in remote place. However, when you are first developing a Seaside application, the server will be running locally, and it is easy to use the ordinary Pharo development tools in the server image.

Figure 12.4: Halting the counter

(☝) *Using the object inspector link in the web browser, open an inspector on the underlying Smalltalk counter object and evaluate* self halt. *The web page will stop loading. Now switch to the Seaside image. You should see a pre-debugger window (Figure 12.4) showing a* WACounter *object executing a* halt. *Examine this execution in the debugger, and then* Proceed. *Go back to the web browser and notice that the counter application is running again.*

Seaside components can be instantiated multiple times and in different contexts.

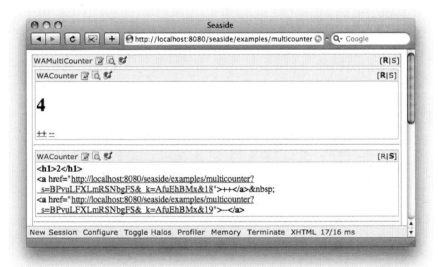

Figure 12.5: Independent subcomponents

(☝) *Point your web browser to http://localhost:8080/seaside/examples/multicounter.*

You will see an application built out of a number of independent instances of the counter component. Increment and decrement several of the counters. Verify that they behave correctly even if you use the "back" button. Toggle the halos to see how the application is built out of nested components. Use the Seaside class browser to view the implementation of WAMultiCounter. *You should see three methods on the class side (*canBeRoot, description, *and* initialize*) and three on the instance side (*children, initialize, *and* renderContentOn:*). Note that an application is simply a component that is willing to be at the root of the component containment hierarchy; this willingness is indicated by defining a class-side method* canBeRoot *to answer* true.

You can use the Seaside web interface to configure, copy or remove individual applications (*i.e.*, root-level components). Try making the following configuration change.

(*!*)   *Point your web browser to* http://localhost:8080/seaside/config. *Supply the login and password (*admin *and* seaside *by default). Select* Configure *next to "examples." Under the heading "Add entry point", enter the new name "counter2" for the type* Application *and click on* Add *(see Figure 12.6). On the next screen, set the* Root Component *to WACounter, then click* Save *and* Close. *Now we have a new counter installed at* http://localhost:8080/seaside/examples/counter2. *Use the same configuration interface to remove this entry point.*

Seaside operates in two modes: *development* mode, which is what we have seen so far, and *deployment* mode, in which the toolbar is not available. You can put Seaside into deployment mode using either the configuration page (navigate to the entry for the application and click on the Configure link) or click the Configure button in the toolbar. In either case, set the deployment mode to *true*. Note that this affects new sessions only. You can also set the mode globally by evaluating WAGlobalConfiguration setDeploymentMode or WAGlobalConfiguration setDevelopmentMode.

The configuration web page is just another Seaside application, so it too can be controlled from the configuration page. If you remove the "config" application, you can get it back by evaluating WADispatcherEditor initialize.

12.3   Seaside components

As we mentioned in the previous section, Seaside applications are built out of *components*. Let's take a closer look at how Seaside works by implementing the *Hello World* component.

Every Seaside component should inherit directly or indirectly from WAComponent, as shown in Figure 12.8.

(*!*)   *Define a subclass of* WAComponent *called* WAHelloWorld.

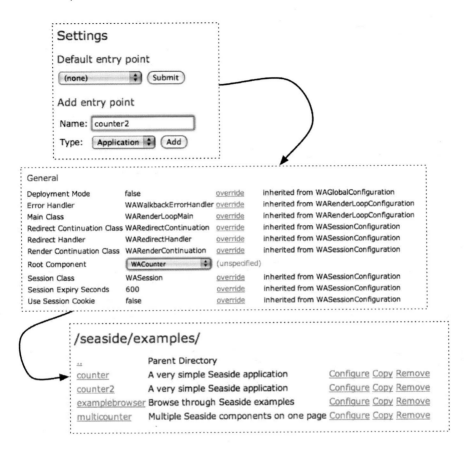

Figure 12.6: Configuring a new application

Components must know how to render themselves. Usually this is done by implementing the method renderContentOn:, which gets as its argument an instance of WAHtmlCanvas, which knows how to render XHTML.

Implement the following method, and put it in a protocol called rendering:

```
WAHelloWorld»renderContentOn: html
    html text: 'hello world'
```

Now we must inform Seaside that this component is willing to be a standalone application.

Implement the following method on the class side of WAHelloWorld.

```
WAHelloWorld class»canBeRoot
```

↑ true

We are almost done!

(i) *Point your web browser at http://localhost:8080/seaside/config, add a new entry point called "hello", and set its root component to be* WAHelloWorld. *Now point your browser to http://localhost:8080/seaside/hello. That's it! You should see a web page like Figure 12.7.*

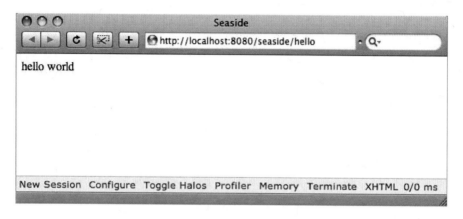

Figure 12.7: "Hello World" in Seaside

State backtracking and the "Counter" Application

The "counter" application is only slightly more complex than the "hello world" application.

The class WACounter is a standalone application, so WACounter class must answer true to the canBeRoot message. It must also register itself as an application; this is done in its class-side initialize method, as shown in Figure 12.8.

WACounter defines two methods, increase and decrease, which will be triggered from the ++ and –– links on the web page. It also defines an instance variable count to record the state of the counter. However, we also want Seaside to synchronize the counter with the browser page: when the user clicks on the browser's "back" button, we want seaside to "backtrack" the state of the WACounter object. Seaside includes a general mechanism for backtracking, but each application has to tell Seaside which parts of its state to track.

A component enables backtracking by implementing the states method on the instance side: states should answer an array containing all the objects to be tracked. In this case, the WACounter object adds itself to Seaside's table of backtrackable objects by returning Array with: self.

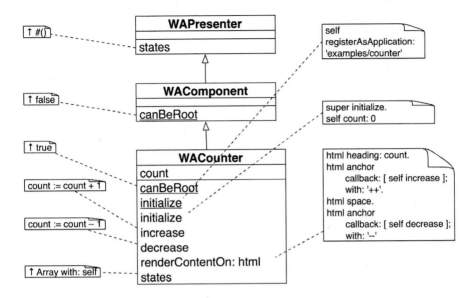

Figure 12.8: The WACounter class, which implements the *counter* application. Methods with underlined names are on the class-side; those with plain-text names are on the instance side.

Caveat. There is a subtle but important point to watch for when declaring objects for backtracking. Seaside tracks state by making a *copy* of all the objects declared in the states array. It does this using a WASnapshot object; WASnapshot is a subclass of IdentityDictionary that records the objects to be tracked as keys and shallow copies of their state as values. If the state of an application is backtracked to a particular snapshot, the state of each object entered into the snapshot dictionary is overwritten by the copy saved in the snapshot.

Here is the point to watch out for: In the case of WACounter, you might think that the state to be tracked is a number — the value of the count instance variable. However, having the states method answer Array with: count won't work. This is because the object named by count is an integer, and integers are immutable. The increase and decrease methods don't change the state of the object 0 into 1 or the object 3 into 2. Instead, they make count name a different integer: every time the count is incremented or decremented, the object named by count is *replaced* by another. This is why WACounter»states must return Array with: self. When the state of a WACounter object is replaced by a previous state, the *value* of each of the instance variable in the object is replaced by a previous value; this correctly replaces the current value of count by a prior value.

12.4   Rendering XHTML

The purpose of a web application is to create, or "render", web pages. As
we mentioned in Section 12.3, each Seaside component is responsible for
rendering itself. So, lets start our exploration of rendering by seeing how the
counter component renders itself.

Rendering the Counter

The rendering of the counter is relatively straightforward; the code is shown
in Figure 12.8. The current value of the counter is displayed as an XHTML
heading, and the increment and decrement operations are implemented as
html anchors (that is, links) with callbacks to blocks that will send increase
and decrease to the counter object.

We will have a closer look at the rendering protocol in a moment. But
before we do, let's have a quick look at the multi-counter.

From Counter to MultiCounter

WAMultiCounter, shown in Figure 12.9 is also a standalone application, so it
overrides canBeRoot to answer true. In addition, it is a *composite* component, so
Seaside requires it to declare its children by implementing a method children
that answers an array of all the components it contains. It renders itself by
rendering each of its subcomponents, separated by a horizontal rule. Aside
from instance and class-side initialization methods, there is nothing else to
the multi-counter!

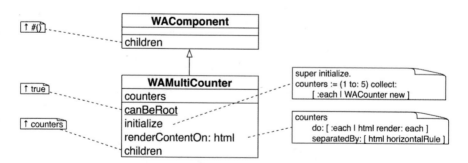

Figure 12.9: WAMultiCounter

More about Rendering XHTML

As you can see from these examples, Seaside does not use templates to generate web pages. Instead it generates XTHML programmatically. The basic idea
is that every Seaside component should override the method renderContentOn:;
this message will be sent by the framework to each component that needs
to be rendered. This renderContentOn: message will have argument that is an
html canvas onto which the component should render itself. By convention,
the html canvas parameter is called html. An html canvas is analogous to the
graphics canvas used by Morphic (and most other drawing frameworks) to
abstract away from the device-dependent details of drawing.

Here are some of the most basic rendering methods:

```
html text: 'hello world'.   "render a plain text string"
html html: '&ndash;'.       "render an XHTML incantation"
html render: 1.             "render any object"
```

The message render: anyObject can be sent to an html canvas to render
anyObject; it is normally used to render subcomponents. anyObject will itself be
sent the message renderContentOn: this is what happens in the multi-counter
(see Figure 12.9).

Using Brushes

A canvas provides a number of *brushes* that can be used to render (*i.e.*, "paint")
content on the canvas. There are brushes for every kind of XHTML element — paragraphs, tables, lists, and so on. To see the full protocol of brushes
and convenience methods, you should browse the class WACanvas and its
subclasses. The argument to renderContentOn: is actually an instance of the
subclass WARenderCanvas.

We have already seen the following brush used in the counter and multi-
counter examples:

```
html horizontalRule.
```

In Figure 12.10 we can see the output of many of the basic brushes
offered by Seaside.[4] The root component SeasideDemo simply renders its
subcomponents, which are instances of SeasideHtmlDemo, SeasideFormDemo,
SeasideEditCallDemo and SeasideDialogDemo, as shown in method 12.1.

---

[4]The source code for method 12.1 is in the package PBE–SeasideDemo in the project http:
//www.squeaksource.com/PharoByExample.

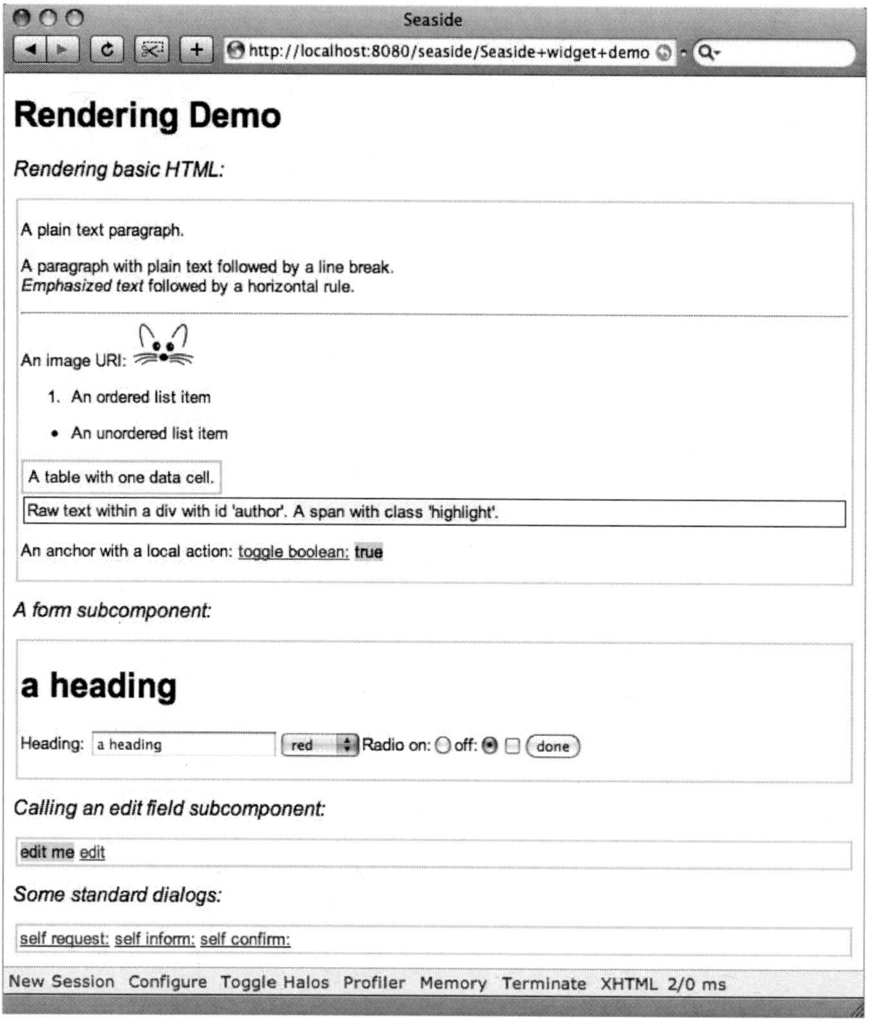

Figure 12.10: RenderingDemo

Method 12.1: SeasideDemo»renderContentOn:

```
SeasideDemo»renderContentOn: html
  html heading: 'Rendering Demo'.
  html heading
    level: 2;
    with: 'Rendering basic HTML: '.
  html div
    class: 'subcomponent';
    with: htmlDemo.
```

"render the remaining components ..."

Recall that a root component must always declare its children, or Seaside will refuse to render them.

```
SeasideDemo»children
  ↑ { htmlDemo . formDemo . editDemo . dialogDemo }
```

Notice that there are two different ways of instantiating the heading brush. The first way is to set the text directly by sending the message heading:. The second way is instantiate the brush by sending heading, and then to send a cascade of messages to the brush to set its properties and render it. Many of the available brushes can be used in these two ways.

> If you send a cascade of messages to a brush including the message with:, then with: should be the *final* message. with: both sets the content and renders the result.

In method 12.1, the first heading is at level 1, since this is the default. We explicitly set the level of the second heading to 2. The subcomponent is rendered as an XHTML *div* with the CSS class "subcomponent". (More on CSS in Section 12.5.) Also note that the argument to the with: keyword message need not be a literal string: it can be another component, or even — as in the next example — a block containing further rendering actions.

The SeasideHtmlDemo component demonstrates many of the most basic brushes. Most of the code should be self-explanatory.

```
SeasideHtmlDemo»renderContentOn: html
  self renderParagraphsOn: html.
  self renderListsAndTablesOn: html.
  self renderDivsAndSpansOn: html.
  self renderLinkWithCallbackOn: html
```

It is common practice to break up long rendering methods into many helper methods, as we have done here.

> Don't put all your rendering code into a single method. Split it into helper methods named using the pattern render *On:. All rendering methods go in the *rendering* protocol. Don't send renderContentOn: from your own code, use render: instead.

Look at the following code. The first helper method, SeasideHtmlDemo» renderParagraphsOn:, shows you how to generate XHTML paragraphs, plain and emphasized text, and images. Note that in Seaside simple elements are rendered by specifying the text they contain directly, whereas complex elements are specified using blocks. This is a simple convention to help you structure your rendering code.

```
SeasideHtmlDemo»renderParagraphsOn: html
    html paragraph: 'A plain text paragraph.'.
    html paragraph: [
      html
        text: 'A paragraph with plain text followed by a line break. ';
        break;
        emphasis: 'Emphasized text ';
        text: 'followed by a horizontal rule.';
        horizontalRule;
        text: 'An image URI: '.
      html image
        url: self squeakImageUrl;
        width: '50']
```

The next helper method, SeasideHtmlDemo»renderListsAndTablesOn:, shows you how to generate lists and tables. A table uses two levels of blocks to display each of its rows and the cells within the rows.

```
SeasideHtmlDemo»renderListsAndTablesOn: html
    html orderedList: [
      html listItem: 'An ordered list item'].
    html unorderedList: [
      html listItem: 'An unordered list item'].
    html table: [
      html tableRow: [
        html tableData: 'A table with one data cell.']]
```

The next example shows how we can specify CSS *div*s and *span*s with *class* or *id* attributes. Of course, the messages class: and id: can also be sent to the other brushes, not just to *div*s and *span*s. The method SeasideDemoWidget»style defines how these XHTML elements should be displayed (see Section 12.5).

```
SeasideHtmlDemo»renderDivsAndSpansOn: html
    html div
      id: 'author';
      with: [
        html text: 'Raw text within a div with id "author". '.
        html span
          class: 'highlight';
          with: 'A span with class "highlight".']
```

Finally we see a simple example of a link, created by binding a simple callback to an "anchor" (*i.e.*, a link). Clicking on the link will cause the subsequent text to toggle between "true" and "false" by toggling the instance variable toggleValue.

```
SeasideHtmlDemo»renderLinkWithCallbackOn: html
    html paragraph: [
        html text: 'An anchor with a local action: '.
        html span with: [
            html anchor
                callback: [toggleValue := toggleValue not];
                with: 'toggle boolean:'].
        html space.
        html span
            class: 'boolean';
            with: toggleValue ]
```

> Note that actions should appear only in callbacks. The code executed while rendering should not change the state of the application!

Forms

Forms are rendered just like the other examples that we have already seen. Here is the code for the SeasideFormDemo component in Figure 12.10.

```
SeasideFormDemo»renderContentOn: html
    | radioGroup |
    html heading: heading.
    html form: [
        html span: 'Heading: '.
        html textInput on: #heading of: self.
        html select
            list: self colors;
            on: #color of: self.
        radioGroup := html radioGroup.
        html text: 'Radio on:'.
        radioGroup radioButton
            selected: radioOn;
            callback: [radioOn := true].
        html text: 'off:'.
        radioGroup radioButton
            selected: radioOn not;
            callback: [radioOn := false].
        html checkbox on: #checked of: self.
        html submitButton
            text: 'done' ]
```

Since a form is a complex entity, it is rendered using a block. Note that all the state changes happen in the callbacks, not as part of the rendering.

There is one Seaside feature used here that is worth special mention, namely the message on:of:. In the example, this message is used to bind a text input field to the variable heading. Anchors and buttons also support this message. The first argument is the name of an instance variable for which accessors have been defined; the second argument is the object to which this instance variable belongs. Both observer (heading) and mutator (heading:) accessor messages must be understood by the object, with the usual naming convention. In the case here of a text input field, this saves us the trouble of having to define a callback that updates the field as well as having to bind the default contents of the html input field to the current value of the instance variable. Using on: #heading of: self, the heading variable is updated automatically whenever the user updates the text input field.

The same message is used twice more in this example, to cause the selection of a colour on the html form to update the color variable, and to bind the result of the checkbox to the checked variable. Many other examples can be found in the functional tests for Seaside. Have a look at the category *Seaside-Tests-Functional*, or just point your browser to http://localhost: 8080/seaside/tests/alltests. Select WAInputTest and click on the Restart button to see most of the features of forms.

Don't forget, if you Toggle Halos, you can browse the source code of the examples directly using the Seaside class browser.

12.5   CSS: Cascading style sheets

Cascading Style Sheets[5], or CSS for short, have emerged as a standard way for web applications to separate style from content. Seaside relies on CSS to avoid cluttering your rendering code with layout considerations.

You can set the CSS style sheet for your web components by defining the method style, which should return a string containing the CSS rules for that component. The styles of all the components displayed on a web page are joined together, so each component can have its own style. A better approach can be to define an abstract class for your web application that defines a common style for all its subclasses.

Actually, for deployed applications, it is more common to define style sheets as external files. This way the look and feel of the component is completely separate from its functionality. (Have a look at WAFileLibrary, which provides a way to serve static files without the need for a standalone server.)

If you already are familiar with CSS, then that's all you need to know.

---

[5]http://www.w3.org/Style/CSS/

```
SeasideDemoWidget»style
   ↑ '
body {
    font: 10pt Arial, Helvetica, sans-serif, Times New Roman;
}
h2 {
    font-size: 12pt;
    font-weight: normal;
    font-style: italic;
}
table { border-collapse: collapse; }
td {
    border: 2px solid #CCCCCC;
    padding: 4px;
}
#author {
    border: 1px solid black;
    padding: 2px;
    margin: 2px;
}
.subcomponent {
    border: 2px solid lightblue;
    padding: 2px;
    margin: 2px;
}
.highlight { background-color: yellow; }
.boolean { background-color: lightgrey; }
.field { background-color: lightgrey; }
   '
```

Figure 12.11: SeasideDemoWidget common style sheet.

Otherwise, read on for a very brief introduction to CSS.

Instead of directly encoding display attributes in the paragraph and text elements of your web pages, with CSS you will define different classes of elements and place all display considerations in a separate style sheet. Paragraph-like entities are called *divs* and text-like entities are *spans*. You would then define symbolic names, like "highlight" (see example below) for text to be highlighted, and specify how highlighted text is to be displayed in your style sheet.

Basically a CSS style sheet consists of a set of rules that specify how to format given XHTML elements. Each rule consists of two parts. There is a *selector* that specifies which XHTML elements the rule applies to, and there is a *declaration* which sets a number of attributes for that element.

Figure 12.11 illustrates a simple style sheet for the rendering demo shown earlier in Figure 12.10. The first rule specifies a preference for the fonts to use for the body of the web page. The next few rules specify properties of second-level headings (h2), tables (table), and table data (td).

The remaining rules have selectors that will match XHTML elements that have the given "class" or "id" attributes. CSS selectors for class attributes start with a "." and those for id attributes with "#". The main difference between class and id attributes is that many elements may have the same class, but only one element may have a given id (*i.e.*, an *identifier*). So, whereas a class attribute, such as highlight, may occur multiple times on any page, an id must identify a *unique* element on the page, such as a particular menu, the modified date, or author. Note that a particular XHTML element may have multiple classes, in which case all the applicable display attributes will be applied in sequence.

Selector conditions may be combined, so the selector div.subcomponent will only match an XHTML element if it is both a div *and* it has a class attribute equal to "subcomponent".

It is also possible to specify nested elements, though this is seldom necessary. For example, the selector "p span" will match a span within a paragraph but not within a div.

There are numerous books and web sites to help you learn CSS. For a dramatic demonstration of the power of CSS, we recommend you to have a look at the CSS Zen Garden[6], which shows how the same content can be rendered in radically different ways simply by changing the CSS style sheet.

12.6   Managing control flow

Seaside makes it particularly easy to design web applications with non-trivial control flow. There are basically two mechanisms that you can use:

1. A component can *call* another component by sending caller call: callee. The caller is temporarily replaced by the callee, until the callee returns control by sending answer:. The caller is usually self, but could also be any other currently visible component.

2. A workflow can be defined as a *task*. This is a special kind of component that subclasses WATask (instead of WAComponent). Instead of defining renderContentOn:, it defines no content of its own, but rather defines a go method that sends a series of call: messages to activate various subcomponents in turn.

---

[6]http://www.csszengarden.com/

Call and answer

Call and answer are used to realize simple dialogues.

There is a trivial example of call: and answer: in the rendering demo of Figure 12.10. The component SeasideEditCallDemo displays a text field and an *edit* link. The callback for the edit link calls a new instance of SeasideEditAnswerDemo initialized to the value of the text field. The callback also updates this text field to the result which is sent as an answer.

(We underline the call: and answer: sends to draw attention to them.)

```
SeasideEditCallDemo»renderContentOn: html
    html span
        class: 'field';
        with: self text.
    html space.
    html anchor
        callback: [self text: (self call: (SeasideEditAnswerDemo new text: self text))];
        with: 'edit'
```

What is particularly elegant is that the code makes absolutely no reference to the new web page that must be created. At run-time, a new page is created in which the SeasideEditCallDemo component is replaced by a SeasideEditAnswerDemo component; the parent component and the other peer components are untouched.

> call: and answer: should never be used while rendering. They may safely be sent from within a callback, or from within the go method of a task.

The SeasideEditAnswerDemo component is also remarkably simple. It just renders a form with a text field. The submit button is bound to a callback that will answer the final value of the text field.

```
SeasideEditAnswerDemo»renderContentOn: html
    html form: [
        html textInput
            on: #text of: self.
        html submitButton
            callback: [ self answer: self text ];
            text: 'ok'.
    ]
```

That's it.

Seaside takes care of the control flow and the correct rendering of all the components. Interestingly, the "back" button of the browser will also work just fine (though side effects are not rolled back unless we take additional steps).

Convenience methods

Since certain call–answer dialogues are very common, Seaside provides some convenience methods to save you the trouble of writing components like SeasideEditAnswerDemo. The generated dialogues are shown in Figure 12.12. We can see these convenience methods being used within SeasideDialogDemo» renderContentOn:

The message request: performs a call to a component that will let you edit a text field. The component answers the edited string. An optional label and default value may also be specified.

```
SeasideDialogDemo»renderContentOn: html
    html anchor
        callback: [ self request: 'edit this' label: 'done' default: 'some text' ];
        with: 'self request:'.
    ...
```

The message inform: calls a component that simply displays the argument message and waits for the user to click "ok". The called component just returns self.

```
...
    html space.
    html anchor
        callback: [ self inform: 'yes!' ];
```

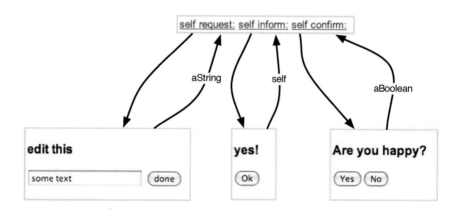

Figure 12.12: Some standard dialogs

```
    with: 'self inform:'.
...
```

The message confirm: asks a questions and waits for the user to select either "Yes" or "No". The component answers a boolean, which can be used to perform further actions.

```
...
  html space.
  html anchor
    callback: [
      (self confirm: 'Are you happy?')
        ifTrue: [ self inform: ':-)' ]
        ifFalse: [ self inform: ':-(' ]
    ];
    with: 'self confirm:'.
```

A few further convenience methods, such as chooseFrom:caption:, are defined in the *convenience* protocol of WAComponent.

Tasks

A task is a component that subclasses WATask. It does not render anything itself, but simply calls other components in a control flow defined by implementing the method go.

WAConvenienceTest is a simple example of a task defined in the category *Seaside-Tests-Functional*. To see its effect, just point your browser to http://localhost: 8080/seaside/tests/alltests, select WAConvenienceTest and click Restart.

```
WAConvenienceTest»go
  [ self chooseCheese.
    self confirmCheese ] whileFalse.
  self informCheese
```

This task calls in turn three components. The first, generated by the convenience method chooseFrom: caption:, is a WAChoiceDialog that asks the user to choose a cheese.

```
WAConvenienceTest»chooseCheese
  cheese := self
    chooseFrom: #('Greyerzer' 'Tilsiter' 'Sbrinz')
    caption: 'What''s your favorite Cheese?'.
  cheese isNil ifTrue: [ self chooseCheese ]
```

The second is a WAYesOrNoDialog to confirm the choice (generated by the convenience method confirm:).

```
WAConvenienceTest»confirmCheese
    ↑self confirm: 'Is ', cheese, ' your favorite cheese?'
```

Finally a WAFormDialog is called (via the convenience method inform:).

```
WAConvenienceTest»informCheese
    self inform: 'Your favorite cheese is ', cheese, '.'
```

The generated dialogues are shown in Figure 12.13.

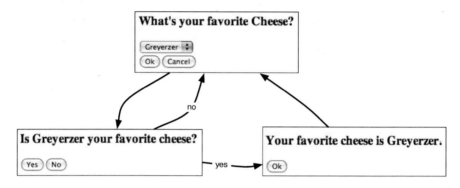

Figure 12.13: A simple task

Transactions

We saw in Section 12.3 that Seaside can keep track of the correspondence between the state of components and individual web pages by having components register their state for backtracking: all that a component need do is implement the method states to answer an array of all the objects whose state must be tracked.

Sometimes, however, we do not want to backtrack state: instead we want to *prevent* the user from accidentally undoing effects that should be permanent. This is often referred to as "the shopping cart problem". Once you have checked-out your shopping cart and paid for the items you have purchased, it should not be possible to go "back" with the browser and add more items to the shopping cart!

Seaside allows you to prevent this by defining a task within which certain actions are grouped together as *transactions*. You can backtrack within a transaction, but once a transaction is complete, you can no longer go back to it. The corresponding pages are *invalidated*, and any attempt to go back to them will cause Seaside to generate a warning and redirect the user to the most recent valid page.

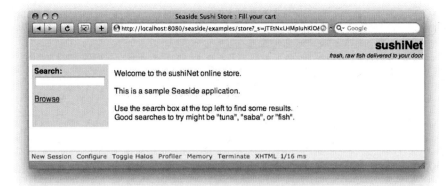

Figure 12.14: The Sushi Store

The Seaside *Sushi Store* is sample application that illustrates many of the features of Seaside, including transactions. This application is bundled with your installation of Seaside, so you can try it out by pointing your browser at http://localhost:8080/seaside/examples/store.[7]

The sushi store supports the following workflow:

1. Visit the store.
2. Browse or search for sushi.
3. Add sushi to your shopping cart.
4. Checkout.
5. Verify your order.
6. Enter shipping address.
7. Verify shipping address.
8. Enter payment information.
9. Your fish is on its way!

If you toggle the halos, you will see that the top-level component of the sushi store is an instance of WAStore. It does nothing but render the title bar, and then it renders task, an instance of WAStoreTask.

```
WAStore»renderContentOn: html
    "... render the title bar ..."
    html div id: 'body'; with: task
```

---

[7]If you cannot find it in your image, there is a version of the sushi store available on Squeak-Source from http://www.squeaksource.com/SeasideExamples/.

WAStoreTask captures this workflow sequence. At a couple of points it is critical that the user not be able to go back and change the submitted information.

(!)   *"Purchase" some sushi and then use the "back" button to try to put more sushi into your cart. You will get the message "That page has expired."*

Seaside lets the programmer say that a certain part of a workflow act like a transaction: once the transaction is complete, the user cannot go back and undo it. You say this by sending isolate: to a task with the transactional block as its argument. We can see this in the sushi store workflow as follows:

```
WAStoreTask»go
  | shipping billing creditCard |
  cart := WAStoreCart new.
  self isolate:
    [[self fillCart.
    self confirmContentsOfCart]
      whileFalse].

  self isolate:
    [shipping := self getShippingAddress.
    billing := (self useAsBillingAddress: shipping)
           ifFalse: [self getBillingAddress]
           ifTrue: [shipping].
    creditCard := self getPaymentInfo.
    self shipTo: shipping billTo: billing payWith: creditCard].

  self displayConfirmation.
```

Here we see quite clearly that there are two transactions. The first fills the cart and closes the shopping phase. (The helper methods fillCart etc. take care of instantiating and calling the right subcomponents.) Once you have confirmed the contents of the cart you cannot go back without starting a new session. The second transaction completes the shipping and payment data. You can navigate back and forth within the second transaction until you confirm payment. However, once both transactions are complete, any attempt to navigate back will fail.

Transactions may also be nested. A simple demonstration of this is found in the class WANestedTransaction. The first isolate: takes as argument a block that contains another, nested isolate:

```
WANestedTransaction»go
  self inform: 'Before parent txn'.
  self isolate:
    [self inform: 'Inside parent txn'.
    self isolate: [self inform: 'Inside child txn'].
    self inform: 'Outside child txn'].
```

> self inform: 'Outside parent txn'

ⓘ *Go to http://localhost:8080/seaside/tests/alltests, select* WATransactionTest *and click on* Restart. *Try to navigate back and forth within the parent and child transaction by clicking the* back *button and then clicking* ok. *Note that as soon as a transaction is complete, you can no longer go back inside the transaction without generating an error upon clicking* ok.

12.7 A complete tutorial example

Let's see how we can build a complete Seaside application from scratch.[8] We will build a RPN (Reverse Polish Notation) calculator as a Seaside application that uses a simple stack machine as its underlying model. Furthermore, the Seaside interface will let us toggle between two displays — one which just shows us the current value on top of the stack, and the other which shows us the complete state of the stack. The calculator with the two display options is shown in Figure 12.15.

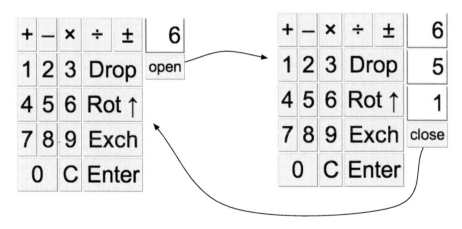

Figure 12.15: RPN calculator and its stack machine

We begin by implementing the stack machine and its tests.

ⓘ *Define a new class called* MyStackMachine *with an instance variable* contents *initialized to a new* OrderedCollection.

---

[8]The exercise should take at most a couple of hours. If you prefer to just look at the completed source code, you can grab it from the SqueakSource project http://www.squeaksource.com/ PharoByExample. The package to load is *PBE-SeasideRPN*. The tutorial that follows uses slightly different class names so that you can compare your implementation with ours.

```
MyStackMachine»initialize
    super initialize.
    contents := OrderedCollection new.
```

The stack machine should provide operations to push: and pop values, view the top of the stack, and perform various arithmetic operations to add, subtract, multiply and divide the top values on the stack.

ⓘ *Write some tests for the stack operations and then implement these operations. Here is a sample test:*

```
MyStackMachineTest»testDiv
    stack
        push: 3;
        push: 4;
        div.
    self assert: stack size = 1.
    self assert: stack top = (4/3).
```

You might consider using some helper methods for the arithmetic operations to check that there are two numbers on the stack before doing anything, and raising an error if this precondition is not fulfilled.[9] If you do this, most of your methods will just be one or two lines long.

You might also consider implementing MyStackMachine»printOn: to make it easier to debug your stack machine implementation with the help of an object inspector. (Hint: just delegate printing to the contents variable.)

ⓘ *Complete the* MyStackMachine *by writing operations* dup *(push a duplicate of the top value onto the stack),* exch *(exchange the top two values), and* rotUp *(rotate the entire stack contents up — the top value will move to the bottom).*

Now we have a simple stack machine implementation. We can start to implement the Seaside RPN Calculator.

We will make use of 5 classes:

- MyRPNWidget — this should be an abstract class that defines the common CSS style sheet for the application, and other common behavior for the components of the RPN calculator. It is a subclass of WAComponent and the direct superclass of the following four classes.

- MyCalculator — this is the root component. It should register the application (on the class side), it should instantiate and render its subcomponents, and it should register any state for backtracking.

---

[9]It's a good idea to use Object»assert: to specify the preconditions for an operation. This method will raise an AssertionFailure if the user tries to use the stack machine in an invalid state.

- MyKeypad — this displays the keys that we use to interact with the calculator.

- MyDisplay — this component displays the top of the stack and provides a button to call another component to display the detailed view.

- MyDisplayStack — this component shows the detailed view of the stack and provides a button to answer back. It is a subclass of MyDisplay.

(!) *Define* MyRPNWidget *in the category* MyCalculator. *Define the common* style *for the application.*

Here is a minimal CSS for the application. You can make it more fancy if you like.

```
MyRPNWidget»style
    ↑ 'table.keypad { float: left; }
td.key {
    border: 1px solid grey;
    background: lightgrey;
    padding: 4px;
    text–align: center;
}
table.stack { float: left; }
td.stackcell {
    border: 2px solid white;
    border–left–color: grey;
    border–right–color: grey;
    border–bottom–color: grey;
    padding: 4px;
    text–align: right;
}
td.small { font–size: 8pt; }'
```

(!) *Define* MyCalculator *to be a root component and register itself as an application* (i.e., *implement* canBeRoot *and* initialize *on the class side). Implement* MyCalculator» renderContentOn: *to render something trivial (such as its name), and verify that the application runs in a browser.*

MyCalculator is responsible for instantiating MyStackMachine, MyKeypad and MyDisplay.

(!) *Define* MyKeypad *and* MyDisplay *as subclasses of* MyRPNWidget. *All three components will need access to a common instance of the stack machine, so define the instance variable* stackMachine *and an initialization method* setMyStackMachine: *in the common parent,* MyRPNWidget. *Add instance variables* keypad *and* display *to* MyCalculator *and initialize them in* MyCalculator»initialize. *(Don't forget to send* super initialize*!)*

Pass the shared instance of the stack machine to the keypad and the display in the same initialize method. Implement MyCalculator»renderContentOn: *to simply render in turn the keypad and the display. To correctly display the subcomponents, you must implement* MyCalculator»children *to return an array with the keypad and the display. Implement placeholder rendering methods for the keypad and the display and verify that the calculator now displays its two subcomponents.*

Now we will change the implementation of the display to show the top value of the stack.

Use a table with class "keypad" containing a row with a single table data cell with class "stackcell". Change the rendering method of the keypad to ensure that the number 0 is pushed on the stack in case it is empty. (Define and use MyKeypad »ensureMyStackMachineNotEmpty.*) Also make it display an empty table with class "keypad". Now the calculator should display a single cell containing the value 0. If you toggle the halos, you should see something like this:*

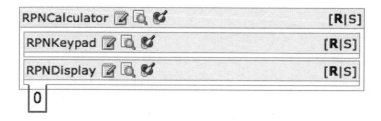

Figure 12.16: Displaying the top of the stack

Now let's implement an interface to interact with the stack.

First define the following helper methods, which will make it easier to script the interface:

```
MyKeypad»renderStackButton: text callback: aBlock colSpan: anInteger on: html
    html tableData
        class: 'key';
        colSpan: anInteger;
        with:
            [html anchor
                callback: aBlock;
                with: [html html: text]]
```

```
MyKeypad»renderStackButton: text callback: aBlock on: html
    self
        renderStackButton: text
        callback: aBlock
        colSpan: 1
```

```
on: html
```

We will use these two methods to define the buttons on the keypad with appropriate callbacks. Certain buttons may span multiple columns, but the default is to occupy just one column.

(💡) *Use the two helper methods to script the keypad as follows: (Hint: start by getting the digit and "Enter" keys working, then the arithmetic operators.)*

```
MyKeypad»renderContentOn: html
 self ensureStackMachineNotEmpty.
 html table
  class: 'keypad';
  with: [
   html tableRow: [
     self renderStackButton: '+' callback: [self stackOp: #add] on: html.
     self renderStackButton: '&ndash;' callback: [self stackOp: #min] on: html.
     self renderStackButton: '&times;' callback: [self stackOp: #mul] on: html.
     self renderStackButton: '&divide;' callback: [self stackOp: #div] on: html.
     self renderStackButton: '&plusmn;' callback: [self stackOp: #neg] on: html ].
   html tableRow: [
     self renderStackButton: '1' callback: [self type: '1'] on: html.
     self renderStackButton: '2' callback: [self type: '2'] on: html.
     self renderStackButton: '3' callback: [self type: '3'] on: html.
     self renderStackButton: 'Drop' callback: [self stackOp: #pop]
      colSpan: 2 on: html ].
" and so on ... "
   html tableRow: [
     self renderStackButton: '0' callback: [self type: '0'] colSpan: 2 on: html.
     self renderStackButton: 'C' callback: [self stackClearTop] on: html.
     self renderStackButton: 'Enter'
      callback: [self stackOp: #dup. self setClearMode]
      colSpan: 2 on: html ]]
```

Check that the keypad displays properly. If you try to click on the keys, however, you will find that the calculator does not work yet...

(💡) *Implement* MyKeypad»type: *to update the top of the stack by appending the typed digit. You will need to convert the top value to a string, update it, and convert it back to an integer, something like this:*

```
MyKeypad»type: aString
   stackMachine push: (stackMachine pop asString, aString) asNumber.
```

Now when you click on the digit keys the display should be updated. (Be sure that MyStackMachine»pop returns the value popped, or this will not work!)

⚖️ *Now we must implement* MyKeypad»stackOp: *Something like this will do the trick:*

```
MyKeypad»stackOp: op
  [ stackMachine perform: op ] on: AssertionFailure do: [ ].
```

The point is that we are not sure that all operations will succeed, for example, addition will fail if we do not have two numbers on the stack. For the moment we can just ignore such errors. If we are feeling more ambitious later on, we can provide some user feedback in the error handler block.

⚖️ *The first version of the calculator should be working now. Try to enter some numbers by pressing the digit keys, hitting* Enter *to push a copy of the current value, and entering* + *to sum the top two values.*

You will notice that typing digits does not behave the way you might expect. Actually the calculator should be aware of whether you are typing a *new* number, or appending to an existing number.

⚖️ *Adapt* MyKeypad»type: *to behave differently depending on the current typing mode. Introduce an instance variable* mode *which takes on one of the three values* #typing *(when you are typing),* #push *(after you have performed a calculator operation and typing should force the top value to be pushed), or* #clear *(after you have performed* Enter *and the top value should be cleared before typing). The new* type: *method might look like this:*

```
MyKeypad»type: aString
  self inPushMode ifTrue: [
    stackMachine push: stackMachine top.
    self stackClearTop ].
  self inClearMode ifTrue: [ self stackClearTop ].
  stackMachine push: (stackMachine pop asString, aString) asNumber.

"
```

Typing might work better now, but it is still frustrating not to be able to see what is on the stack.

⚖️ *Define* MyDisplayStack *as a subclass of* MyDisplay. *Add a button to the rendering method of* MyDisplay *which will call a new instance of* MyDisplayStack. *You will need an html anchor that looks something like this:*

```
html anchor
  callback: [ self call: (MyDisplayStack new setMyStackMachine: stackMachine)];
  with: 'open'
```

The callback will cause the current instance of MyDisplay to be temporarily replaced by a new instance of MyDisplayStack whose job it is to display the complete stack. When this component signals that it is done (*i.e.*, by sending self answer), then control will return to the original instance of MyDisplay.

ⓘ *Define the rendering method of* MyDisplayStack *to display all of the values on the stack. (You will either need to define an accessor for the stack machine's* contents *or you can define* MyStackMachine»do: *to iterate over the stack values.) The stack display should also have a button labelled "close" whose callback will simply perform* self answer.

```
html anchor
    callback: [ self answer];
    with: 'close'
```

Now you should be able to *open* and *close* the stack while you are using the calculator.

There is, however, one thing we have forgotten. Try to perform some operations on the stack. Now use the "back" button of your browser and try to perform some more stack operations. (For example, open the stack, type 1, Enter twice and +. The stack should display "2" and "1". Now hit the "back" button. The stack now shows three times "1" again. Now if you type + the stack shows "3". Backtracking is not yet working.

ⓘ *Implement* MyCalculator»states *to return an array with the contents of the stack machine. Check that backtracking now works correctly!*

Sit back and enjoy a tall glass of something cool!

12.8   A quick look at AJAX

AJAX (Asynchronous JavaScript and XML) is a technique to make web applications more interactive by exploiting JavaScript functionality on the client side.

Two well-known JavaScript libraries are Prototype (http://www.prototypejs.org) and script.aculo.us (http://script.aculo.us). Prototype provides a framework to ease writing JavaScript. script.aculo.us provides some additional features to support animations and drag-and-drop on top of Prototype. Both frameworks are supported in Seaside through the package "Scriptaculous".

All ready-made images have the Scriptaculous package extensions already loaded. The latest version is available from http://www.squeaksource.com/Seaside. An online demo is available at http://scriptaculous.seasidehosting.st. Alternatively, if you have a enabled image running, simply go to http://localhost:8080/seaside/tests/scriptaculous.

The Scriptaculous extensions follow the same approach as Seaside itself—simply configure Smalltalk objects to model your application, and the needed Javascript code will be generated for you.

Let us look at a simple example of how client-side Javascript support can make our RPN calculator behave more naturally. Currently every keystroke to enter a digit generates a request to refresh the page. We would like instead to handle editing of the display on the client-side by updating the display in the existing page.

(!) *To address the display from JavaScript code we must first give it a unique id. Update the calculator's rendering method as follows:*[10]

```
MyCalculator»renderContentOn: html
    html div id: 'keypad'; with: keypad.
    html div id: 'display'; with: display.
```

(!) *To be able to re-render the display when a keyboard button is pressed, the keyboard needs to know the display component. Add a* display *instance variable to* MyKeypad, *an initialize method* MyKeypad»setDisplay:, *and call this from* MyCalculator >>initialize. *Now we are able to assign some JavaScript code to the buttons by updating* MyKeypad»renderStackButton:callback:colSpan:on: *as follows:*

```
MyKeypad»renderStackButton: text callback: aBlock colSpan: anInteger on: html
    html tableData
        class: 'key';
        colSpan: anInteger;
        with: [
            html anchor
                callback: aBlock;
                onClick:            "handle Javascript event"
                    (html updater
                        id: 'display';
                        callback: [ :r |
                            aBlock value.
                            r render: display ];
                        return: false);
                with: [ html html: text ] ]
```

onClick: specifies a JavaScript event handler. html updater returns an instance of SUUpdater, a Smalltalk object representing the JavaScript Ajax.Updater object (http://www.prototypejs.org/api/ajax/updater). This object performs an AJAX request and updates a container's contents based on the response text. id: tells the updater what XHTML DOM element to update, in this case the

---

[10]If you have not implemented the tutorial example yourself, you can simply load the complete example (PBE-SeasideRPN) from http://www.squeaksource.com/PharoByExample and apply the suggested changes to the classes RPN* instead of My*.

contents of the div element with the id 'display'. callback: specifies a block that is triggered when the user presses the button. The block argument is a new renderer r, which we can use to render the display component. (Note: Even though html is still accessible, it is not valid anymore at the time this callback block is evaluated). Before rendering the display component we evaluate aBlock to perform the desired action.

return: false tells the JavaScript engine to not trigger the original link callback, which would cause a full refresh. We could instead remove the original anchor callback:, but like this the calculator will still work even if JavaScript is disabled.

(⚙) *Try the calculator again, and notice how a full page refresh is triggered every time you press a digit key. (The URL of the web page is updated at each keystroke.)*

Although we have implemented the client-side behavior, we have not yet activated it. Now we will enable the Javascript event handling.

(⚙) *Click on the* Configure *link in the toolbar of the calculator. Select "Add Library:"* SULibrary, *click the* Add *button and* Close.

Instead of manually adding the library, you may also do it programmatically when you register the application:

```
MyCalculator class»initialize
  (self registerAsApplication: 'rpn')
    addLibrary: SULibrary}}
```

(⚙) *Try the revised application. Note that the feedback is much more natural. In particular, a new URL is not generated with each keystroke.*

You may well ask, *yes, but how does this work?* Figure 12.17 shows how the RPN applications would both without and with AJAX. Basically AJAX short-circuits the rendering to *only* update the display component. Javascript is responsible both for triggering the request and updating the corresponding DOM element. Have a look at the generated source-code, especially the JavaScript code:

```
new Ajax.Updater(
  'display',
  'http://localhost/seaside/RPN+Calculator',
  {'evalScripts': true,
    'parameters': ['_s=zcdqfonqwbeYzkza', '_k=jMORHtqr','9'].join('&')});
return false
```

For more advanced examples, have a further look at http://localhost:8080/seaside/tests/scriptaculous.

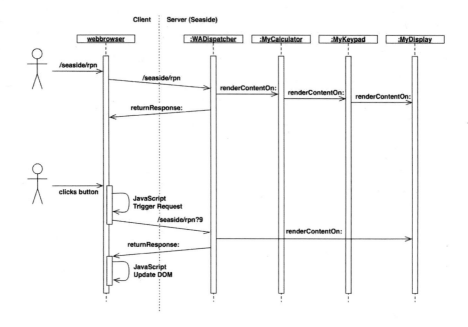

Seaside: AJAX Processing (simplified)

Lukas Renggli, 2007

Figure 12.17: Seaside AJAX processing (simplified)

Hints. In case of server side problems use the Smalltalk debugger. In case of client side problems use FireFox (http://www.mozilla.com) with the JavaScript debugger FireBug (http://www.getfirebug.com/) plugin enabled.

12.9 Chapter summary

- The easiest way to get started is to download the "Seaside One-Click Experience" from http://seaside.st

- Turn the server on and off by evaluating WAKom startOn: 8080 and WAKom stop.

- Reset the administrator login and password by evaluating WADispatcherEditor initialize.

- Toggle Halos to directly view application source code, run-time objects, CSS and XHTML.

- Send WAGlobalConfiguration setDeploymentMode to hide the toolbar.

- Seaside web applications are composed of components, each of which is an instance of a subclass of WAComponent.

- Only a root component may be registered as an application. It should implement canBeRoot on the class side. Alternatively it may register itself as an application in its class-side initialize method by sending self registerAsApplication: *application path*. If you override description it is possible to return a descriptive application name that will be displayed in the configuration editor.

- To backtrack state, a component must implement the states method to answer an array of objects whose state will be restored if the user clicks the browser's "back" button.

- A component renders itself by implementing renderContentOn:. The argument to this method is an XHTML rendering *canvas* (usually called html).

- A component can render a subcomponent by sending self render: *subcomponent*.

- XHTML is generated programmatically by sending messages to *brushes*. A brush is obtained by sending a message, such as paragraph or div, to the html canvas.

- If you send a cascade of messages to a brush that includes the message with:, then with: should be the last message sent. The with: message sets the contents *and* renders the result.

- Actions should appear only in callbacks. You should not change the state of the application while you are rendering it.

- You can bind various form widgets and anchors to instance variables with accessors by sending the message on: *instance variable* of: *object* to the brush.

- You can define the CSS for a component hierarchy by defining the method style, which should return a string containing the style sheet. (For deployed applications, it is more usual to refer to a style sheet located at a static URL.)

- Control flows can be programmed by sending x call: y, in which case component x will be replaced by y until y answers by sending answer: with a result in a callback. The receiver of call: is usually self, but may in general be any visible component.

- A control flow can also be specified as a *task* — a instance of a subclass of WATask. It should implement the method go, which should call: a series of components in a workflow.

- Use WAComponents's convenience methods request:, inform:, confirm: and chooseFrom:caption: for basic interactions.

- To prevent the user from using the browser's "back" button to access a previous execution state of the web application, you can declare portions of the workflow to be a *transaction* by enclosing them in an isolate: block.

Part III

Advanced Pharo

Chapter 13

Classes and metaclasses

As we saw in Chapter 5, in Smalltalk, everything is an object, and every object is an instance of a class. Classes are no exception: classes are objects, and class objects are instances of other classes. This object model captures the essence of object-oriented programming: it is lean, simple, elegant and uniform. However, the implications of this uniformity may confuse newcomers. The goal of this chapter is to show that there is nothing complex, "magic" or special here: just simple rules applied uniformly. By following these rules you can always understand why the situation is the way that it is.

13.1 Rules for classes and metaclasses

The Smalltalk object model is based on a limited number of concepts applied uniformly. Smalltalk's designers applied Occam's razor: any consideration leading to a model more complex than necessary was discarded.

To refresh your memory, here are the rules of the object model that we explored in Chapter 5.

Rule 1. Everything is an object.

Rule 2. Every object is an instance of a class.

Rule 3. Every class has a superclass.

Rule 4. Everything happens by sending messages.

Rule 5. Method lookup follows the inheritance chain.

As we mentioned in the introduction to this chapter, a consequence of Rule 1 is that *classes are objects too*, so Rule 2 tells us that classes must also be instances of classes. The class of a class is called a *metaclass*. A metaclass is created automatically for you whenever you create a class. Most of the time you do not need to care or think about metaclasses. However, every time that you use the browser to browse the "class side" of a class, it is helpful to recall that you are actually browsing a different class. A class and its metaclass are two separate classes, even though the former is an instance of the latter.

To properly explain classes and metaclasses, we need to extend the rules from Chapter 5 with the following additional rules.

Rule 6. Every class is an instance of a metaclass.

Rule 7. The metaclass hierarchy parallels the class hierarchy.

Rule 8. Every metaclass inherits from Class and Behavior.

Rule 9. Every metaclass is an instance of Metaclass.

Rule 10. The metaclass of Metaclass is an instance of Metaclass.

Together, these 10 rules complete Smalltalk's object model.

We will first briefly revisit the 5 rules from Chapter 5 with a small example. Then we will take a closer look at the new rules, using the same example.

13.2 Revisiting the Smalltalk object model

Since everything is an object, the color blue in Smalltalk is also an object.

```
Color blue  ⟶  Color blue
```

Every object is an instance of a class. The class of the color blue is the class Color:

```
Color blue class  ⟶  Color
```

Interestingly, if we set the *alpha* value of a color, we get an instance of a different class, namely TranslucentColor:

```
(Color blue alpha: 0.4) class  ⟶  TranslucentColor
```

We can create a morph and set its color to this translucent color:

```
EllipseMorph new color: (Color blue alpha: 0.4); openInWorld
```

You can see the effect in Figure 13.1.

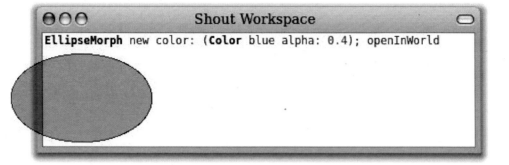

Figure 13.1: A translucent ellipse

By Rule 3, every class has a superclass. The superclass of TranslucentColor is Color, and the superclass of Color is Object:

| TranslucentColor superclass | $\longrightarrow$ | Color |
| Color superclass | $\longrightarrow$ | Object |

Everything happens by sending messagess (Rule 4), so we can deduce that blue is a message to Color, class and alpha: are messages to the color blue, openInWorld is a message to an ellipse morph, and superclass is a message to TranslucentColor and Color. The receiver in each case is an object, since everything is an object, but some of these objects are also classes.

Method lookup follows the inheritance chain (Rule 5), so when we send the message class to the result of Color blue alpha: 0.4, the message is handled when the corresponding method is found in the class Object, as shown in Figure 13.2.

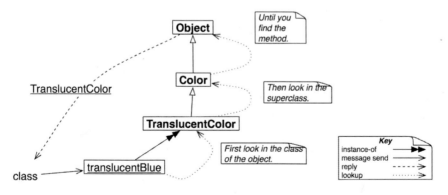

Figure 13.2: Sending a message to a translucent color

The figure captures the essence of the *is-a* relationship. Our translucent blue object *is a* TranslucentColor instance, but we can also say that it *is a* Color and that it *is an* Object, since it responds to the messages defined in all of these classes. In fact, there is a message, isKindOf:, that you can send to any object to find out if it is in an *is a* relationship with a given class:

```
translucentBlue := Color blue alpha: 0.4.
translucentBlue isKindOf: TranslucentColor    ⟶    true
translucentBlue isKindOf: Color               ⟶    true
translucentBlue isKindOf: Object              ⟶    true
```

13.3   Every class is an instance of a metaclass

As we mentioned in Section 13.1, classes whose instances are themselves classes are called metaclasses.

Metaclasses are implicit.   Metaclasses are automatically created when you define a class. We say that they are *implicit* since as a programmer you never have to worry about them. An implicit metaclass is created for each class you create, so each metaclass has only a single instance.

Whereas ordinary classes are named by global variables, metaclasses are anonymous. However, we can always refer to them through the class that is their instance. The class of Color, for instance, is Color class, and the class of Object is Object class:

```
Color class     ⟶    Color class
Object class    ⟶    Object class
```

Figure 13.3 shows how each class is an instance of its (anonymous) metaclass.

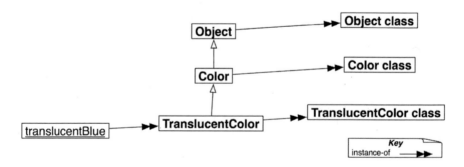

Figure 13.3: The metaclasses of Translucent and its superclasses

The fact that classes are also objects makes it easy for us to query them by sending messages. Let's have a look:

Color subclasses	⟶	{TranslucentColor}
TranslucentColor subclasses	⟶	#()
TranslucentColor allSuperclasses	⟶	an OrderedCollection(Color Object ProtoObject)
TranslucentColor instVarNames	⟶	#('alpha')
TranslucentColor allInstVarNames	⟶	#('rgb' 'cachedDepth' 'cachedBitPattern' 'alpha')
TranslucentColor selectors	⟶	an IdentitySet(#pixelValueForDepth: #pixelWord32 #convertToCurrentVersion:refStream: #isTransparent #scaledPixelValue32 #bitPatternForDepth: #storeArrayValuesOn: #setRgb:alpha: #alpha #isOpaque #pixelWordForDepth: #isTranslucentColor #hash #isTranslucent #alpha: #storeOn: #asNontranslucentColor #privateAlpha #balancedPatternForDepth:)

13.4 The metaclass hierarchy parallels the class hierarchy

Rule 7 says that the superclass of a metaclass cannot be an arbitrary class: it is constrained to be the metaclass of the superclass of the metaclass's unique instance.

TranslucentColor class superclass	⟶	Color class
TranslucentColor superclass class	⟶	Color class

This is what we mean by the metaclass hierarchy being parallel to the class hierarchy; Figure 13.4 shows how this works in the TranslucentColor hierarchy.

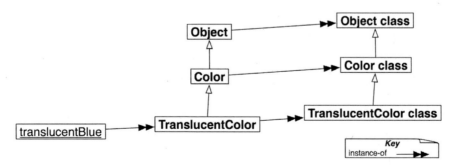

Figure 13.4: The metaclass hierarchy parallels the class hierarchy.

TranslucentColor class	⟶	TranslucentColor class
TranslucentColor class superclass	⟶	Color class
TranslucentColor class superclass superclass	⟶	Object class

Uniformity between Classes and Objects. It is interesting to step back a moment and realize that there is no difference between sending a message to an object and to a class. In both cases the search for the corresponding method starts in the class of the receiver, and proceeds up the inheritance chain.

Thus, messages sent to classes must follow the metaclass inheritance chain. Consider, for example, the method blue, which is implemented on the class side of Color. If we send the message blue to TranslucentColor, then it will be looked-up the same way as any other message. The lookup starts in TranslucentColor class, and proceeds up the metaclass hierarchy until it is found in Color class (see Figure 13.5).

TranslucentColor blue	⟶	Color blue

Note that we get as a result an ordinary Color blue, and not a translucent one — there is no magic!

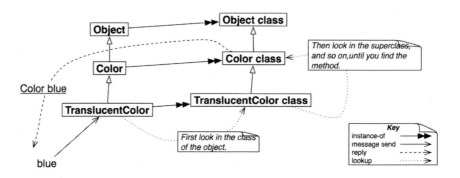

Figure 13.5: Message lookup for classes is the same as for ordinary objects.

Thus we see that there is one uniform kind of method lookup in Smalltalk. Classes are just objects, and behave like any other objects. Classes have the power to create new instances only because classes happen to respond to the message new, and because the method for new knows how to create new instances. Normally, non-class objects do not understand this message, but if you have a good reason to do so, there is nothing stopping you from adding a new method to a non-metaclass.

Since classes are objects, we can also inspect them.

(❗)   *Inspect* Color blue *and* Color.

Notice that in one case you are inspecting an instance of Color and in the other case the Color class itself. This can be a bit confusing, because the title bar of the inspector names the *class* of the object being inspected.

The inspector on Color allows you to see the superclass, instance variables, method dictionary, and so on, of the Color class, as shown in Figure 13.6.

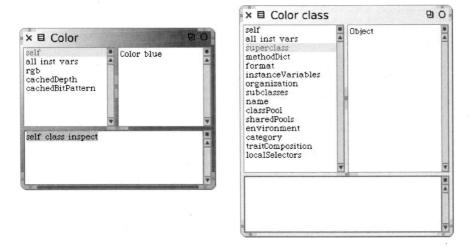

Figure 13.6: Classes are objects too.

13.5   Every metaclass Inherits from Class and Behavior

Every metaclass *is-a* class, hence inherits from Class. Class in turn inherits from its superclasses, ClassDescription and Behavior. Since everything in Smalltalk *is-an* object, these classes all inherit eventually from Object. We can see the complete picture in Figure 13.7.

Where is new defined?   To understand the importance of the fact that metaclasses inherit from Class and Behavior, it helps to ask where new is defined

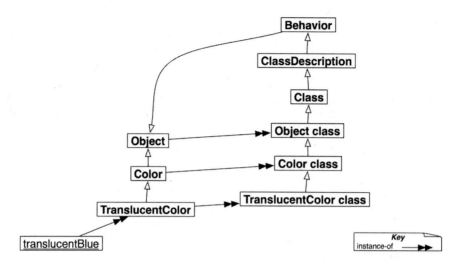

Figure 13.7: Metaclasses inherit from Class and Behavior

and how it is found. When the message new is sent to a class it is looked up in its metaclass chain and ultimately in its superclasses Class, ClassDescription and Behavior as shown in Figure 13.8.

The question *"Where new is defined?"* is crucial. new is first defined in the class Behavior, and it can be redefined in its subclasses, including any of the metaclass of the classes we define, when this is necessary. Now when a message new is sent to a class it is looked up, as usual, in the metaclass of this class, continuing up the superclass chain right up to the class Behavior, if it has not been redefined along the way.

Note that the result of sending TranslucentColor new is an instance of TranslucentColor and *not* of Behavior, even though the method is looked-up in the class Behavior! new always returns an instance of self, the class that receives the message, even if it is implemented in another class.

TranslucentColor new class $\longrightarrow$ TranslucentColor *"not Behavior"*

A common mistake is to look for new in the superclass of the receiving class. The same holds for new:, the standard message to create an object of a given size. For example, Array new: 4 creates an array of 4 elements. You will not find this method defined in Array or any of its superclasses. Instead you should look in Array class and its superclasses, since that is where the lookup will start.

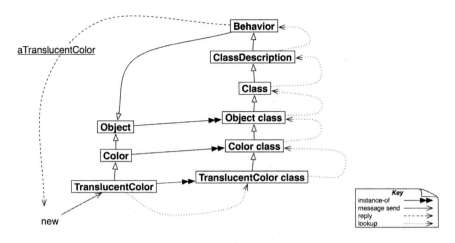

Figure 13.8: new is an ordinary message looked up in the metaclass chain.

Responsibilities of Behavior, ClassDescription and Class.   Behavior provides the minimum state necessary for objects that have instances: this includes a superclass link, a method dictionary, and a description of the instances (*i.e.*, representation and number). Behavior inherits from Object, so it, and all of its subclasses, can behave like objects.

Behavior is also the basic interface to the compiler. It provides methods for creating a method dictionary, compiling methods, creating instances (*i.e.*, new, basicNew, new:, and basicNew:), manipulating the class hierarchy (*i.e.*, superclass:, addSubclass:), accessing methods (*i.e.*, selectors, allSelectors, compiledMethodAt:), accessing instances and variables (*i.e.*, allInstances, instVarNames . . .), accessing the class hierarchy (*i.e.*, superclass, subclasses) and querying (*i.e.*, hasMethods, includesSelector, canUnderstand:, inheritsFrom:, isVariable).

ClassDescription is an abstract class that provides facilities needed by its two direct subclasses, Class and Metaclass. ClassDescription adds a number of facilities to the basis provided by Behavior: named instance variables, the categorization of methods into protocols, the notion of a name (abstract), the maintenance of change sets and the logging of changes, and most of the mechanisms needed for filing-out changes.

Class represents the common behaviour of all classes. It provides a class name, compilation methods, method storage, and instance variables. It provides a concrete representation for class variable names and shared pool variables (addClassVarName:, addSharedPool:, initialize). Class knows how to create instances, so all metaclasses should inherit ultimately from Class.

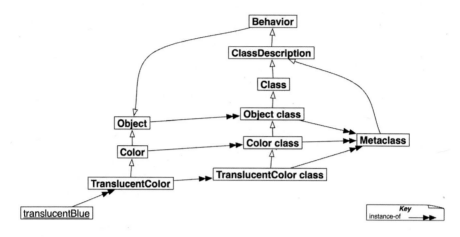

Figure 13.9: Every metaclass is a Metaclass.

13.6   Every metaclass is an instance of Metaclass

Metaclasses are objects too; they are instances of the class Metaclass as shown in Figure 13.9. The instances of class Metaclass are the anonymous metaclasses, each of which has exactly one instance, which is a class.

Metaclass represents common metaclass behaviour. It provides methods for instance creation (subclassOf:) creating initialized instances of the metaclass's sole instance, initialization of class variables, metaclass instance, method compilation, and class information (inheritance links, instance variables, etc.).

13.7   The metaclass of Metaclass is an Instance of Metaclass

The final question to be answered is: what is the class of Metaclass class?

The answer is simple: it is a metaclass, so it must be an instance of Metaclass, just like all the other metaclasses in the system (see Figure 13.10).

The figure shows how all metaclasses are instances of Metaclass, including the metaclass of Metaclass itself. If you compare Figures 13.9 and 13.10 you

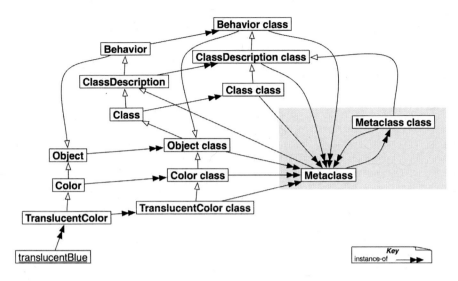

Figure 13.10: All metaclasses are instances of the class Metaclass, even the metaclass of Metaclass.

will see how the metaclass hierarchy perfectly mirrors the class hierarchy, all the way up to Object class.

The following examples show us how we can query the class hierarchy to demonstrate that Figure 13.10 is correct. (Actually, you will see that we told a white lie — Object class superclass $\longrightarrow$ ProtoObject class, not Class. In Pharo, we must go one superclass higher to reach Class.)

Example 13.1: *The class hierarchy*

TranslucentColor superclass	$\longrightarrow$	Color
Color superclass	$\longrightarrow$	Object

Example 13.2: *The parallel metaclass hierarchy*

TranslucentColor class superclass	$\longrightarrow$	Color class
Color class superclass	$\longrightarrow$	Object class
Object class superclass superclass	$\longrightarrow$	Class *"NB: skip ProtoObject class"*
Class superclass	$\longrightarrow$	ClassDescription
ClassDescription superclass	$\longrightarrow$	Behavior
Behavior superclass	$\longrightarrow$	Object

Example 13.3: *Instances of Metaclass*

TranslucentColor class class	$\longrightarrow$	Metaclass
Color class class	$\longrightarrow$	Metaclass
Object class class	$\longrightarrow$	Metaclass
Behavior class class	$\longrightarrow$	Metaclass

Example 13.4: *Metaclass class is a Metaclass*

Metaclass class class	$\longrightarrow$	Metaclass
Metaclass superclass	$\longrightarrow$	ClassDescription

13.8   Chapter summary

Now you should understand better how classes are organized and the impact of a uniform object model. If you get lost or confused, you should always remember that message passing is the key: you look for the method in the class of the receiver. This works on *any* receiver. If the method is not found in the class of the receiver, it is looked up in its superclasses.

- Every class is an instance of a metaclass. Metaclasses are implicit. A Metaclass is created automatically when you create the class that is its sole instance.

- The metaclass hierarchy parallels the class hierarchy. Method lookup for classes parallels method lookup for ordinary objects, and follows the metaclass's superclass chain.

- Every metaclass inherits from Class and Behavior. Every class *is a* Class . Since metaclasses are classes too, they must also inherit from Class. Behavior provides behaviour common to all entities that have instances.

- Every metaclass is an instance of Metaclass. ClassDescription provides everything that is common to Class and Metaclass.

- The metaclass of Metaclass is an instance of Metaclass. The *instance-of* relation forms a closed loop, so Metaclass class class $\longrightarrow$ Metaclass.

Chapter 14

Reflection

Smalltalk is a reflective programming language. In a nutshell, this means that programs are able to "reflect" on their own execution and structure. More technically, this means that the *metaobjects* of the runtime system can be *reified* as ordinary objects, which can be queried and inspected. The metaobjects in Smalltalk are classes, metaclasses, method dictionaries, compiled methods, the run-time stack, and so on. This form of reflection is also called *introspection*, and is supported by many modern programming languages.

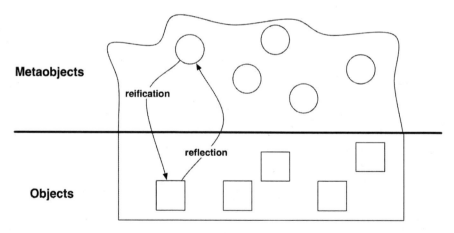

Figure 14.1: Reification and reflection.

Conversely, it is possible in Smalltalk to modify reified metaobjects and *reflect* these changes back to the runtime system (see Figure 14.1). This is also called *intercession*, and is supported mainly by dynamic programming languages, and only to a very limited degree by static languages.

A program that manipulates other programs (or even itself) is a *metapro-*

gram. For a programming language to be reflective, it should support both introspection and intercession. Introspection is the ability to *examine* the data structures that define the language, such as objects, classes, methods and the execution stack. Intercession is the ability to *modify* these structures, in other words to change the language semantics and the behavior of a program from within the program itself. *Structural reflection* is about examining and modifying the structures of the run-time system, and *behavioural reflection* is about modifying the interpretation of these structures.

In this chapter we will focus mainly on structural reflection. We will explore many practical examples illustrating how Smalltalk supports introspection and metaprogramming.

14.1 Introspection

Using the inspector, you can look at an object, change the values of its instance variables, and even send messages to it.

(!) *Evaluate the following code in a workspace:*

```
w := Workspace new.
w openLabel: 'My Workspace'.
w inspect
```

This will open a second workspace and an inspector. The inspector shows the internal state of this new workspace, listing its instance variables in the left part (dependents, contents, bindings...) and the value of the selected instance variable in the right part. The contents instance variable represents whatever the workspace is displaying in its text area, so if you select it, the right part will show an empty string.

(!) *Now type* 'hello' *in place of that empty string, then* accept *it.*

The value of the contents variable will change, but the workspace window will not notice it, so it does not redisplay itself. To trigger the window refresh, evaluate self contentsChanged in the lower part of the inspector.

Accessing instance variables

How does the inspector work? In Smalltalk, all instance variables are protected. In theory, it is impossible to access them from another object if the class doesn't define any accessor. In practice, the inspector can access instance variables without needing accessors, because it uses the reflective abilities of Smalltalk. In Smalltalk, classes define instance variables either by name or

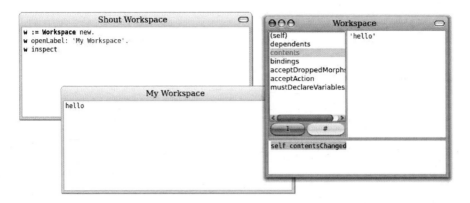

Figure 14.2: Inspecting a Workspace.

by numeric indices. The inspector uses methods defined by the Object class to access them: instVarAt: *index* and instVarNamed: *aString* can be used to get the value of the instance variable at position *index* or identified by *aString*, respectively; to assign new values to these instance variables, it uses instVarAt:put: and instVarNamed:put:.

For instance, you can change the value of the w binding of the first workspace by evaluating:

```
w instVarNamed: 'contents' put: 'howdy'; contentsChanged
```

> *Caveat:* Although these methods are useful for building development tools, using them to develop conventional applications is a bad idea: these reflective methods break the encapsulation boundary of your objects and can therefore make your code much harder to understand and maintain.

Both instVarAt: and instVarAt:put: are primitive methods, meaning that they are implemented as primitive operations of the Pharo virtual machine. If you consult the code of these methods, you will see the special pragma syntax <primitive: N> where N is an integer.

```
Object»instVarAt: index
    "Primitive. Answer a fixed variable in an object. ..."
    <primitive: 73>
    "Access beyond fixed variables."
    ↑self basicAt: index – self class instSize
```

Typically, the code after the primitive invocation is not executed. It is executed only if the primitive fails. In this specific case, if we try to access a variable that does not exist, then the code following the primitive will be tried. This also allows the debugger to be started on primitive methods. Although it is possible to modify the code of primitive methods, beware that this can be risky business for the stability of your Pharo system.

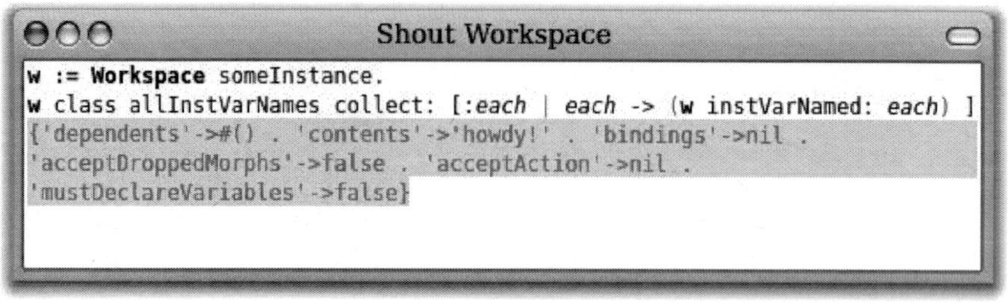

```
⊖ ⊖ ⊖                        Shout Workspace                              ⊜
w := Workspace someInstance.
w class allInstVarNames collect: [:each | each -> (w instVarNamed: each) ]
{'dependents'->#() . 'contents'->'howdy!' . 'bindings'->nil .
'acceptDroppedMorphs'->false . 'acceptAction'->nil .
'mustDeclareVariables'->false}
```

Figure 14.3: Displaying all instance variables of a Workspace.

Figure 14.3 shows how to display the values of the instance variables of an arbitrary instance (w) of class Workspace. The method allInstVarNames returns all the names of the instance variables of a given class.

In the same spirit, it is possible to gather instances that have specific properties. For instance, to get all instances of class SketchMorph whose instance variable owner is set to the world morph (*i.e.*, images currently displayed), try this expression:

```
SketchMorph allInstances select: [:c | (c instVarNamed: 'owner') isWorldMorph]
```

Iterating over instance variables

Let us consider the message instanceVariableValues, which returns a collection of all values of instance variables defined by this class, excluding the inherited instance variables. For instance:

```
(1@2) instanceVariableValues  ⟶  an OrderedCollection(1 2)
```

The method is implemented in Object as follows:

```
Object»instanceVariableValues
    "Answer a collection whose elements are the values of those instance variables of the
        receiver which were added by the receiver's class."
    | c |
    c := OrderedCollection new.
    self class superclass instSize + 1
        to: self class instSize
        do: [ :i | c add: (self instVarAt: i)].
    ↑ c
```

This method iterates over the indices of instance variables that the class defines, starting just after the last index used by the superclasses. (The method instSize returns the number of all named instance variables that a class defines.)

Querying classes and interfaces

The development tools in Pharo (code browser, debugger, inspector...) all use the reflective features we have seen so far.

Here are a few other messages that might be useful to build development tools:

isKindOf: *aClass* returns true if the receiver is instance of *aClass* or of one of its superclasses. For instance:

```
1.5 class              ⟶   Float
1.5 isKindOf: Number   ⟶   true
1.5 isKindOf: Integer  ⟶   false
```

respondsTo: *aSymbol* returns true if the receiver has a method whose selector is *aSymbol*. For instance:

```
1.5 respondsTo: #floor   ⟶   true   "since Number implements floor"
1.5 floor                ⟶   1
Exception respondsTo: #,  ⟶   true   "exception classes can be grouped"
```

> *Caveat:* Although these features are especially useful for defining development tools, they are normally not appropriate for typical applications. Asking an object for its class, or querying it to discover which messages it understands, are typical signs of design problems, since they violate the principle of encapsulation. Development tools, however, are not normal applications, since their domain is that of software itself. As such these tools have a right to dig deep into the internal details of code.

Code metrics

Let's see how we can use Smalltalk's introspection features to quickly extract some code metrics. Code metrics measure such aspects as the depth of the inheritance hierarchy, the number of direct or indirect subclasses, the number of methods or of instance variables in each class, or the number of locally defined methods or instance variables. Here are a few metrics for the class Morph, which is the superclass of all graphical objects in Pharo, revealing that it is a huge class, and that it is at the root of a huge hierarchy. Maybe it needs some refactoring!

```
Morph allSuperclasses size.      ⟶      2 "inheritance depth"
Morph allSelectors size.         ⟶   1378 "number of methods"
Morph allInstVarNames size.      ⟶      6 "number of instance variables"
Morph selectors size.            ⟶    998 "number of new methods"
Morph instVarNames size.         ⟶      6 "number of new variables"
Morph subclasses size.           ⟶     45 "direct subclasses"
Morph allSubclasses size.        ⟶    326 "total subclasses"
Morph linesOfCode.               ⟶   5968 "total lines of code!"
```

One of the most interesting metrics in the domain of object-oriented languages is the number of methods that extend methods inherited from the superclass. This informs us about the relation between the class and its superclasses. In the next sections we will see how to exploit our knowledge of the runtime structure to answer such questions.

14.2 Browsing code

In Smalltalk, everything is an object. In particular, classes are objects that provide useful features for navigating through their instances. Most of the messages we will look at now are implemented in Behavior, so they are understood by all classes.

As we saw previously, you can obtain an instance of a given class by sending it the message #someInstance.

```
Point someInstance    ⟶    0@0
```

You can also gather all the instances with #allInstances, or the number of alive instances in memory with #instanceCount.

```
ByteString allInstances        ⟶   #('collection' 'position' ...)
ByteString instanceCount       ⟶   104565
String allSubInstances size    ⟶    101675
```

These features can be very useful when debugging an application, because you can ask a class to enumerate those of its methods exhibiting specific properties.

- whichSelectorsAccess: returns the list of all selectors of methods that read or write the instance variable named by the argument

- whichSelectorsStoreInto: returns the selectors of methods that modify the value of an instance variable

- whichSelectorsReferTo: returns the selectors of methods that send a given message

- crossReference associates each message with the set of methods that send it.

```
Point whichSelectorsAccess: 'x'      ⟶    an IdentitySet(#'\\' #= #scaleBy: ...)
Point whichSelectorsStoreInto: 'x'   ⟶    an IdentitySet(#setX:setY: ...)
Point whichSelectorsReferTo: #+      ⟶    an IdentitySet(#rotateBy:about: ...)
Point crossReference    ⟶    an Array(
    an Array('*' an IdentitySet(#rotateBy:about: ...))
    an Array('+' an IdentitySet(#rotateBy:about: ...))
    ...)
```

The following messages take inheritance into account:

- whichClassIncludesSelector: returns the superclass that implements the given message

- unreferencedInstanceVariables returns the list of instance variables that are neither used in the receiver class nor any of its subclasses

```
Rectangle whichClassIncludesSelector: #inspect   ⟶    Object
Rectangle unreferencedInstanceVariables          ⟶    #()
```

SystemNavigation is a facade that supports various useful methods for querying and browsing the source code of the system. SystemNavigation default returns an instance you can use to navigate the system. For example:

```
SystemNavigation default allClassesImplementing: #yourself   ⟶    {Object}
```

The following messages should also be self-explanatory:

```
SystemNavigation default allSentMessages size        ⟶    24930
SystemNavigation default allUnsentMessages size      ⟶    6431
SystemNavigation default allUnimplementedCalls size  ⟶    270
```

Note that messages implemented but not sent are not necessarily useless, since they may be sent implicitly (*e.g.*, using perform:). Messages sent but not implemented, however, are more problematic, because the methods sending these messages will fail at runtime. They may be a sign of unfinished implementation, obsolete APIs, or missing libraries.

SystemNavigation default allCallsOn: #Point returns all messages sent explicitly to Point as a receiver.

All these features are integrated in the programming environment of Pharo, in particular in the code browsers. As you are surely already aware, there are convenient keyboard shortcuts for browsing all implementors (CMD−m) and senders (CMD−n) of a given message. What is perhaps not so well known is that there are many such pre-packaged queries implemented as methods of the SystemNavigation class in the *browsing* protocol. For example, you can programmatically browse all implementors of the message ifTrue: by evaluating:

SystemNavigation default browseAllImplementorsOf: #ifTrue:

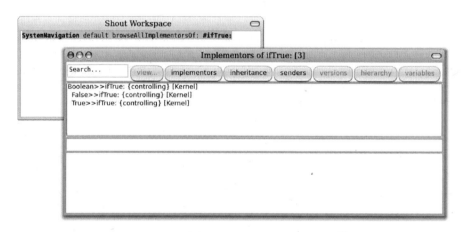

Figure 14.4: Browse all implementations of #ifTrue:.

Particularly useful are the methods browseAllSelect: and browseMethodsWith-SourceString:. Here are two different ways to browse all methods in the system that perform super sends (the first way is rather brute force; the second way is better and eliminates some false positives):

SystemNavigation default browseMethodsWithSourceString: 'super'.
SystemNavigation default browseAllSelect: [:method | method sendsToSuper].

14.3   Classes, method dictionaries and methods

Since classes are objects, we can inspect or explore them just like any other object.

Evaluate Point explore.

In Figure 14.5, the explorer shows the structure of class Point. You can see that the class stores its methods in a dictionary, indexing them by their selector. The selector #∗ points to the decompiled bytecode of Point»∗.

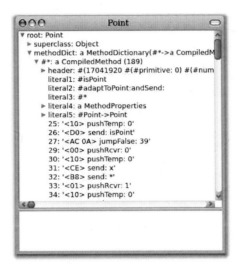

Figure 14.5: Explorer class Point and the bytecode of its #∗ method.

Let us consider the relationship between classes and methods. In Figure 14.6 we see that classes and metaclasses have the common superclass Behavior. This is where new is defined, amongst other key methods for classes. Every class has a method dictionary, which maps method selectors to compiled methods. Each compiled method knows the class in which it is installed. In Figure 14.5 we can even see that this is stored in an association in literal5.

We can exploit the relationships between classes and methods to pose queries about the system. For example, to discover which methods are newly introduced in a given class, *i.e.*, do not override superclass methods, we can navigate from the class to the method dictionary as follows:

```
[:aClass| aClass methodDict keys select: [:aMethod |
   (aClass superclass canUnderstand: aMethod) not ]] value: SmallInteger
   ⟶    an IdentitySet(#threeDigitName #printStringBase:nDigits: ...)
```

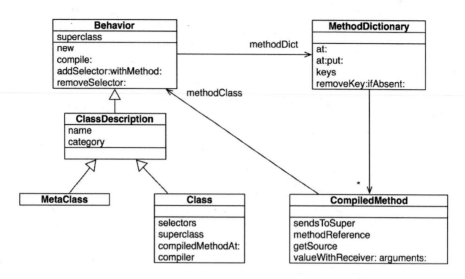

Figure 14.6: Classes, method dictionaries and compiled methods

A compiled method does not simply store the bytecode of a method. It is also an object the provides numerous useful methods for querying the system. One such method is isAbstract (which tells if the method sends subclassResponsibility). We can use it to identify all the abstract methods of an abstract class

```
[:aClass| aClass methodDict keys select: [:aMethod |
 (aClass>>aMethod) isAbstract ]] value: Number
    ⟶   an IdentitySet(#storeOn:base: #printOn:base: #+ #- #* #/ ...)
```

Note that this code sends the >> message to a class to obtain the compiled method for a given selector.

To browse the super-sends within a given hierarchy, for example within the Collections hierarchy, we can pose a more sophisticated query:

```
class := Collection.
SystemNavigation default
  browseMessageList: (class withAllSubclasses gather: [:each |
    each methodDict associations
    select: [:assoc | assoc value sendsToSuper]
    thenCollect: [:assoc | MethodReference class: each selector: assoc key]])
  name: 'Supersends of ' , class name , ' and its subclasses'
```

Note how we navigate from classes to method dictionaries to compiled methods to identify the methods we are interested in. A MethodReference is a lightweight proxy for a compiled method that is used by many tools. There is a convenience method CompiledMethod»methodReference to return the method reference for a compiled method.

```
(Object>>#=) methodReference methodSymbol   ⟶   #=
```

14.4 Browsing environments

Although SystemNavigation offers some useful ways to programmatically query and browse system code, there is a better way. The Refactoring Browser, which is integrated into Pharo, provides both interactive and programmatic ways to pose complex queries.

Suppose we are interested to discover which methods in the Collection hierarchy send a message to super which is different from the method's selector. This is normally considered to be a bad code smell, since such a super-send should normally be replaced by a self-send. (Think about it — you only *need* super to extend a method you are overriding; all other inherited methods can be accessed by sending to self!)

The refactoring browser provides us with an elegant way to restrict our query to just the classes and methods we are interested in.

(?) *Open a browser on the class* Collection. *action-click on the class name and select* refactoring scope>subclasses with . *This will open a new Browser Environment on just the* Collection *hierarchy. Within this restricted scope select* refactoring scope>super-sends *to open a new environment with all methods that perform super-sends within the* Collectuon *hierarchy. Now click on any method and select* refactor>code critics . *Navigate to* Lint checks>Possible bugs>Sends different super message *and action-click to select* browse .

In Figure 14.7 we can see that 19 such methods have been found within the Collection hierarchy, including Collection»printNameOn:, which sends super printOn:.

Browser environments can also be created programmatically. Here, for example, we create a new BrowserEnvironment for Collection and its subclasses, select the super-sending methods, and open the resulting environment.

```
((BrowserEnvironment new forClasses: (Collection withAllSubclasses))
   selectMethods: [:method | method sendsToSuper])
   label: 'Collection methods sending super';
   open.
```

Note how this is considerably more compact than the earlier, equivalent example using SystemNavigation.

Finally, we can find just those methods that send a different super message programmatically as follows:

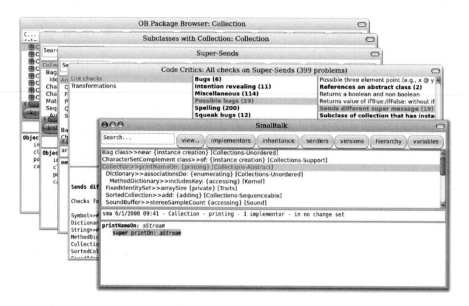

Figure 14.7: Finding methods that send a different super message.

```
((BrowserEnvironment new forClasses: (Collection withAllSubclasses))
    selectMethods: [:method |
      method sendsToSuper
      and: [(method parseTree superMessages includes: method selector) not]])
    label: 'Collection methods sending different super';
    open
```

Here we ask each compiled method for its (Refactoring Browser) parse tree, in order to find out whether the super messages differ from the method's selector. Have a look at the *querying* protocol of the class RBProgramNode to see some the things we can ask of parse trees.

14.5 Accessing the run-time context

We have seen how Smalltalk's reflective capabilities let us query and explore objects, classes and methods. But what about the run-time environment?

Method contexts

In fact, the run-time context of an executing method is in the virtual machine — it is not in the image at all! On the other hand, the debugger obviously has access to this information, and we can happily explore the run-time context, just like any other object. How is this possible?

Actually, there is nothing magical about the debugger. The secret is the pseudo-variable thisContext, which we have encountered only in passing before. Whenever thisContext is referred to in a running method, the entire run-time context of that method is reified and made available to the image as a series of chained MethodContext objects.

We can easily experiment with this mechanism ourselves.

Ⓘ *Change the definition of* Integer»factorial *by inserting the underlined expression as shown below:*

```
Integer»factorial
    "Answer the factorial of the receiver."
    self = 0 ifTrue: [thisContext explore. self halt. ↑ 1].
    self > 0 ifTrue: [↑ self * (self – 1) factorial].
    self error: 'Not valid for negative integers'
```

Ⓘ *Now evaluate* 3 factorial *in a workspace. You should obtain both a debugger window and an explorer, as shown in Figure 14.8.*

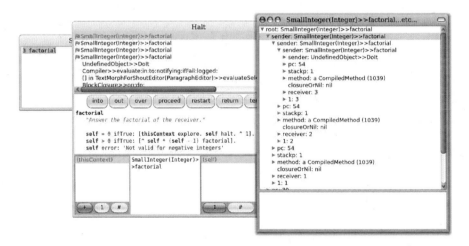

Figure 14.8: Exploring thisContext.

Welcome to the poor-man's debugger! If you now browse the class of the explored object (*i.e.*, by evaluating self browse in the bottom pane of the explorer) you will discover that it is an instance of the class MethodContext, as is each sender in the chain.

thisContext is not intended to be used for day-to-day programming, but it is essential for implementing tools like debuggers, and for accessing information about the call stack. You can evaluate the following expression to discover which methods make use of thisContext:

```
SystemNavigation default browseMethodsWithSourceString: 'thisContext'
```

As it turns out, one of the most common applications is to discover the sender of a message. Here is a typical application:

```
Object»subclassResponsibility
    "This message sets up a framework for the behavior of the class' subclasses.
    Announce that the subclass should have implemented this message."

    self error: 'My subclass should have overridden ', thisContext sender selector
        printString
```

By convention, methods in Smalltalk that send self subclassResponsibility are considered to be abstract. But how does Object»subclassResponsibility provide a useful error message indicating which abstract method has been invoked? Very simply, by asking thisContext for the sender.

Intelligent breakpoints

The Smalltalk way to set a breakpoint is to evaluate self halt at an interesting point in a method. This will cause thisContext to be reified, and a debugger window will open at the breakpoint. Unfortunately this poses problems for methods that are intensively used in the system.

Suppose, for instance, that we want to explore the execution of OrderedCollection»add:. Setting a breakpoint in this method is problematic.

🕮 *Take a* fresh *image and set the following breakpoint:*

```
OrderedCollection»add: newObject
    self halt.
    ↑self addLast: newObject
```

Notice how your image immediately freezes! We do not even get a debugger window. The problem is clear once we understand that (i) OrderedCollection »add: is used by many parts of the system, so the breakpoint is triggered very soon after we accept the change, but (ii) *the debugger itself* sends add: to an instance of OrderedCollection, preventing the debugger from opening! What we need is a way to *conditionally halt* only if we are in a context of interest. This is exactly what Object»haltIf: offers.

Suppose now that we only want to halt if add: is sent from, say, the context of OrderedCollectionTest»testAdd.

🕮 *Fire up a fresh image again, and set the following breakpoint:*

```
OrderedCollection»add: newObject
    self haltlf: #testAdd.
    ↑self addLast: newObject
```

This time the image does not freeze. Try running the OrderedCollectionTest. (You can find it in the *CollectionsTests-Sequenceable* category.)

How does this work? Let's have a look at Object»haltlf::

```
Object»haltlf: condition
    | cntxt |
    condition isSymbol ifTrue: [
        "only halt if a method with selector symbol is in callchain"
        cntxt := thisContext.
        [cntxt sender isNil] whileFalse: [
            cntxt := cntxt sender.
            (cntxt selector = condition) ifTrue: [Halt signal]. ].
        ↑self.
    ].
    ...
```

Starting from thisContext, haltlf: goes up through the execution stack, checking if the name of the calling method is the same as the one passed as parameter. If this is the case, then it raises an exception which, by default, summons the debugger.

It is also possible to supply a boolean or a boolean block as an argument to haltlf:, but these cases are straightforward and do not make use of thisContext.

14.6 Intercepting messages not understood

So far we have used the reflective features of Smalltalk mainly to query and explore objects, classes, methods and the run-time stack. Now we will look at how to use our knowledge of the Smalltalk system structure to intercept messages and modify behaviour at run-time.

When an object receives a message, it first looks in the method dictionary of its class for a corresponding method to respond to the message. If no such method exists, it will continue looking up the class hierarchy, until it reaches Object. If still no method is found for that message, the object will *send itself* the message doesNotUnderstand: with the message selector as its argument. The process then starts all over again, until Object»doesNotUnderstand: is found, and the debugger is launched.

But what if doesNotUnderstand: is overridden by one of the subclasses of Object in the lookup path? As it turns out, this is a convenient way of realizing certain kinds of very dynamic behaviour. An object that does not understand a message can, by overriding doesNotUnderstand:, fall back to an alternative strategy for responding to that message.

Two very common applications of this technique are (1) to implement lightweight proxies for objects, and (2) to dynamically compile or load missing code.

Lightweight proxies

In the first case, we introduce a "minimal object" to act as a proxy for an existing object. Since the proxy will implement virtually no methods of its own, any message sent to it will be trapped by doesNotUnderstand:. By implementing this message, the proxy can then take special action before delegating the message to the real subject it is the proxy for.

Let us have a look at how this may be implemented[1].

We define a LoggingProxy as follows:

```
ProtoObject subclass: #LoggingProxy
    instanceVariableNames: 'subject invocationCount'
    classVariableNames: ''
    poolDictionaries: ''
    category: 'PBE-Reflection'
```

Note that we subclass ProtoObject rather than Object because we do not want our proxy to inherit over 400 methods (!) from Object.

```
Object methodDict size    ⟶    408
```

Our proxy has two instance variables: the subject it is a proxy for, and a count of the number of messages it has intercepted. We initialize the two instance variables and we provide an accessor for the message count. Initially the subject variable points to the proxy object itself.

```
LoggingProxy»initialize
    invocationCount := 0.
    subject := self.
```

```
LoggingProxy»invocationCount
    ↑ invocationCount
```

We simply intercept all messages not understood, print them to the Transcript, update the message count, and forward the message to the real subject.

```
LoggingProxy»doesNotUnderstand: aMessage
    Transcript show: 'performing ', aMessage printString; cr.
```

---

[1]You can also load *PBE-Reflection* from http://www.squeaksource.com/PharoByExample/

```
invocationCount := invocationCount + 1.
↑ aMessage sendTo: subject
```

Here comes a bit of magic. We create a new Point object and a new LoggingProxy object, and then we tell the proxy to become: the point object:

```
point := 1@2.
LoggingProxy new become: point.
```

This has the effect of swapping all references in the image to the point to now refer to the proxy, and vice versa. Most importantly, the proxy's subject instance variable will now refer to the point!

```
point invocationCount   ⟶   0
point + (3@4)           ⟶   4@6
point invocationCount   ⟶   1
```

This works nicely in most cases, but there are some shortcomings:

```
point class   ⟶   LoggingProxy
```

Curiously, the method class is not even implemented in ProtoObject but in Object, which LoggingProxy does not inherit from! The answer to this riddle is that class is never sent as a message but is directly answered by the virtual machine.[2]

Even if we can ignore such special message sends, there is another fundamental problem which cannot be overcome by this approach: self-sends cannot be intercepted:

```
point := 1@2.
LoggingProxy new become: point.
point invocationCount   ⟶   0
point rect: (3@4)       ⟶   1@2 corner: 3@4
point invocationCount   ⟶   1
```

Our proxy has been cheated out of two self-sends in the rect: method:

```
Point»rect: aPoint
    ↑ Rectangle origin: (self min: aPoint) corner: (self max: aPoint)
```

---

[2]yourself is also never truly sent. Other messages that may be directly interpreted by the VM, depending on the receiver, include: +– < > <= >= = ~= * / == @ bitShift: // bitAnd: bitOr: at: at:put: size next nextPut: atEnd blockCopy: value value: do: new new: x y. Selectors that are never sent, because they are inlined by the compiler and transformed to comparison and jump bytecodes: ifTrue: ifFalse: ifTrue:ifFalse: ifFalse:ifTrue: and: or: whileFalse: whileTrue: whileFalse whileTrue to:do: to:by:do: caseOf: caseOf:otherwise: ifNil: ifNotNil: ifNil:ifNotNil: ifNotNil:ifNil: Attempts to send these messages to non-boolean objects can be intercepted and execution can be resumed with a valid boolean value by overriding mustBeBoolean in the receiver or by catching the NonBooleanReceiver exception.

Although messages can be intercepted by proxies using this technique, one should be aware of the inherent limitations of using a proxy. In Section 14.7 we will see another, more general approach for intercepting messages.

Generating missing methods

The other most common application of intercepting not understood messages is to dynamically load or generate the missing methods. Consider a very large library of classes with many methods. Instead of loading the entire library, we could load a stub for each class in the library. The stubs know where to find the source code of all their methods. The stubs simply trap all messages not understood, and dynamically load the missing methods on-demand. At some point, this behaviour can be deactivated, and the loaded code can be saved as the minimal necessary subset for the client application.

Let us look at a simple variant of this technique where we have a class that automatically adds accessors for its instance variables on-demand:

```
DynamicAcccessors»doesNotUnderstand: aMessage
  | messageName |
  messageName := aMessage selector asString.
  (self class instVarNames includes: messageName)
    ifTrue: [
      self class compile: messageName, String cr, ' ↑ ', messageName.
      ↑ aMessage sendTo: self ].
  ↑ super doesNotUnderstand: aMessage
```

Any message not understood is trapped here. If an instance variable with the same name as the message sent exists, then we ask our class to compile an accessor for that instance variables and we re-send the message.

Suppose the class DynamicAcccessors has an (uninitialized) instance variable x but no pre-defined accessor. Then the following will generate the accessor dynamically and retrieve the value:

```
myDA := DynamicAccessors new.
myDA x    ⟶    nil
```

Let us step through what happens the first time the message x is sent to our object (see Figure 14.9).

(1) We send x to myDA, (2) the message is looked up in the class, and (3) not found in the class hierarchy. (4) This causes self doesNotUnderstand: #x to be sent back to the object, (5) triggering a new lookup. This time doesNotUnderstand: is found immediately in DynamicAccessors, (6) which asks its class to compile the string 'x ↑ x'. The compile method is looked up (7), and (8) finally found in Behavior, which (9-10) adds the new compiled method

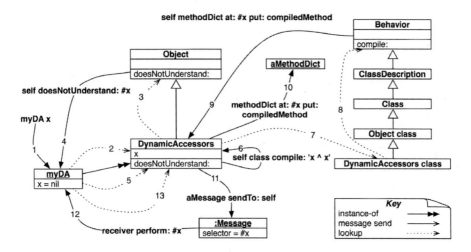

Figure 14.9: Dynamically creating accessors.

to the method dictionary of DynamicAccessors. Finally, (11-13) the message is resent, and this time it is found.

The same technique can be used to generate setters for instance variables, or other kinds of boilerplate code, such as visiting methods for a Visitor.

Note the use of Object»perform: in step (13) which can be used to send messages that are composed at run-time:

```
5 perform: #factorial                         ⟶    120
6 perform: ('fac', 'torial') asSymbol          ⟶    720
4 perform: #max: withArguments: (Array with: 6)  ⟶  6
```

14.7   Objects as method wrappers

We have already seen that compiled methods are ordinary objects in Smalltalk, and they support a number of methods that allow the programmer to query the run-time system. What is perhaps a bit more surprising, is that *any object* can play the role of a compiled method. All it has to do is respond to the method run:with:in: and a few other important messages.

ⓘ *Define an empty class* Demo. *Evaluate* Demo new answer42 *and notice how the usual "Message Not Understood" error is raised.*

Now we will install a plain Smalltalk object in the method dictionary of our Demo class.

ⓘ *Evaluate* Demo methodDict at: #answer42 put: ObjectsAsMethodsExample new.

Now try again to print the result of Demo new answer42. *This time we get the answer* 42.

If we take look at the class ObjectsAsMethodsExample we will find the following methods:

```
answer42
    ↑42
```

```
run: oldSelector with: arguments in: aReceiver
    ↑self perform: oldSelector withArguments: arguments
```

When our Demo instance receives the message answer42, method lookup proceeds as usual, however the virtual machine will detect that in place of a compiled method, an ordinary Smalltalk object is trying to play this role. The VM will then send this object a new message run:with:in: with the original method selector, arguments and receiver as arguments. Since ObjectsAsMethodsExample implements this method, it intercepts the message and delegates it to itself.

We can now remove the fake method as follows:

```
Demo methodDict removeKey: #answer42 ifAbsent: []
```

If we take a closer look at ObjectsAsMethodsExample, we will see that its superclass also implements the methods flushcache, methodClass: and selector:, but they are all empty. These messages may be sent to a compiled methods, so they need to be implemented by an object pretending to be a compiled method. (flushcache is the most important method to be implemented; others may be required depending on whether the method is installed using Behavior »addSelector:withMethod: or directly using MethodDictionary»at:put:.)

Using methods wrappers to perform test coverage

Method wrappers are a well-known technique for intercepting messages[3]. In the original implementation[4], a method wrapper is an instance of a subclass of CompiledMethod. When installed, a method wrapper can perform special actions before or after invoking the original method. When uninstalled, the original method is returned to its rightful position in the method dictionary.

In Pharo, method wrappers can be implemented more easily by implementing run:with:in: instead of by subclassing CompiledMethod. In fact, there exists a lightweight implementation of objects as method wrappers[5], but it is not part of standard Pharo at the time of this writing.

---

[3]John Brant et al., Wrappers to the Rescue. In Proceedings European Conference on Object Oriented Programming (ECOOP'98). Volume 1445, Springer-Verlag 1998.

[4]http://www.squeaksource.com/MethodWrappers.html

[5]http://www.squeaksource.com/ObjectsAsMethodsWrap.html

Nevertheless, the Pharo Test Runner uses precisely this technique to evaluate test coverage. Let's have a quick look at how it works.

The entry point for test coverage is the method TestRunner»runCoverage:

```
TestRunner»runCoverage
   | packages methods |
   ... "identify methods to check for coverage"
   self collectCoverageFor: methods
```

The method TestRunner»collectCoverageFor: clearly illustrates the coverage checking algorithm:

```
TestRunner»collectCoverageFor: methods
   | wrappers suite |
   wrappers := methods collect: [ :each | TestCoverage on: each ].
   suite := self
      reset;
      suiteAll.
   [ wrappers do: [ :each | each install ].
   [ self runSuite: suite ] ensure: [ wrappers do: [ :each | each uninstall ] ] ]
      valueUnpreemptively.
   wrappers := wrappers reject: [ :each | each hasRun ].
   wrappers isEmpty
      ifTrue:
         [ UIManager default inform: 'Congratulations. Your tests cover all code under
         analysis.' ]
      ifFalse: ...
```

A wrapper is created for each method to be checked, and each wrapper is installed. The tests are run, and all wrappers are uninstalled. Finally the user obtains feedback concerning the methods that have not been covered.

How does the wrapper itself work? The TestCoverage wrapper has three instance variables, hasRun, reference and method. They are initialized as follows:

```
TestCoverage class»on: aMethodReference
   ↑ self new initializeOn: aMethodReference

TestCoverage»initializeOn: aMethodReference
   hasRun := false.
   reference := aMethodReference.
   method := reference compiledMethod
```

The install and uninstall methods simply update the method dictionary in the obvious way:

```
TestCoverage»install
   reference actualClass methodDictionary
      at: reference methodSymbol
```

```
    put: self

TestCoverage»uninstall
   reference actualClass methodDictionary
      at: reference methodSymbol
      put: method
```

and the run:with:in: method simply updates the hasRun variable, uninstalls the wrapper (since coverage has been verified), and resends the message to the original method

```
run: aSelector with: anArray in: aReceiver
   self mark; uninstall.
     ↑ aReceiver withArgs: anArray executeMethod: method

mark
   hasRun := true
```

(Have a look at ProtoObject»withArgs:executeMethod: to see how a method displaced from its method dictionary can be invoked.)

That's all there is to it!

Method wrappers can be used to perform any kind of suitable behaviour before or after the normal operation of a method. Typical applications are instrumentation (collecting statistics about the calling patterns of methods), checking optional pre- and post-conditions, and memoization (optionally cacheing computed values of methods).

14.8   Pragmas

A *pragma* is an annotation that specifies data about a program, but is not involved in the execution of the program. Pragmas have no direct effect on the operation of the method they annotate. Pragmas have a number of uses, among them:

- Information for the compiler: pragmas can be used by the compiler to make a method call a primitive function. This function has to be defined by the virtual machine or by an external plugging.

- Runtime processing: Some pragmas are available to be examined at runtime.

Pragmas can be applied to a program's method declarations only. A method may declare one or more pragmas, and the pragmas have to be declared prior any Smalltalk statement. Each pragma is in effect a static message send with literal arguments.

We briefly saw pragmas when we introduced primitives earlier in this chapter. A primitive is nothing more than a pragma declaration. Consider <primitive: 73> as contained in instVarAt:. The pragma's selector is primitive: and its arguments is an immediate literal value, 73.

The compiler is probably the bigger user of pragmas. SUnit is another tool that makes use of annotations. SUnit is able to estimate the coverage of an application from a test unit. One may want to exclude some methods from the coverage. This is the case of the documentation method in SplitJointTest class:

```
SplitJointTest class»documentation
    <ignoreForCoverage>
    "self showDocumentation"

    ↑ 'This package provides function.... "
```

By simply annotating a method with the pragma <ignoreForCoverage> one can control the scope of the coverage.

As instances of the class Pragma, pragmas are first class objects. A compiled method answers to the message pragmas. This method returns an array of pragmas.

```
(SplitJoinTest class >> #showDocumentation) pragmas
     ⟶    an Array(<ignoreForCoverage>)
(Float>>#+) pragmas      ⟶    an Array(<primitive: 41>)
```

Methods defining a particular query may be retrieved from a class. The class side of SplitJoinTest contains some methods annotated with < ignoreForCoverage>:

```
Pragma allNamed: #ignoreForCoverage in: SplitJoinTest class     ⟶    an Array(<
    ignoreForCoverage> <ignoreForCoverage> <ignoreForCoverage>)
```

A variant of allNamed:in: may be found on the class side of Pragma.

A pragma knows in which method it is defined (using method), the name of the method (selector), the class that contains the method (methodClass), its number of arguments (numArgs), about the literals the pragma has for arguments (hasLiteral: and hasLiteralSuchThat:).

14.9 Chapter summary

Reflection refers to the ability to query, examine and even modify the metaobjects of the run-time system as ordinary objects.

- The Inspector uses instVarAt: and related methods to query and modify "private" instance variables of objects.

- Send Behavior»allInstances to query instances of a class.

- The messages class, isKindOf:, respondsTo: etc. are useful for gathering metrics or building development tools, but they should be avoided in regular applications: they violate the encapsulation of objects and make your code harder to understand and maintain.

- SystemNavigation is a utility class holding many useful queries for navigation and browsing the lass hierarhy. For example, use SystemNavigation default browseMethodsWithSourceString: 'pharo'. to find and browse all methods with a given source string. (Slow, but thorough!)

- Every Smalltalk class points to an instance of MethodDictionary which maps selectors to instances of CompiledMethod. A compiled method knows its class, closing the loop.

- MethodReference is a leightweight proxy for a compiled method, providing additional convenience methods, and used by many Smalltalk tools.

- BrowserEnvironment, part of the Refactoring Browser infrastructure, offers a more refined interface than SystemNavigation for querying the system, since the result of a query can be used as a the scope of a new query. Both GUI and programmatic interfaces are available.

- thisContext is a pseudo-variable that reifies the run-time stack of the virtual machine. It is mainly used by the debugger to dynamically construct an interactive view of the stack. It is also especially useful for dynamically determining the sender of a message.

- Intelligent breakpoints can be set using haltIf:, taking a method selector as its argument. haltIf: halts only if the named method occurs as a sender in the run-time stack.

- A common way to intercept messages sent to a given target is to use a "minimal object" as a proxy for that target. The proxy implements as few methods as possible, and traps all message sends by implementing doesNotunderstand:. It can then perform some additional action and then forward the message to the original target.

- Send become: to swap the references of two objects, such as a proxy and its target.

- Beware, some messages, like class and yourself are never really sent, but are interpreted by the VM. Others, like +, − and ifTrue: may be directly interpreted or inlined by the VM depending on the receiver.

- Another typical use for overriding doesNotUnderstand: is to lazily load or compile missing methods.

- doesNotUnderstand: cannot trap self-sends.

- A more rigorous way to intercept messages is to use an object as a method wrapper. Such an object is installed in a method dictionary in place of a compiled method. It should implement run:with:in: which is sent by the VM when it detects an ordinary object instead of a compiled method in the method dictionary. This technique is used by the SUnit Test Runner to collect coverage data.

Part IV

Appendices

Appendix A

Frequently Asked Questions

A.1   Getting started

FAQ 1 *Where do I get the latest Pharo?*

Answer   http://www.pharo-project.org/

FAQ 2 *Which Pharo image should I use with this book?*

Answer   You should be able to use any Pharo image, but we recommend you to use the prepared image on the Pharo by Example web site: http://PharoByExample.org. You should also be able to use most other images, but you may find that the hands-on exercises behave differently in surprising ways.

A.2 · Collections

FAQ 3 *How do I sort an* OrderedCollection?

Answer   Send it the message asSortedCollection.
```
#(7 2 6 1) asSortedCollection    ⟶    a SortedCollection(1 2 6 7)
```

FAQ 4 *How do I convert a collection of characters to a* String?

Answer
```
String streamContents: [:str | str nextPutAll: 'hello' asSet]    ⟶    'hleo'
```

A.3 Browsing the system

FAQ 5 *The browser does not look like the one described in the book. What gives?*

Answer   You are probably using an image in which a different version of
the OmniBrowser is installed as the default browser. In this book we assume
that the OmniBrowser *Package Browser* is installed as the default. You can
change the default by clicking on the menu bar of the browser. Just click on
the gray lozenge in the top right corner of the window, select "Choose new
default Browser", and then pick the O2PackageBrowserAdaptor. The next
browser you open will be the Package Browser.

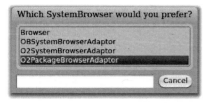

    (a) Choose a new browser   (b) Select the OB Package Browser

Figure A.1: Changing the default browser

FAQ 6 *How do I search for a class?*

Answer   CMD−b (browse) on the class name, or CMD−f in the category pane
of the browser.

FAQ 7 *How do I find/browse all sends to super?*

Answer   The second solution is much faster:

```
SystemNavigation default browseMethodsWithSourceString: 'super'.
SystemNavigation default browseAllSelect: [:method | method sendsToSuper ].
```

FAQ 8 *How do I browse all super sends within a hierarchy?*

Answer

```
browseSuperSends := [:aClass | SystemNavigation default
    browseMessageList: (aClass withAllSubclasses gather: [ :each |
      (each methodDict associations
        select: [ :assoc | assoc value sendsToSuper ])
          collect: [ :assoc | MethodReference class: each selector: assoc key ] ])
    name: 'Supersends of ' , aClass name , ' and its subclasses'].
browseSuperSends value: OrderedCollection.
```

FAQ 9 *How do I find out which new methods are introduced by a class? (I.e., not including overridden methods.)*

Answer   Here we ask which methods are introduced by True:

```
newMethods := [:aClass| aClass methodDict keys select:
    [:aMethod | (aClass superclass canUnderstand: aMethod) not ]].
newMethods value: True    ⟶     an IdentitySet(#asBit)
```

FAQ 10 *How do I tell which methods of a class are abstract?*

Answer

```
abstractMethods :=
    [:aClass | aClass methodDict keys select:
      [:aMethod | (aClass>>aMethod) isAbstract ]].
abstractMethods value: Collection    ⟶     an IdentitySet(#remove:ifAbsent: #add: #do:)
```

FAQ 11 *How do I generate a view of the AST of an expression?*

Answer   Load AST from squeaksource.com. Then evaluate:

```
(RBParser parseExpression: '3+4') explore
```

(Alternatively *explore it.*)

FAQ 12 *How do I find all the Traits in the system?*

Answer

```
Smalltalk allTraits
```

FAQ 13 *How do I find which classes use traits?*

Answer

Smalltalk allClasses select: [:each | each hasTraitComposition and: [each
    traitComposition notEmpty]]

A.4   Using Monticello and SqueakSource

FAQ 14 *How do I load a SqueakSource project?*

Answer

1. Find the project you want in http://squeaksource.com
2. Copy the registration code snippet
3. Select open ▷ Monticello browser
4. Select +Repository ▷ HTTP
5. Paste and accept the Registration code snippet; enter your password
6. Select the new repository and Open it
7. Select and load the latest version

FAQ 15 *How do I create a SqueakSource project?*

Answer

1. Go to http://squeaksource.com
2. Register yourself as a new member
3. Register a project (name = category)
4. Copy the Registration code snippet
5.   open ▷ Monticello browser
6.   +Package to add the category
7. Select the package
8.   +Repository ▷ HTTP
9. Paste and accept the Registration code snippet; enter your password
10. Save to save the first version

FAQ 16 *How do I extend* Number *with* Number»chf *but have Monticello recognize it as being part of my* Money *project?*

Answer   Put it in a method-category named *Money. Monticello gathers all methods that are in other categories named like *package and includes them in your package.

A.5   Tools

FAQ 17 *How do I programmatically open the SUnit TestRunner?*

Answer   Evaluate TestRunner open.

FAQ 18 *Where can I find the Refactoring Browser?*

Answer   Load AST then Refactoring Engine from squeaksource.com: http://www.squeaksource.com/AST http://www.squeaksource.com/RefactoringEngine

FAQ 19 *How do I register the browser that I want to be the default?*

Answer   Click the menu icon in the top right of the Browser window.

A.6   Regular expressions and parsing

FAQ 20 *Where is the documentation for the RegEx package?*

Answer   Look at the DOCUMENTATION protocol of RxParser class in the VB-Regex category.

FAQ 21 *Are there tools for writing parsers?*

Answer   Use SmaCC — the Smalltalk Compiler Compiler. You should install at least SmaCC-lr.13.   Load it from http://www.squeaksource.com/SmaccDevelopment.html. There is a nice tutorial online: http://www.refactory.com/Software/SmaCC/Tutorial.html

FAQ 22 *Which packages should I load from SqueakSource SmaccDevelopment to write parsers?*

Answer   Load the latest version of SmaCCDev — the runtime is already there. (SmaCC-Development is for Squeak 3.8)

Bibliography

Sherman R. Alpert, Kyle Brown and Bobby Woolf: The Design Patterns Smalltalk Companion. Addison Wesley, 1998, ISBN 0–201–18462–1

Kent Beck: Smalltalk Best Practice Patterns. Prentice-Hall, 1997

Kent Beck: Test Driven Development: By Example. Addison-Wesley, 2003, ISBN 0–321–14653–0

John Brant et al.: Wrappers to the Rescue. In Proceedings European Conference on Object Oriented Programming (ECOOP'98). Volume 1445, Springer-Verlag 1998, 396–417

Erich Gamma et al.: Design Patterns: Elements of Reusable Object-Oriented Software. Reading, Mass.: Addison Wesley, 1995, ISBN 0–201–63361–2– (3)

Adele Goldberg and David Robson: Smalltalk 80: the Language and its Implementation. Reading, Mass.: Addison Wesley, May 1983, ISBN 0–201–13688–0

Dan Ingalls et al.: Back to the Future: The Story of Squeak, a Practical Smalltalk Written in Itself. In Proceedings of the 12th ACM SIGPLAN conference on Object-oriented programming, systems, languages, and applications (OOPSLA'97). ACM Press, November 1997 ⟨URL: http://www.cosc.canterbury.ac.nz/~wolfgang/cosc205/squeak.html⟩, 318–326

Wilf LaLonde and John Pugh: Inside Smalltalk: Volume 1. Prentice Hall, 1990, ISBN 0–13–468414–1

Alec Sharp: Smalltalk by Example. McGraw-Hill, 1997 ⟨URL: http://stephane.ducasse.free.fr/FreeBooks/ByExample/⟩

Bobby Woolf: Null Object. In **Robert Martin, Dirk Riehle and Frank Buschmann, editors:** Pattern Languages of Program Design 3. Addison Wesley, 1998, 5–18

Index

*, *see* package, dirty
:=, *see* assignment
;, *see* cascade
←, *see* assignment
[ ], *see* block
#( ), *see* Array, literal
#, *see* literal symbol
_, *see* assignment
., *see* statement separator
==, *see* Object, identity
=, *see* Object, equality
>>, *see* Behavior, >>
become:, *see* ProtoObject»become:
{ }, *see* Array, dynamic
↑, *see* return

abstract class, *see* class, abstract
abstract method, *see* method, abstract
accept it, *see* keyboard shortcut, accept
accessing (protocol), 40, 80, 183
accessing untypeable characters (protocol), 175
accessor, 40, 79
ActiveHand (global), 97
adding (protocol), 183
Agile software development, 145
AJAX, 267
all (protocol), 31, 37, 106, 116
AlphaBlendingCanvas (class), 234
Array
    (class), 185, 187
    at:, 187, 188
    at:put:, 187, 188
    copy, 188
    dynamic, 51, 165
    literal, 51, 165, 188

Array (class), 184, 186, 187
Array class
    new:, 187
    with:, 187
as yet unclassified (protocol), 38
assignment, 51, 90
association, *see* Object, ->
AST, 317
at:, *see* Collection, at:
at:put:, *see* Collection, at:put:
attribute, *see* instance variable

Bag
    (class), 185, 191
Bag (class), 184
BalloonCanvas (class), 234
Beck, Kent, 92, 145
Behavior
    >>, 23, 38
    addSelector:withMethod:, 306
    addSubclass:, 283
    allInstances, 283, 292
    allInstVarNames, 279, 292
    allSelectors, 283, 292
    allSubclasses, 292
    allSubInstances, 292
    allSuperclasses, 279, 292
    basicNew, 283
    basicNew:, 283
    canUnderstand:, 283
    compiledMethodAt:, 283
    crossReference, 293
    hasMethods, 283
    includesSelector, 283
    inheritsFrom:, 283
    instanceCount, 292

instVarNames, 279, 283, 292
isVariable, 283
methodDict, 295
new, 58, 171, 282, 283, 295
new:, 58, 283
selectors, 279, 283, 292
someInstance, 292
subclasses, 283, 292
superclass, 277, 283
superclass:, 283
unreferencedInstanceVariables, 293
whichClassIncludesSelector:, 293
whichSelectorsAccess:, 293
whichSelectorsReferTo:, 293
whichSelectorsStoreInto:, 293
Behavior (class), 88, 276, 281, 282
Behavior Driven Development, *see* Test
        Driven Development
behavioural reflection, 288
binary message, *see* message, binary
Bitmap (class), 181
block, 49, 51, 55, 73, 152, 169
BlockClosure
        value, 55
        value:, 55
        value:value:, 55
        valueWithArguments:, 55
        whileFalse:, 56
        whileTrue:, 56
BlockClosure (class), 52, 56
Blue Book, 181
blue button, 6, 218
Boolean
        &, 179
        (class), 177
        and:, 179
        ifFalse:, 56, 178
        ifFalse:ifTrue, 178
        ifTrue:, 56, 178
        ifTrue:ifFalse:, 56, 177
Boolean (class), 16, 49, 52, 168, 170, 171
BorderedMorph
        fullPrintOn:, 94
BorderedMorph (class), 34, 231
Browser (class), 164
browser, 14, 16, 28, 80, 104
        browse button, 109
        class side, 80, 82, 84, 100, 276, 280
        defining a class, 30, 108

defining a method, 31, 108
finding classes, *see* class, finding
finding methods, *see* method,
        finding
hierarchy button, 110, 112
implementors, 111
instance side, 80, 81, 84
senders, 109, 111
variables, 112
versions button, 111
view, 114
BrowserEnvironment (class), 297
browsing programmatically, 116, 316
brushes, 247
Bryant, Avi, 237
Bykov, Vassili, 177
ByteArray (class), 214
bytecode, 295
ByteString
        (class), 176
ByteString (class), 128, 193

C++, 61, 65, 79, 82, 84
camelCase, 49, 118
Canvas
        (class), 234
Canvas (class), 221
canvas, *see* html canvas
caret, *see* return
cascade, 52, 54, 73, 199, 249
Cascading Style Sheets, *see* CSS
category, 15, 29
        creating, 28
        filing in, *see* file, filing in
        filing out, *see* file, filing out
change set, *see* file, filing out
change sorter, 137
changes, 4, 10, 141
Character
        (class), 175
        asString, 176
        asUppercase, 19
        isAlphaNumeric, 175
        isCharacter, 175
        isDigit, 175
        isLowercase, 175
        isVowel, 175
        printOn:, 175
        printString, 176

Character (class), 19, 51, 87, 168, 172, 193
Character class
    backspace, 175
    cr, 100, 175
    escape, 175
    euro, 175
    space, 51, 175
    tab, 51, 175
    value:, 175
CharacterArray (class), 184
CharacterTable (class variable), 176
Class
    addClassVarName:, 283
    addSharedPool:, 283
    initialize, 283
    subclasses, 279
Class (class), 276, 281, 283
class
    abstract, 86, 170, 177
    comment, 17, 31
    creation, 30, 108
    filing in, *see* file, filing in
    filing out, *see* file, filing out
    finding, 16, 115
    initialization, 100
    instance variable, 80, 82
    invariant, 172
    method, 80, 82, 85
    recent, 115
    variable, 50, 96, 98, 99
class browser, *see* browser
ClassDescription
    linesOfCode, 292
ClassDescription (class), 281, 283
closure, *see* block
code smell, 297
Collection
    (class), 181
    add:, 186
    addAll:, 186
    asOrderedCollection, 189
    asSet, 191
    asSortedCollection, 192, 315
    at:, 186
    at:put:, 186
    collect:, 57, 183, 186, 197
    comma operator, 24, 193, 194, 209
    common errors, 199
    count:, 199

    detect:, 57
    detect:ifNone:, 183, 198
    do:, 57, 157, 183, 186, 196, 197
    do:separatedBy:, 196
    do:without:, 196
    include:, 186
    includes:, 183, 191, 199
    inject:into:, 57, 183, 198
    intersection:, 191
    isEmpty, 183, 186
    iteration, 195
    occurrencesOf:, 183
    reject:, 57, 183, 198
    remove:, 171, 186, 200
    select:, 57, 183, 186, 198
    size, 186
    sorting, *see* Collection,
        asSortedCollection
    union:, 191
    weak, 185
Collection (class), 297
Collection class
    new:, 186
    newFrom:, 186
    with:, 186
    with:with:, 186
    withAll:, 186
Collections-Streams (category), 181
Collections-Strings (category), 175, 176
Color
    alpha:, 277
    name, 99
    printOn:, 164
Color (class), 81, 98, 218, 276–278
Color class
    blue, 82, 277, 280
    colorNames, 100
    initialize, 100
    initializeNames, 99
    showColorCube, 82
Color class (class), 278
ColorNames (class variable), 99
comma, *see* Collection, comma operator
comment, 51
comparing (protocol), 177
compiled methods, 295
CompiledMethod
    methodReference, 296
    pragmas, 309

CompiledMethod (class), 181
Complex
=, 166
hash, 166
Complex (class), 172, 173
constant methods, 38
control constructs, *see* iteration
converting (protocol), 183
copy, *see* Object, copy
CR (global), 100
creation (protocol), 86, 183
CrossMorph (class), 221
CSS, 238, 240, 249, 252
CVS, 44

Dabble DB, 237
debug (protocol), 170
debugger, 23, 41, 104, 126, 169, 298, 300
declaration, *see* variable declaration
deep copy, *see* Object, deepCopy
dependents (protocol), 106
deprecation, 170
design by contract, 169
Dictionary
(class), 190
associationsDo:, 196
at:, 190
at:ifAbsent:, 190
at:put:, 190
do:, 196
keys, 190
keysDo:, 196
overriding = and hash, 190, 200
removeKey:, 171
values, 190
valuesDo:, 196
Dictionary (class), 166, 171, 184, 186
Dictionary class
newFrom:, 187
withAll:, 187
DieMorph (class), 231
dirty package, *see* package, dirty
do:, *see* Collection, do:
download, 3, 4, 315
Duration
(class), 173
Duration (class), 125, 172

EllipseMorph

defaultColor, 91
EllipseMorph (class), 229
encapsulation boundary, 79
enumerating (protocol), 183, 197
enumeration, *see* iteration
equality, *see* Object, equality
EventSensor (class), 97
execution context, 41
explorer, 14, 125, 295
exponent, 51
extension, *see* method, extension
extension package, *see* package, extension
eXtreme Programming, 145, 147

False
(class), 177
ifTrue:, 178
False (class), 52
false (pseudo variable), 49, 52
Feathers, Michael, 160
field, *see* instance variable
file
browsing, *see* file list browser
change set, 137
filing in, 44, 115
filing out, 43, 103, 115, 138
file list browser, 139
FileStream
(class), 213
binary, 214
close, 213
localName, 214
FileStream (class), 181
FileStream class
fileNamed:, 213
fileNamed:do:, 205
forceNewFileNamed:, 213
forceNewFileNamed:do:, 214
newFileNamed:, 213
oldFileNamed:, 213
readOnlyFileNamed:, 213
fixture, *see* SUnit, fixture
Float
(class), 174
Float (class), 172
Float class
e, 174
infinity, 174
nan, 174

pi, 174
FloatArray (class), 184
floating point number, 51
fold, *see* Collection»inject:into
FormCanvas (class), 234
Fraction
    numerator:denominator:, 174
Fraction (class), 168, 172
Fractions (class), 174
full stop, *see* statement separator

geometry (protocol), 220
getter method, *see* accessor
global variable, *see* variable, global

HandMorph (class), 97
Haskell, 182
hook method, 171
html canvas, 247

identity, *see* Object, identity
IdentityDictionary
    (class), 190
IdentityDictionary (class), 245
image, 3, 5, 10
ImageMorph
    drawOn:, 112
ImageMorph (class), 112
inheritance, 85, 90
    canceling, 171
initialization, 32, 84, 93
initialization (protocol), 38, 80
inspector, 13, 33, 79, 124, 281
instance variable, 33, 79, 90
instance variable definition, 35
Integer
    (class), 174
    atRandom, 174
    bitAnd:, 58
    bitOr:, 58
    bitShift:, 58
    factorial, 174
    gcd:, 174
    isPrime, 174
    timesRepeat:, 56, 175
Integer (class), 172
IntegerArray (class), 184
intercession, 288
Interval

(class), 185, 189
    at:, 184
    printOn:, 165
Interval (class), 57, 184, 186
Interval class
    from:to:, 189
    from:to:by:, 189
    printString, 189
introspection, 287, 288
is-a, 278, 281
iteration, 56, *see also* Collection, iteration

Java, 65, 79, 82, 84, 92, 145
JavaScript, 267, 268

Kernel (category), 15
Kernel-Classes (category), 86
Kernel-Numbers (category), 172
Kernel-Objects (category), 17, 163
keyboard events, 225
keyboard shortcut, 16, 109
    accept, 21, 30
    browse it, 16, 17, 109, 316
    cancel, 129
    do it, 13
    explore it, 14, 125, 129
    find ..., 17, 316
    inspect it, 124, 129
    print it, 13
keyboard shortcuts, 12, 21, 26
KeyboardEvent (class), 226
keys, *see* Dictionary, keys
keyword message, *see* message, keyword
Knight, Alan, x

lambda expression, 183
LargeNegativeInteger (class), 172, 175
LargePositiveInteger (class), 172, 175
launching Pharo, 4
lexical closure, *see* block
LF (global), 100
Lights Out, 27
lightweight proxies, 302
LinkedList
    (class), 184, 185
LinkedList (class), 184
Linux, 238
Lisp, 182
literal, 50

array, 51
character, 51
number, 50
string, 51
symbol, 51
literal arrays, 188
literal objects, 49
LOCell
    initialize, 32
    mouseAction:, 40
    mouseUp:, 40
LOCell (class), 29
LOGame
    cellsPerSide, 38
    initialize, 35, 42
    newCellAt:at:, 39, 43
    toggleNeighboursOfCellAt:at:, 39
LOGame (class), 34
loops, *see* iteration

Mac OS X Finder, 107
Mac OSX, 238
Magnitude
    <, 87, 173, 192
    <=, 192
    =, 173, 192
    >, 173, 192
    >=, 87, 192
    (class), 172
    between:and:, 192
Magnitude (class), 86, 170, 172, 175, 177, 192
Matrix
    free will, *see* Oracle
Matrix (class), 36, 39
Matrix class
    new:tabulate:, 36
    rows:columns:, 37
message
    binary, 52, 53, 61
    evaluation order, 65
    keyword, 52, 53, 61
    not understood, 95
    receiver, 62
    selector, 61
    send, 62, 89
    unary, 51, 53, 61
message name finder, 104
message names browser, 136
message selector, 52

Metaclass (class), 276, 283, 284
metaclass, 78, 80, 276, 278, 281
    anonymous, 278
    hierarchy, 276, 279, 285
    implicit, 278
Metaclass class (class), 284
metaobjects, 287
metaprogram, 287
method
    abstract, 86
    byte code, 114
    categorize, 38, 40
    creation, 31, 108
    decompile, 114
    dictionary, 281
    extension, 93
    filing in, *see* file, filing in
    filing out, *see* file, filing out
    finding, 18, 116
    lookup, 90, 280
    overriding, 93
    pretty-print, 114
    public, 80
    returning self, 42
    selector, 78
    value, 43
    version, 111
method dictionary, 295
method finder, 18, 104
method lookup, 93
method wrappers, 306
MethodContext (class), 52, 299
MethodDictionary
    at:put:, 306
metrics, 292
minimal object, 302
ML, 182
Model
    myDependents, 106
Monticello, 27, 44, 103, 104, 117, 118, 138, 318
Morph
    addMorph:, 220
    bounds, 221
    center:, 220
    color:, 219
    composing, 220
    constructorString, 94
    drawOn:, 109, 221

extent, 219
handleKeystroke:, 225, 226
handlesMouseDown:, 224, 226
handlesMouseOver:, 225
mouseDown:, 224
mouseEnter:, 226
mouseLeave:, 226
mouseUp:, 224
openInWorld, 91, 218, 219, 222, 277
position, 219
repelsMorph:event:, 229
subclassing, 221
wantsDroppedMorph:event:, 229
Morph (class), 34, 112
Morphic, 30, 97, 217
animation, 227, 234
halo, 6, 7, 11, 34, 43, 218
isStepping, 227
startStepping, 227
step, 227
stepTime, 227
stopStepping, 227
morphic halo, *see* Morphic, *see* Morphic
MorphicEvent
hand, 230
MorphicEvent (class), 226
mouse events, 225
MouseEvent
redButtonPressed, 225
yellowButtonPressed, 225
MouseEvent (class), 224, 225
MyTestCase class
buildSuiteFromSelectors, 159

.Net, 145
new, *see* Behavior»new
NeXTstep, 105
nil (pseudo variable), 49, 52
notifier, 41
Null Object (pattern), 171
Number
∗, 173
+, 173
−, 173
/, 173
(class), 172, 173
asFloat, 173
asInteger, 173
ceiling, 173

day, 173
even, 173
floor, 173
fractionPart, 173
hour, 173
i, 173
integerPart, 173
isInfinite, 173
log, 173
negative, 173
odd, 173
positive, 173
printOn:, 173
raiseTo:, 173
sin, 173
sqrt, 173
squared, 173
to:, 189
to:by:, 189
to:do:, 57
week, 173
Number (class), 168, 170, 172

Object
–>, 190
=, 166
(class), 163
∼=, 166
asMorph, 218
assert:, 169
asString, 195
at:, 58
at:put:, 58
class, 167, 277, 291
copy, 168, 169
copyTwoLevel, 168
deepCopy, 168
deprecated:, 170
doesNotUnderstand:, 96, 170, 301
equality, 166
error, 170
error:, 170
explore, 295
halt, 169, 299, 300
haltIf:, 300, 301
hash, 166
identity, 166
initialization, *see* initialization
instanceVariableValues, 290

instVarAt:, 289
instVarAt:put:, 289
instVarNamed:, 289
instVarNamed:put:, 289
isArray, 171
isBlock, 171
isBoolean, 171
isCollection, 171
isComplex, 171
isKindOf:, 167, 278, 291
isMemberOf:, 167
notNil, 171
perform:, 233, 305
postCopy, 169
printOn:, 262
printOn:, 164
printString, 16, 164, 195
respondsTo:, 168, 291
shallow copy, 168
shallowCopy, 168
shouldNotImplement, 171
storeOn:, 165
subclassResponsibility, 86, 87, 170, 300
yourself, 199
Object (class), 14, 15, 29, 86, 95, 277
Object class (class), 278
ObjectsAsMethodsExample (class), 306
OmniBrowser, 14, 316
on the fly variable definition, 35
Oracle, 145
OrderedCollection
(class), 188
add:, 188, 199
addAll:, 188
addFirst:, 184, 188
addLast:, 184, 188
anySatisfy:, 199
at:, 184
at:put:, 184
detect:, 198
do:, 204
remove:, 189
remove:ifAbsent:, 189
removeAt:, 116
reverseDo:, 196
OrderedCollection (class), 184, 186, 204, 315
OrderedCollections (class), 185
overriding, *see* method, overriding

package, 27, 29, 44, 117
cache, 119, 122
creating, 28, 107
dirty, 45
extension, 117
package browser, *see* Monticello
package cache, 45
parentheses, 61, 65, 68
PasteUpMorph (class), 97
Pelrine, Joseph, 89, 145
period, *see* statement separator
Perl, 145
Pluggable collections, 184
Point
dist:, 79
printOn:, 165
Point (class), 32, 295
pool dictionary, *see* variable, pool
PositionableStream
atEnd, 207
contents, 207
isEmpty, 207
peek, 206
peekFor:, 206
position, 206
position:, 206
reset, 203, 207
setToEnd, 207
skip:, 207
skipTo:, 207
PositionableStream (class), 203
PositionableStream class
on:, 206
Pragma (class), 309
pragma, 289, 308
pragmas, 308
pre-debugger, 135
PreDebugWindow (class), 41, 127
preference browser, 170
primitive, 58, 90
primitive methods, 289
primitive., 51
printing (protocol), 15
private (protocol), 80
process
browser, 135
interrupting, 104, 134
process browser, 104
protocol, 15, 37

ProtoObject
  ==, 190
  become:, 303
  initialize, 171
  isNil, 171
  withArgs:executeMethod:, 308
ProtoObject (class), 86, 95, 163, 167
ProtoObject class (class), 285
Prototype, 267
pseudo-variable, *see* variable, pseudo
Python, 145

radix notation, 50
RBParser
  (class), 317
ReadStream
  (class), 205
  next, 205
  next:, 205
  upToEnd, 206
ReadStream (class), 204
ReadWriteStream (class), 204, 210
ReceiverMorph (class), 229
Rectangle
  containsPoint:, 222
Rectangle (class), 32, 221
red button, 6
refactoring, 31
Refactoring Browser, 297, 319
reflection, 79, 146, 164, 233, 287
Regex (package), 177, 194
regular expression package, 177
removing (protocol), 183
resource, *see* test, resource
restore display, 82
return, 43, 52, 55, 90, 92
  implicit, 55

saving code, *see* categories
script.aculo.us, 267
Seaside, 237
  administrator login, 238
  backtracking state, 237, 245
  callback, 250, 255
  components, 237, 242
  configuration, 242
  control flow, 254
  convenience methods, 256
  counter, 238

deployment mode, 242
development mode, 242
halos, 240, 259
multi-counter, 242, 246
One-Click Experience, 238
rendering, 243
Sushi Store, 259
task, 254, 257
toolbar, 239
transactions, 237
web site, 238
XHTML forms, 251
Self, 217
self
  send, 93
self (pseudo variable), 32, 36, 49, 50, 52,
    55, 90
self-evaluating objects, 165
sending messages, 277
Sensor (class), 97
SequenceableCollection
  doWithIndex:, 196
  first, 183
  last, 183
  readStream, 206
SequenceableCollection (class), 183
SequenceableCollection class
  streamContents:, 209
Set
  (class), 191
  add:, 191
  intersection, *see* Collection,
    intersection:
  membership, *see* Collection, includes:
  union, *see* Collection, union:
Set (class), 184, 186, 190
Set class
  newFrom:, 191
setter method, *see* accessor
shallow copy, *see* Object, shallowCopy
Sharp, Alex, x
shortcut constructor methods, 173, 177
SimpleSwitchMorph (class), 29
Singleton (pattern), 177
Singleton pattern, 84
SkipList
  (class), 184
slot, *see* instance variable
SmaCC, 319

SmaCCDev, 319
SmallInteger
    +, 58
    (class), 174
    maxVal, 174
    minVal, 174
SmallInteger (class), 14, 168, 172
Smalltalk (global), 97, 98, 191
SortedCollection
    (class), 192
SortedCollection (class), 184, 186
SortedCollection class
    sortBlock:, 193
SortedCollections (class), 185
SourceForge, 46
sources, 3, 4
SqueakSource, 237, 318
SqueakSource, 46, 123
Stack
    pop, 169
stack trace, 127
StandardFileStream
    fullName, 214
statement, 53
    separator, 52, 53, 73
Stream
    (class), 203
    nextPut:, 204
    print:, 209
Stream (class), 164, 181, 203
String
    (class), 176, 193
    anySatisfy:, 194
    asDate, 177
    asFileName, 177
    asLowercase, 195
    asUppercase, 19, 195
    at:put:, 193
    capitalized, 177, 195
    comma, *see* Collection, comma
        operator
    concatenation, *see* Collection,
        comma operator
    copyReplaceAll:, 194
    expandMacros, 195
    expandMacrosWith:, 195
    format:, 195
    includes:, 194
    isEmpty, 194

lineCount, 54
match:, 177, 194
pattern matching, 194
replaceAll:with:, 194
replaceFrom:to:with:, 194
templating, 195
translateToLowercase, 177
String (class), 19, 21, 23, 54, 164, 184, 195,
        315
StringTest
    testShout, 22
StringTest (class), 21, 135
structural reflection, 288
Subversion, 44
SUnit, 21, 22, 104, 132, 145, 319
    fixture, 149
    set up method, 148
super
    initialize, 93
    send, 93, 110, 316
super (pseudo variable), 49, 52, 90
superclass, 85, 90
Symbol
    (class), 177, 184
Symbol (class), 108, 168, 184, 190, 195
symbol, 30
syntax, 49
SystemDictionary (class), 97, 191
SystemNavigation
    (class), 316
    allCallsOn:, 294
    allClassesImplementing:, 293
    allSentMessages, 293
    allUnimplementedCalls, 293
    allUnsentMessages, 293
    browseAllImplementorsOf:, 294
    browseAllSelect:, 294
    browseMethodsWithSourceString:, 294
SystemNavigation (class), 293, 297
SystemNavigation (global), 116
SystemNavigation class
    default, 293
SystemOrganization (global), 98
SystemOrganizer (class), 98

template method, 164
Test Driven Development, 20, 145
Test Runner, 104, 150
TestCase

(class), 154
assert:, 151, 170
assert:description:, 152, 156
deny:, 150
deny:description:, 152, 156
failureLog, 156
isLogging, 156
run, 157
run:, 157, 158
runCase, 158
setUp, 148, 154, 159
should:description:, 156
should:raise:, 152
shouldnt:description:, 156
shouldnt:raise:, 152
tearDown, 154, 159
TestCase (class), 148, 153
testing, 21, *see* SUnit
testing (protocol), 171, 183
TestResource
(class), 155
setUp, 160
TestResource (class), 153, 160
TestResource class
current, 160
isAvailable, 160
TestResult
(class), 155
runCase:, 158
TestResult (class), 153, 157
TestResult class
error, 152
TestRunner, 22, 319
collectCoverageFor:, 307
runCoverage, 307
TestSuite
(class), 154
run, 159
run:, 159
TestSuite (class), 153
Text (class), 100
thisContext (pseudo variable), 49, 52, 299
three button mouse, 6
Timespan (class), 172
TimeStamp
(class), 124
Trait (class), 87
trait, 86, 87
Transcript (global), 54, 97, 104, 226

transcript, 11
TranscriptStream (class), 97
TranslucentColor (class), 99, 276, 277, 279, 282
True
(class), 177
ifTrue:, 178
not, 178
True (class), 52
true (pseudo variable), 49, 52, 179

UIManager
request:initialAnswer:, 227
UIManager (class), 227, 228
unary message, *see* message, unary
Undeclared (global), 98
UndefinedObject
(class), 128
UndefinedObject (class), 52, 168

value, *see* BlockClosure
values, *see* Dictionary, values
variable
class, *see* class, variable
class instance, *see* class, instance variable
declaration, 51, 55, 90
global, 50, 96
instance, *see* instance variable
pool, 50, 96, 100
pseudo, 50, 52, 92
shared, 96
versions browser, 111, 112
virtual machine, 3, 10, 51, 58, 90, 95

WAAnchorTag
on:of:, 252
WABrush
with:, 249
WACanvas (class), 247
WAChoiceDialog (class), 257
WAComponent
answer:, 255
call:, 255
chooseFrom: caption:, 257
chooseFrom:caption:, 257
confirm:, 257
inform:, 256, 258
isolate:, 260

request:, 256
WAComponent (class), 242, 254, 257
WAComponent class
    canBeRoot, 244, 246
WAConvenienceTest (class), 257
WACounter (class), 242, 244
WADispatcherEditor (class), 238, 242
WAFileLibrary (class), 252
WAFormDialog (class), 258
WAGlobalConfiguration (class), 242
WAHtmlCanvas (class), 243
WAKom (class), 238
WANestedTransaction (class), 260
WAPresenter
    renderContentOn:, 243, 247
    states, 245
WARenderCanvas (class), 247
WASnapshot (class), 245
WAStore (class), 259
WAStoreTask (class), 259, 260
WATagBrush
    onClick:, 268
WATask
    go, 255, 257
WATask (class), 254, 257
WAYesOrNoDialog (class), 257
weak collections, 185
web application development, 237
WebServer (class), 84
WideString (class), 193
Windows, 238
workspace, 11, 104
World (global), 97
world menu, 5, 7
WriteStream
    (class), 208
    cr, 209
    ensureASpace, 209
    nextPut:, 209
    nextPutAll:, 209
    space, 209
    tab, 209
WriteStream (class), 204

XML, 267
xUnit, 145

yellow button, 6